Youth Sport, Physical Activity and Play

Sport, physical activity and play are key constituents of social life, impacting such diverse fields as health care, education and criminal justice. Over the past decade, governments around the world have begun to place physical activity at the heart of social policy, providing increased opportunities for participation for young people. This groundbreaking text explores the various ways in which young people experience sport, physical activity and play as part of their everyday lives, and the interventions and outcomes that shape and define those experiences.

The book covers a range of sporting and physical activities across an array of social contexts, providing insight into the way in which sport, physical activity and play are interpreted by young people and how these interpretations relate to broader policy objectives set by governments, sporting organisations and other NGOs. In the process, it attempts to answer a series of key questions, including:

- How has sport policy developed over the last decade?
- How do such policy developments reflect changes at the broader political level?
- How have young people experienced these changes in and through their sporting lives?

By locating sport, physical activity and play within the context of recent policy developments, and exploring the moral and ethical dimensions of sports participation, the book fills a significant gap in the sport studies literature. It is an important reference for students and scholars from a wide range of sub-disciplines, including sports pedagogy, sports development, sport and leisure management, sports coaching, physical education, play and playwork, and health studies.

Andrew Parker is Professor of Sport and Christian Outreach and Director of the Centre for Sport, Spirituality and Religion (CSSR) in the Faculty of Applied Sciences at the University of Gloucestershire, UK.

Don Vinson is Senior Lecturer in Sports Coaching in the Faculty of Applied Sciences at the University of Gloucestershire, UK.

Routledge research in sport, culture and society

Youth Sport, Physical Activity and Play

Policy, intervention and participation

Andrew Parker and Don Vinson

Routledge
Taylor & Francis Group

LONDON AND NEW YORK

First published 2013
by Routledge
2 Park Square, Milton Park, Abingdon, Oxon OX14 4RN

Simultaneously published in the USA and Canada
by Routledge
711 Third Avenue, New York, NY 10017

Routledge is an imprint of the Taylor & Francis Group, an informa business

British Library Cataloguing in Publication Data
A catalogue record for this book is available from the British Library

Library of Congress Cataloging in Publication Data
Youth sport, physical activity and play : policy, interventions and
participation / edited by Andrew Parker and Don Vinson.
p. cm.
1. Sports for children. 2. Exercise for children. 3. Child psychology.
4. Adolescent psychology. I. Parker, Andrew. II. Vinson, Don.
GV709.2.Y67 2013
796.0835--dc23
2012041589

ISBN: 978-0-415-69493-3 (hbk)
ISBN: 978-0-203-14743-6 (ebk)

Typeset in Times New Roman
by Taylor & Francis Books

Andrew: For Lily

Don: For Mum and Dad

Contents

Figures and tables

Figures

Tables

Contributors

Elizabeth Annett is founding Director of Sport Malawi, a sport-for-development initiative based at the University of Gloucestershire, UK. Elizabeth has a strong research interest in the sustainability of sport and development programmes, the complexity of their partnerships and the 'decolonising' not only of the programmes themselves but the research that surrounds them. Her interests also include the more general intersection between sport, development and religion.

Celia Brackenridge is Professorial Research Fellow at Brunel University, London, UK. She chaired the Organising Committee for the pre-Olympic Convention in 2012 and, before that, led two major research projects for The Football Association. She was awarded an OBE in the 2012 Queen's New Year Honours.

Mike Collins, a geographer and town planner, was Head of Research Strategy and Planning at the Sports Council for many years, after which he has taught and researched at the Universities of Loughborough and Gloucestershire, UK as well as being active in the professional institute, CIMSPA. His interests focus on planning in sport, sport social capital and social exclusion, sports development (see *Examining Sports Development*, Routledge, 2009) and currently sport and religion. He is Visiting Professor in the Faculty of Applied Sciences and in the Centre for Sport, Spirituality and Religion at the University of Gloucestershire.

Diane Crone is Professor in the Faculty of Applied Sciences at the University of Gloucestershire, UK. Her research focuses on the role of physical activity in and for mental health services, the evaluation of exercise referral schemes and cohort studies in physical activity referral. Published outputs have appeared in: the *British Journal of Clinical Psychology*, the *International Journal of Mental Health Nursing*, the *Journal of Public Health*, and the *Journal of Sports Sciences.*

Tom Davenport completed his MSc by Research at the University of Gloucestershire, UK in 2010. His thesis examined the impact of physical activity on self-esteem and academic behaviours. Tom is an advocate of the role of outdoor education for young people and currently works as a Royal Yacht Association (RYA) OnBoard Development Officer and Regional Club Coach.

Mark Elliot is Senior Lecturer in Sports Development in the Faculty of Applied Sciences at the University of Gloucestershire, UK. Mark's research interests include sport and social identity, grass-roots association football, and student employability.

Samaya Farooq is Lecturer at the University of Derby, UK. Her research interests include the sociology of 'race', culture and identity; sport, Muslims and Islam; sport in south Asian diaspora; and the sociology of self/bodywork, physical education and schooling. Published outputs have focused primarily on the social construction of religious masculine identities and Independent faith schooling in the UK.

Denise M. Hill is Subject Group Lead for the School of Sport and Exercise in the Faculty of Applied Sciences at the University of Gloucestershire, UK. As a BASES-accredited Sport and Exercise Scientist, Denise has completed a wide range of research projects in the area of sport and exercise psychology. Her primary research interests lie within performance psychology, body image and self-esteem, athletic self-identity and exercise motivational theory.

David V. B. James is Professor and Deputy Dean in the Faculty of Applied Sciences at the University of Gloucestershire, UK. David's research interests include the application of study design and quantitative techniques to commissioned evaluations of physical activity, lifestyle and community interventions, and laboratory assessment techniques in human exercise physiology. He has published widely on these topics in periodicals such as the *Journal of Sports Sciences*, the *Journal of Public Health*, and the *International Journal of Sports Medicine*.

Lindsey Kilgour is Senior Lecturer in Exercise Psychology at the University of Gloucestershire, UK and Programme Leader for postgraduate qualifications in Physical Activity and Health. She has extensive and wide-ranging practitioner and research experience within the area of physical activity and health, including health policy, community nursing practice, student perceptions of safety, contemporary practices in sport and exercise psychology, health literacy in schools, gender issues in sport and physical activity referral schemes.

Stuart Lester is Senior Lecturer in Play and Playwork at the University of Gloucestershire, UK and an Independent Play Consultant and Trainer. His research interests include the nature and value of children's play, the everyday playful production of time/space and the conditions under which playfulness thrives. Publications include *Play, Naturally* (with Martin Maudsley, 2007), *Play for a Change: Play, Policy and Practice: A review of* *contemporary perspectives* (2008) and *Children's Right to Play: An examination of the importance of play in the lives of children worldwide* (2010) (both with Wendy Russell). He has also contributed to a number of other play and playwork publications.

Matt Lloyd is Head of Physical Education at Springfield's Academy in Wiltshire, UK. He began teaching 15 years ago, before becoming Partnership Development Manager in Mid-Wilts School Sports Partnership. Matt then took up a post as Senior Lecturer in Sport Education at the University of Gloucestershire, UK before moving into his current role. Matt specialises in leading innovative approaches to PE and shifting ownership to students to make outstanding progress.

Nic Matthews is Subject Group Lead for the School of Leisure in the Faculty of Applied Sciences at the University of Gloucestershire, UK. Nic has a research background in the role of the European Union and local government in the development of sports and leisure policy. She has conducted further research on issues of health literacy and subjective well-being amongst children and young people, the role of active play on childhood health and fair play in sport and has also completed pedagogic research on the role of feedback and support in student learning.

Hannah Mawson is Work-based Learning Coordinator for the Division of Sport, Health and Exercise in the Faculty of Health, Sport and Science at the University of Glamorgan, Wales, UK. Her research interests include volunteering and leadership in sport. Hannah has experience of working in industry and in sport development. Her current role at the University of Glamorgan involves working closely with sports organisations to provide work-based voluntary experience for students.

Samuel Mayuni is the National Director of Sport Malawi based in Malawi. He is also part of the leadership team of the Student Christian Organisation of Malawi (SCOM). Samuel is a graduate of the Sport and Christian Outreach postgraduate programme at the University of Gloucestershire, UK. His research interests focus on the theology of sports mission and ministry.

Rosie Meek is a Chartered Psychologist and Professor of Criminological Psychology in the School of Social Sciences and Law, Teesside University, UK. Her primary research interests include prison and community interventions and their evaluation, identity processes, resettlement and desistance. She carries out research across the prison estate, with a particular focus on children and young people. Rosie completed her doctorate at the University of Sussex and was previously lecturer at the University of Southampton and a Fulbright Distinguished Scholar at the University of California, San Diego.

Ben Moreland is Lecturer in Sports Development and Coaching in the Faculty of Applied Sciences at the University of Gloucestershire, UK. His research interests sit within the areas of sport for development, social inequality and alternative/innovative teaching pedagogies. Ben's current research focuses on the use of sport as a medium to engage 'hard to reach' and 'at risk' young people.

Christopher S. Owens is Lecturer in Public Health in the Faculty of Medicine and Health Sciences at the University of Nottingham, UK. His main research interests are in the areas of sport and physical activity participation and sedentary behaviour among adolescent populations. Christopher also has broader research interests in mental health and well-being.

Simon Padley is Senior Lecturer in Sport Education and Coaching and Head of Hockey at the University of Gloucestershire, UK. His research interests include sport and morality, coaching pedagogy and sport and faith. Simon plays National League hockey with Cheltenham Hockey Club and enjoys participating in any and all sports.

Andrew Parker is Professor of Sport and Christian Outreach and Director of the Centre for Sport, Spirituality and Religion (CSSR) in the Faculty of Applied Sciences at the University of Gloucestershire, UK. His research interests include sport and social identity, sport and spirituality, and physical activity and schooling. Andrew has served on the editorial boards of the *Sociology of Sport Journal* (2005–2008) (Human Kinetics) and *Qualitative Research* (2001–present) (Sage) and was co-editor of the *International Journal of Religion and Sport* between 2010 and 2012.

Andy Pitchford is Director of Sport at the University of Gloucestershire, UK. He has a background in teaching, research and community engagement in higher education, and in a previous life was a Sports Development Officer in London. He has a particular interest in youth football and cultural change on which he has published widely.

Wendy Russell is Senior Lecturer in Play and Playwork in the Faculty of Applied Sciences at the University of Gloucestershire, UK. She has worked often in collaboration with Stuart Lester, most notably on the commissioned literature review *Play for a Change* for Play England (2008) and *Children's Right to Play* for the International Play Association published by the Bernard van Leer Foundation (2010). Her research interests in children's play and playwork are interdisciplinary, with a particular focus on social theory, geography, policy and politics.

Don Vinson is Senior Lecturer in Sports Coaching at the University of Gloucestershire, UK. His research interests include: sports and higher education pedagogy, performance analysis and the maintenance of physical activity programmes. His research outputs have appeared in *Qualitative Research in Sport, Exercise and Health, Active Learning in Higher Education* and the *Journal of Sports Sciences*. Don is also Head Coach at Sutton Coldfield Ladies Hockey Club.

Kara Wilcox is a graduate of the MSc in Physical Activity and Public Health in the School of Sport and Exercise at the University of Gloucestershire, UK. Her thesis examined the impact of physical activity on self-esteem. Kara currently works within a health promotion role for NHS Cornwall.

Acknowledgements

Writing projects of this kind are always a collective venture, and ones which sometimes take longer than we might first imagine. We wish to record our grateful thanks to those who have helped us to produce this volume. We are especially indebted to our contributors: for agreeing to be involved in the first place, for their attention to detail on editorial queries and for their patience concerning final publication. We are also grateful to friends and colleagues who have offered encouragement and support along the way and who have endured our endless mummerings and questions. We are extremely thankful to Simon Whitmore and Joshua Wells at Routledge who have given generously of their time and to those who provided insightful comments on earlier drafts of various chapters, especially Nick Watson, Phil Mizen, David Baker and Jon Cryer. Last, but by no means least, we would like to thank our partners, Beckie and Cheryl, for their love, patience and support, and for taking care of all the things that we should have been doing whilst we were working on what follows. Needless to say, the inadequacies and inconsistencies found herein are entirely our own.

Introduction

Youth sport, physical activity and play

Andrew Parker and Don Vinson

Whether structured or spontaneous, sport, physical activity and play are key constituents of modern-day life and a fundamental part of the social reality in which we live. As a consequence, they are subject to the ebb and flow of political priorities and wider economic conditions. Over the past 50 years this proposition has been clearly borne out within the UK context, especially with regard to the experiences of young people. During that time government intervention and policy initiatives involving sport, physical activity and play have been utilised to address a whole series of issues concerning health, education, employment and social exclusion (Collins, 2003; Green, 2006; Grix, 2010). In the late 1950s and early '60s, the Albermarle (1959) and Wolfenden (1960) reports began to explicitly promote sport's potential to engender positive lifestyle choice, with youth being identified as a priority (McIntosh and Charlton, 1985). The 1970s and '80s subsequently saw sporting provision framed as a necessity in the battle to reduce urban unrest and to aid policy planning: issues which were poignantly reflected in the Sports Council's earliest 'Sport for all' campaign.

More recently, physical activity has been associated with having a positive impact on a range of personal conditions and characteristics, particularly where young people are concerned: self-confidence, self-esteem, elevated levels of motivation and well-being, and reduced fatigue and depression (Coalter, 2004, 2008; Holt, 2011; Malina, 2011). It has also been embraced as something which has the capacity to nurture a sense of active citizenship and to promote social interaction and exchange (Nichols, 2007; Muncie, 2009; Theeboom *et al.*, 2010). These claims highlight the extent to which sport and physical activity can bring benefit to individuals and communities. In turn, such qualities and attributes have been widely recognised and acclaimed in government policies and strategies concerning children and young people (see, for example, Social Exclusion Unit, 2002; Department of Education, 2003; Department for Education and Skills, 2005). Of late there has also been particular interest in the way that sport might contribute to the lives of vulnerable groups (International Olympic Committee, 2000; European Commission, 2007; Kay, 2009; Kelly, 2011).

The promotion of physically active lifestyles and the restructuring of sporting governance during the post-1997 era has, of course, been well documented (see Collins, 2011; Grix, 2009; Grix and Phillpots, 2011). Yet, despite heavy investment by the former (New) Labour government to address this and a range of other social issues, the advent of economic downturn in recent years has led to a climate of fiscal austerity amidst which the continued resourcing of sport has been placed at risk. It is in this way, and a host of others, that young people are said to be 'bearing the brunt' of the current financial crisis. Government cuts to public spending and welfare provision mean that certain groups are now at even greater risk of social exclusion. Cuts to Jobseeker's Allowance, Educational Maintenance Grants and soaring Higher Education tuition fees are just some examples of the way in which young people are experiencing the conditions and consequences of economic instability.

How then, we might ask, does government intend to address these issues and what part will sport and physical activity play in the grander scheme of things? The Coalition government has been clear in its intentions with regard to sport policy, favouring investment in elite performance and the promotion of competitive games in schools over and above mass participation (Department for Culture, Media and Sport, 2012). At a wider level, policy initiatives have an altogether more 'collective' feel. On 19 July 2010, David Cameron launched the idea of the 'Big Society' as an innovative way of dealing with issues affecting local communities. Despite widespread confusion and criticism, the concept rests, it seems, on the notion of promoting the empowerment of individuals to help themselves (Stott, 2011; McAll, 2011) rather than on interventionist techniques (Waring and Mason, 2010) or, indeed, the model adopted by the previous Labour government which relied on increasing income levels, welfare rights and access to socio-economic provision. Public promotion of the Big Society has witnessed the Prime Minister campaigning passionately about devolving power to local communities so as to better enable local people to have a voice in decisions that affect their everyday lives and the services that they access, such as post offices, public libraries, parks, community centres and housing regeneration projects – almost all of which have been subject to recent public funding cuts.

Although the focus on building sustainable and cohesive communities in and through collective action exposes the social communitarian aspect of the Big Society, a central strand of its overall agenda rests on the regeneration of social, moral and civic responsibility and a sense of altruism (Haugh, 2011; Knoxx, 2011). According to David Cameron, empowering communities through collective action is fundamentally aimed at supporting the most disadvantaged. Localised practices that rely on cross-sector collaboration between private, public, voluntary and community stakeholders and social enterprises can certainly offer benefits, such as promoting attachments to one's neighbourhood, boosting community morale and fostering a greater sense of cohesion and belonging (Chanan and Miller, 2011; Haugh, 2011; Knoxx, 2011). There is a dearth of empirical evidence surrounding the outworking of Big Society rhetoric and only time will tell whether or not it will manifest itself in productive social action. Likewise, the extent to which such political ideals will shape policy on sport, physical activity and play, and how these elements of everyday life might be seen as vehicles through which to achieve a renewed sense of social cohesion, will be borne out over the coming months and years.

Of course, what all of this highlights is that sport does not exist in a social vacuum. On the contrary, it evolves and develops in accordance with a variety of broader factors and forces. Modern-day sports policy looks like it does because it has been (and continues to be) shaped and formed in line with the turbulence of social existence (economics, politics, etc.), which, in turn, makes it what it is. The relationship between sport and young people is no different. This, too, is a reflection of the way in which sport has increasingly impacted wider society and has progressed from being a marginal social concern to an established feature of political decision-making. It is neither the intention nor the remit of this book to debate the pros and cons of such matters, nor to unpack the precise content or chronology of policy-making in this area. But what our respective contributors do illustrate is the way in which related policy has developed over time and how, with this in mind, we might think further about young people's experiences of sport. It is our view that the volume and breadth of policy impacting the lives of children and young people in the UK warrants further consideration, and it is against this backdrop that the following chapters have been written.

Chapter structure

The book is divided into three parts which correspond to its main themes: policy, intervention and participation. Tracking the historical trajectory of UK sport policy has been a central preoccupation for a number of scholars over the years. That said, relatively few have explored in detail either the broader social factors impacting policy formulation or the international comparisons available. Fewer still have been written by those who have experienced life at the forefront of policy change. In achieving all these objectives, Mike Collins kick-starts proceedings in Chapter 1 with an overview of UK policy development in youth sport, physical activity and play since the 1960s. Crucial here is not only Collins's analysis of the different ways in which succesive governments have engaged with sport but how wider political motives and decisions have shaped the contours of policy outcomes.

One of the things which is often absent from discussions surrounding the construction of domestic social policy is a broader sense of why such decisions are made and how they relate (or not) to what is going on elsewhere. Building upon the international snapshots outlined by Collins, in Chapter 2 Nic Matthews provides a detailed analysis of European policy in sport and cognate fields. As a specialist scholar in the area, Matthews presents a detailed overview of how, since the European Union established the political and social prerequisites for an economic union across Europe in 1992, subsequent Treaties and Declarations have facilitated a developing dialogue between European member states concerning sport, physical activity and play. For Matthews, the key point about these developments is that, in impacting the interdependencies between member states, altering the dynamics between governing bodies and changing the way that policies are framed, agreements at the European level have led to a whole series of benefits, in relation not only to institutional practice but also the promotion and protection of individual rights.

Of course, nowhere is this notion of 'rights' more important than in the lives of children and young people, and in Chapter 3 we look at how social policy formulation has accommodated such issues, specifically in the area of play. Over the years, much has been written about sport and physical activity, but less about play, especially within the context of playwork. This book sets out to offer some kind of corrective in this respect. More specifically, this chapter showcases the work of Stuart Lester and Wendy Russell, two established academics and practitioners in the field. Drawing on their wealth of experience and expertise, Lester and Russell provide a critique of traditional notions of playwork as commonly articulated in policy objectives and propose, in their place, an altogether new way of conceptualising play in the interests of a renewed sense of sponteneity and informality in terms of its delivery. At a time when the policy landscape in this area appears to be contracting, such debates are not only key to broadening public understandings of the scope and remit of playwork but also to highlighting the philosophical underpinnings of its practices.

And so to Part 2, where we take a slightly different tack – one which is concerned with examples of sporting intervention. We begin in Chapter 4 with the work of Denise Hill and colleagues who, from a practitioner perspective, present a psychological analysis of the ways in which school sport provision might be shaped to accommodate the needs of young people who have disengaged from physical activity and who demonstrate low self-esteem. Hill *et al.*'s account provides a classic example of sporting intervention whereby incentive, innovation and empowerment come together to facilitate visible change in the lives of participants. Acknowledging the benefits of physical activity in relation to levels of self-esteem, the authors argue that government policy-makers should not simply adopt a 'one-size-fits-all' model of school sport but should instead attempt to better understand why particular activities engage or disengage young people in order to capture the interest and imagination of those marginalised by traditional forms of curricular provision.

Discussions of marginalisation necessarily bring with them notions of exclusion, which are also central to Andrew Parker and Rosie Meek's contribution in Chapter 5. Whilst the sport-related literature is replete with examples of intervention in community settings, to date few researchers have explored the impact of sport in custody. Parker and Meek report on the findings of one such study. As we have seen, sport has long been considered an antidote to a range of social ills, but custodial environments operate in line with significant levels of regulation and, for this reason, the facilitation and delivery of physical activity within them is often subject to a variety of constraints. Nevertheless, what Parker and Meek show is that, where there is a commitment on the part of the host institution to utilise sport both as a form of personal engagement and as a broader educational pathway, participants may respond positively to this. As a consequence, individual experiences of such interventions may not only prove rewarding in a cognitive, physical and social sense, but they may also hold longer lasting potential in terms of hightened aspirations, changing value structures and improved lifestyle choices.

One of the things that often comes into question when debates surrounding physical activity surface is the notion of morality – closely followed by discussions of integrity and character. Amidst more general suggestions of moral decomposition, should we not be able to look to modern-day sport as promoter of positive values and qualities? Alas, sport does not always manage to live up to its historical (and philosophical) roots: fair play, respect (both for oneself and others), physical and emotional strength, discipline, loyalty, co-operation, self-control. British society has long since engendered an affinity for sport and, in particular, its character-building qualities. Hence, it is highly appropriate that in Chapter 6 Mark Elliot, Andy Pitchford and Celia Brackenridge present findings from their research into The Football Association's (FA) 'Respect' programme, which is designed to address anti-social behaviour within professional and amateur football in the UK. Set against the backdrop of broader policy measures, the chapter examines the rationale behind the introduction of the programme and draws upon qualitative data to map the reaction of young people to the series of interventions that have been central to its cause. The chapter concludes by assessing the extent to which the 'Respect' initiative may impact on social relations in football in a way that might engender a more respectful and civil participatory climate.

In Chapter 7 we move overseas, yet we do so in line with the focus of the preceding discussion, respect: this time, the cultural variety. In this chapter we are presented with sporting intervention in its broadest sense, whereby its associated characteristics and attributes are used to carry a series of wider messages in order to aid development goals. With the benefit of their extensive experience in the field of international (sport for) development, Elizabeth Annett and Samuel Mayuni present an overview of how one sporting initiative, 'Sport Malawi', seeks to bring about social transformation as a consequence of its work with young people around the issue of HIV/ AIDS. Utilising notions of partnership and personal empowerment, the chapter draws upon contemporary conceptions of development practice to illustrate how the building of in-depth, reciprocal relationships with local stakeholders (individuals and agencies) can provide a basis upon which to achieve cultural acceptance and social impact. In conclusion, Annett and Mayuni reiterate the need for sport-for-development workers to consider the broader social norms, customs and traditions in play during programme design and implementation, emphasising that, without an appropriate appreciation and understanding of cultural heritage, such initiatives may fail to relate to the everyday needs of those whom they are originally designed to reach.

All of this takes us into section three, where we move to the practicalities of participant experience. We begin this section in Chapter 8 with a look at one of the key debates of our time, physical activity amongst adolescents. Here Christopher Owens and his co-authors explore contemporary concerns, surrounding not only the perceived shortfall in the activity levels of children and young people but also associated sedentary behaviours. Drawing on research findings both from the UK and overseas, what Owens *et al.* present is a series of explanations as to why it is important to have an understanding of physical activity and sedentary behaviour during adolescence. At the same time they examine current recommendations and policies aimed at reducing the decline in physical activity levels and the increase in sedentary behaviour through the course of adolescence. In closing, they articulate the need for further longitudinal studies examining the effects of such behaviours and the factors associated with subsequent behaviour change.

In Chapter 9 we return to the school setting, this time for an analysis of the way in which decisions at the policy level might impact curricular provision and shape the contours of participant experience. By way of their examination of key philosophical shifts in Physical Education and School Sport (PESS) over the last 10 years, Don Vinson and Matt Lloyd present an overview of two areas of practice which PESS teachers, coaches and support staff have developed during that period, namely Fundamental Motor Skills (FMS) and Physical Literacy, both of which, the authors contend, have the potential to promote holistic and lifelong learning. On the basis of the evidence presented, Vinson and Lloyd suggest that, contrary to recent policy developments, a more diverse physical education curriculum benefits, rather than detracts from, the sporting competence of young people and the likelihood of continued participation. For them, PESS has made significant progress in the post-1997 period and there is a very real danger that a return to an emphasis on traditional competitive sports and team games within schools will have a negative impact on pupil experience.

Physical education is not the only context to experience a more recent shift away from performance-oriented sporting provision. Coaching, too, has witnessed similar change. In Chapter 10, Simon Padley and Don Vinson stay with the theme of holistic development to present a series of arguments as to why policy moves of this nature should be viewed as highly desirable given the wider benefits for children and young people in terms of skill acquisition and personal progression. By way of an analysis of contemporary learning theory and a philosophical critique of twenty-first-century sports coaching, the chapter challenges coach practitioners to reflect on the methods of delivery which they adopt and to consider the experiences of the young people with whom they work. Padley and Vinson conclude by suggesting that, by embracing contemporary pedagogic theory, it is possible for coaches to meet the demands of competitively based UK sport policy whilst at the same time adopting holistically focussed coaching strategies.

Coaching, of course, is one area which has undergone significant transformation in recent years, particularly in terms of accreditation pathways, a process which continues to evolve amidst the quest for professionalisation. Representing something of a historical (and, some would say, outdated) juxtaposition to this is the sporting volunteer, a role which has been in rapid decline in the UK. Given that British sport has long since relied on volunteers to facilitate the activities of amateur clubs, and given that such altruisic contributions are at the heart of contemporary government thinking, where, we might ask, will the next generation of sports volunteers come from? This is the question posed by Hannah Mawson and Andrew Parker in Chapter 11 as they assess the role of one sports leadership organisation, Sports Leaders UK (SLUK), in the perpetuation of these volunteer roles. Through a case study examination of the work of SLUK, Mawson and Parker provide an overview of the current position with regard to youth sport volunteering in Britain and an analysis of the demographic profiles of those who typically undertake SLUK awards. The authors go on to state that, whilst in recent years there appears to have been a reduction in the number of young people taking up volunteer roles, there is evidence to suggest a reversal of this trend. In turn, they argue that the 'Big Society' policy model provides an ideal platform for sport development initiatives to flourish, particularly those which focus on volunteers and community empowerment.

In Chapter 12, we draw our foray into empirical research to a close with a further look at volunteering, this time in connection with marginalised and vulnerable young people. Taking up some of the key themes explored in the previous chapter, here Samaya Farooq and colleagues report on findings from a recent study of two groups of British migrants, both of which see their engagement in sport-based volunteering in what might be regarded as non-traditional terms, that is, as a means by which to increase their social networks and employment opportunities and to generate a greater sense of personal stability and security. Farooq *et al.* conclude that, whilst the adoption of a proactive approach to volunteering may have its benefits, such activities alone do not always serve to empower young people, particularly those experiencing multiple social deprivations. The authors reveal a series of practical barriers and constraints relating to the recruitment of marginalised young people as volunteers, especially around issues of personal background and identification. Needless to say, when such groups experience problems accessing opportunities which are designed to help them, there is a danger that their sense of social exclusion and marginalisation may be exacerbated rather than alleviated.

In sum, *Youth Sport, Physical Activity and Play* aims not only to reflect on the ways in which modern-day policy, intervention and participation manifest themselves and how they might intersect, but also to consider and challenge the underlying values upon which policy objectives are formulated and how this impacts participant experience. We believe that it is by way of such reflection that our understandings of the sporting landscape can continue to develop and that the desire for ongoing empirical scholarship in this area will be stimulated and encouraged.

References

Albermarle Report (1959). *Youth Service in England and Wales*. London: HMSO.

Chanan, G. and Miller, C. (2011). 'The Big Society: How Could it Work?' In M. Stott *The Big Society Challenge*. London: Keystone Development Trust Publications, pp. 52–64.

Coalter, F. (2004). *The Social Benefits of Sport: An Overview to Inform the Community Planning Process*. Edinburgh: Sport Scotland.

——(2008). *A Wider Social Role for Sport: Who's Keeping the Score?* Oxon: Routledge.

Collins, M. (2011). 'Children's Sport in Policy Contexts'. In I. Stafford (Ed.) *Coaching Children in Sport*. London: Routledge, pp. 276–277.

Collins, M.F. with Kay, T. (2003). *Sport and Social Exclusion*. London, Routledge.

Department for Culture, Media and Sport (2012). *Creating a Sporting Habit for Life: New Youth Sport Strategy 2012*. London: DCMS.

Department for Education and Skills (2005). *Youth Matters*. London: HMSO.

Department of Education (2003). *Every Child Matters*. London: HMSO.

European Commission (2007). *White Paper on Sport*. Luxembourg: Office for Official Publications of the European Communities.

Green, M. (2006). 'From "Sport for All" to Not About "Sport" at All? Interrogating Sport Policy Interventions in the United Kingdom'. *European Sport Management Quarterly*. 6 (3): 217–38.

Grix, J. (2009). 'The Impact of UK Sport Policy on the Governance of Athletics'. *International Journal of Sport Policy*. 1 (1): 31–49.

——(2010). 'From Hobbyhorse to Mainstream: Using Sport to Understand British Politics'. *British Politics*. 5 (1): 114–129.

Grix, J. and Phillpots, L. (2011). 'Revisiting the "Governance Narrative": "Asymmetrical Network Governance" and the Deviant Case of the Sports Policy Sector'. *Public Policy and Administration*. 26 (1): 3–19.

Haugh, H. (2011). 'Community and Big Society'. In M. Stott *The Big Society Challenge*. Keystone Development Trust Publications, pp. 95–99.

Holt, N.L. (2011), 'Sport and Positive Youth Development'. In I. Stafford (Ed.) *Coaching Children in Sport*. London: Routledge, pp. 256–266.

International Olympic Committee (2000). *Sport for All*. Lausanne: International Olympic Committee, Sport for All Commission.

Kay, T. (2009), *Fathering through Sport and Leisure*, London: Routledge.

Kelly, L. (2011). '"Social Inclusion" through Sports-based Interventions?' *Critical Social Policy*. 31 (1): 126–150.

Knoxx, K. (2011). 'The Big Society and Sustainable Communities'. In M. Stott *The Big Society Challenge*. London: Keystone Development Trust Publications, pp. 75–81.

McAll, B. (2011). 'Big Society and the Devolution of Power'. In M. Stott *The Big Society Challenge*. London: Keystone Development Trust Publications, pp. 65–74.

McIntosh, P. and Charlton, V. (1985). *The Impact of Sport for All Policy 1966–1984 and a Way Forward*. London: Sports Council.

Malina, R.M. (2011). 'The Health of Young Athletes'. In I. Stafford (Ed.) *Coaching Children in Sport*. London: Routledge, pp. 240–253.

Muncie, J. (2009). *Youth and Crime*. London: Sage.

Nichols, G. (2007). *Sport and Crime Reduction*. London: Routledge.

Social Exclusion Unit (2002). *Preventing Social Exclusion*. London: SEU.

Stott, M. (2011). (Ed.) *The Big Society Challenge*. London: Keystone Development Trust Publications.

Theeboom, M., Haudenhuyse, R. and De Knop, P. (2010). 'Community Sports Development for Socially Deprived Groups: A Wider Role for the Commercial Sports Sector? A look at the Flemish Situation'. *Sport in Society*. 13 (9): 1392–1410.

Waring, A. and Mason, C. (2010). 'Opening Doors: Promoting Social Inclusion through Increased Sports Opportunities'. *Sport in Society*. 13 (3): 517–529.

Wolfenden, J. (1960). *Sport and the Community*. London: Central Council of Physical Recreation.

Part I
Policy

1 Youth sport and UK sport policy

Mike Collins

Introduction

In this chapter I begin by looking at recent and current sports participation in school and community by youth, and then at how sport policy interacts with other social factors, producing a kaleidoscope of groups and needs to which there are no simple policy responses: as stated by Macdonald *et al.* (2012: 21) 'the discourses of sport clash and intersect with other discourses related to, for example, gender, religion, family, ethnicity, school achievement, work and the like'. I then summarise phases of UK youth sport policy and conclude the chapter with the short-term prospects for sport under the present Coalition government.

Youth sports participation

Numerous studies from around the world show four common patterns in terms of young people and sport: (i) post-school drop-out; (ii) a narrowing of activity choices; (iii) lower participation by women and girls; and (iv) a marked income/status gradient. Downward and Rasciute (2012) reworked data from three recent British surveys which demonstrated these continuing features in England. Those data also show a large gap for children with disabilities, despite nearly two decades of attempts at mainstreaming disabled children in local state (rather than special) schools (see also Department for Culture, Media and Sport (DCMS), 2011).

Over the years, many sociologists have argued that education would level out the class legacy gaps, but recent research on social mobility following up 1946, 1958 and 1970 birth cohorts in Britain (Bukodi and Goldthorpe, 2011) shows little evidence of this. Rowe, Sport England's Head of Research (Rowe *et al.*, 2004) admitted that this was the most resistant of gaps. Other national occupational mobility studies from Germany, Italy, Sweden and the Netherlands found similar patterns to Britain. Thus, the UK government's Game Plan (DCMS, 2002) strategy of trying to make British sports participation like that of Finland, thereby closing the gap from the fourth most unequal situation in the developed world to the third most equal (Wilkinson and Pickett, 2009) in 16 years, never stood the slightest chance of succeeding (Collins, 2010).

Income and status reinforcing other social structural features in sport

I reiterate my argument (Collins, 2003) that the basis of most social exclusion is poverty/income inequality, but that other social features can ally and reinforce this in youth sport, including gender, sexuality, disability, ethnicity and social cohesion/disaffection. Interestingly, it is structural enough to appear also in expressions of sporting ability.

Gender

The 1989 National Curriculum was introduced with a premise that it would ensure 'equal opportunities for all pupils', but this did not happen, with still a wider range of sports for boys than girls, a majority policy attitude favouring team games, many of which are unpopular with girls, and competition promoted above recreation, embedding stereotypes of male masculinity. Clearly there is still gender inequality in coaching and in sports administration nationally and internationally, though countries like Norway have passed regulations to counter this (Ottesen *et al.*, 2010), and the International Olympic Committee (IOC) set a target of 20 per cent female membership of National Olympic Committees (NOC) by 2005. Henry and Robinson (2010) reported that the IOC's target had been met, in that 21.3 per cent of members of NOC commissions were, by then, female and were usually very well qualified and active, but some saw this as a norm or maximum. To this end, there appears to be an 'illusion of achieved gender equality' (Azzarito, 2012: 77). Sport England is still concerned about this issue, having launched a £10m programme for Active Women in 2010, including £2.29m of Streetsports in various cities.

Sexuality

Sexuality is still a developing facet of sports research (Collins, 2012). Wellard (2012) spoke of a dominant adult, male, heteronormative model, based on dualist male and female roles, overshadowing other norms of sexuality, and not allowing sexuality in schoolchildren to be properly addressed, who often feel they cannot raise related issues (Dismore, 2007).

Disability

As already stated, children with disability have lower provision than the majority of schoolchildren (Collins, 2012; Sport England, 2001). Thomas and Smith (2009) and Goodwin and Peers (2012), however, have pointed to the plethora of domestic and international rules and classifications that make both participation and competition a maze, and reify differences. Improvements in teacher training provision, buildings and equipment planning, and the choice and design of activities are still needed to facilitate developments in this area.

Ethnicity and religion

Collins (2012) demonstrates that, while curricular provision includes all ethnicities, the gaps widen in club competition and in adult sport, particularly for Asian groups (and women). Religion has become part of the Equality and Human Rights Commission's portfolio of statutory equality policies, including for Sport England, but is only now being opened up by research. As for Muslim girls and women, Dagkas and Benn (2012: 112) have spoken of the 'racialisation of religion' (i.e. currently, Islam); there are popular misconceptions that Muslim girls and young women lack interest in sport, yet two in five mosques and Muslim centres provide multisport programmes for them as well as for boys and men (see also Farooq and Parker, 2009). The Koran neither forbids segregation of the sexes nor physical activity, but there are varying interpretations within Islamic groups over practical issues of single-sex provision and bodily modesty. This provides challenges for those in positions of leadership and management in schools, clubs and public facilities, and to pupils, parents and teachers alike. In schools this is hindered by the fact that PE has the lowest recruitment and retention of black and ethnic minority teachers (Flintoff, 2008). There are places in the UK, e.g. Birmingham, where Muslim girls are frequently withdrawn from PE, and the city has had to devise specific strategies to balance this (Jawad, Benn and Dagkas, 2012).

Youth sport and social cohesion

One strong focus of youth sport policy since 1980 has been the issue of socially costly outcomes of misbehaviour either on the pitch or in wider society by disaffected and delinquent youth (Collins, 2003). It is clear that many interventions are grossly under-resourced, poorly focused and with overambitious delivery, too short term and often returning youth to the toxic contexts that originally produced anti-social rather than pro-social behaviour (Coalter, 2007; Collins, 2012; Audit Commission, 2009; Nichols, 2007). In terms of wider social cohesion, Spaaij (2011) portrays the different ways in which, in Amsterdam, Rio de Janeiro and Melbourne, local agencies and clubs have opened up opportunities for disadvantaged and immigrant youth in an attempt to build social capital.

Ability and performance

As a result of the 'world-wide arms race for medals' (De Bosscher *et al.*, 2008), coaching for adults and children has received much attention and investment over the last 20 years. Bruner *et al.* (2011) have identified three important transitions in youth sport coaching:

- entry into sport (at around 5–7 years of age);
- movement into performance-based sports participation (around 12–14 years of age, though younger in gymnastics and trampolining) and;
- movement into recreational sports participation (also around 12–14 years of age).

Côté *et al.* (2012) continue by contrasting an efficient process of transmitting motor skills without any thought to allied costs to young athletes, and effective programmes focusing on developing appropriate competencies. Their concerns are that too much specialisation and coaching occurs at too young an age, driving out spontaneity and enjoyment. Hay (2012) has further suggested that coaching focuses too much on the anthropometric, physiological and psychological aspects of youth performance that can be measured and can act in exclusionary ways (see also Padley and Vinson, Chapter 10).

The social gradient in elite sport showed strongly in the national squads of 12 sports in the Development of Sporting Talent study (English Sports Council (ESC), 1998: 13):

> the opportunity to realise sporting potential is significantly influenced by an individual's social background. So for example, a precociously talented youngster born in an affluent family with sport-loving parents, one of whom has (probably) achieved high levels of sporting success, and attending an independent/private school, has a 'first-class' ticket to the sporting podium. His or her counterpart, equally talented but born into less favoured social circumstances has, at best a third class ticket and at worst no ticket at all. The chances of the former achieving high levels of sporting success are very good while the chances of the latter are minimal. The differences in opportunity clearly affect the country's ability to compete and win in international competition.

It would be timely to repeat this study, but there is no reason to believe that the differences will have lessened. I now go on to consider how PE has been treated since 1960.

Phases of policy for youth sport in school and community

Collins (2011) identified three key phases in the development of policy in this area. These comprise:

- the Sports Council going solo: 1960s–1980s;
- the challenges of the 1990s;
- a double priority under New Labour: 1997–2010.

Table 1.1 sets out a chronology of major events in each period, on which I offer brief commentaries. Youth has been a constant policy priority, often to the exclusion of mature adults and older people who can derive health-related benefits at lower unit costs than their younger counterparts (Collins, 2010).

The Sports Council going solo: 1960s–1980s

PE has been a core subject in secondary schools since 1945, but it has often been looked down upon by teachers of academic subjects and administrators as 'not a serious subject' (Peters, 1966). Its resourcing is not cheap and, when public sports facilities were lacking, it made economic sense for communities and schools to share sites and equipment and to invest jointly (Department for Education (DfE), 1965). However, there was little or no contact between the DfE and the growing provision for sport by the Sports Council and local government before the 1990s – what Houlihan and White (2002: 63) called, first, 'disdain' and then, 'neglect'. In the meantime, PE continued with basic movement learning and then games-based teaching – almost a hangover from Edwardian muscular Christianity; then some suggested a wider range of activities to meet the growing demand for individual and countryside pursuits and, from the 1980s, others sought a fitness and health-related diet. Squabbles between various factions did not endear PE to the education mandarins and, despite PE bodies merging, such tensions rumble on behind the scenes.

School populations and budgets had shrunk; pupil profiling and other stewardship tasks squeezed the time of non-specialist teachers supporting school sport; the Labour Party niggled at the idea of competitive sport. School sports facilities needed improving, there was no proper talent identification method, and coaching was very amateur, but the Sports Council promoted the National Coaching Foundation (NCF) in 1993, and Sue Campbell became its Head. Sebastian (now Lord) Coe, who was vice-chair of the Sports Council 1986–1989, constantly complained that British elite athletes were badly underfunded compared to their competitors.

The challenges of the 1990s

The 1990s saw some real changes in youth sport policy. Prime Minister John Major was the first to back elite sport, with a new national strategy Raising the Game (Department of National Heritage (DNH), 1995); sports science and medicine support started to develop, and the new National Lottery provided what Coe had wanted: income support for individual athletes' training and support for their National Governing Body training programmes, in the Talented Athletes Scheme, leading in a few years to major improvements in medal-winning in several sports. The Lottery funded major provision at universities, which formed a distributed network of bases for the English Institute for Sport. The NCF – rebranded into Sports Coach UK in 2001 – developed an ambitious programme for a UK-wide professional structure (North, 2009),

Table 1.1 Major events for PE and youth sport in the UK (1960–2012)

The Sports Council going solo: 1960s–1980s

1960	Lord Wolfenden reported Britain lagging in facilities, support for elite; advisory Sports Council formed 1965; major progress in 1970s in sports halls, pools, golf courses through grant aid and advice to local authorities
1965	DfE *A Chance to Share* school facilities with communities
1983	National Coaching foundation formed, CEO Sue Campbell develops Champion Coaching to support PE teachers, coaches
1987	BBC Panorama documentary *Is Your Child Fit for Life?* provides early warning bell about 'couch potato' children – electronic games/computing give a growing threat to fitness (see Burrows and McCormack, 2012)
1988	Education Reform Act
1989	National Curriculum supposedly providing equal opportunities for all pupils; PE made a foundation subject 1991.

The challenges of the 1990s

1994	YST formed, with sponsorship then exchequer money for TOPs teacher programmes; *faute de mieux*, huge take-up
1995	DNH *Sport: Raising the Game*
1997	National Lottery provides new support for community and elite sport.

A double priority under New Labour: 1997–2008

1997	*Sporting Future for All* (DCMS, 2000) targets for 110 Specialist Sports Colleges (SSCs) to develop elite, 600 School Sport Coordinators (SSCos) to link to primaries, clubs
1999	Home Office, Sport England and others set up *Positive Futures* to help youth most at risk of crime/drugs in most deprived areas – successful in over 100 places, transferred to charity in 2009
2002	Minister's working party on coaching leads in 2004 to Sports Coach UK and a professionalisation strategy for coaching
2002	*Game Plan* (DCMS targets 1m new participants to be like Finland; New Labour committed to investment plan – *Building Schools for the Future*)
2003	*PE, School Sport and Club Links* policy promoted jointly by DCMS, DfE with target for 2 curricular hours, achieved ahead of time
2008	DCMS Secretary Andy Burnham launches new strategy document, *Playing to Win: A new era for sport*. Minister switches from 'Sport for (social) good' to 'Sport for sport's sake'; physical activity left to Department of Health; Sport England *Strategy 2008–11* decides to use NGBs and HEIs as delivery agents for delivering 700,000 participants
2009	Short-term legacy programmes for adult and youthful participants, volunteers developed in wake of award of London 2012.

Con-dem (nation)

2010	Coalition Secretary of State Michael Gove cuts BSF, threatens to cut PESSYP, Sports Colleges and other specialists abolished, switch to competitive sport
2011	DCMS Secretary Jeremy Hunt abandons 1 million participation target, but continues to threaten NGB grant cuts for non-delivery
2012	DCMS Secretary Jeremy Hunt launches first Coalition strategy document on sport, *Creating a Sporting Habit for Life: A new youth sport strategy*.

including specialist coaches for children; basic and increasing numbers of intermediate grade coaches were going into schools to support PE teachers. Sue Campbell identified a need for support for teachers of PE, including non-specialist primary teachers and, with patron Sir John Beckwith, started the Youth Sport Trust (YST) in 1994, which rapidly attracted funds and provided a wide suite of training, obtaining support from the Department for Education and Skills (DfES), DCMS and Sport England, despite some minor frictions. A Lottery programme, Space for Sport and the Arts, started to improve school facilities from 1999.

Houlihan and Green (2006) explained how multiple streams of interest (but not mainstream PE) changed policy around.

A double priority under New Labour: 1997–2010

In stark contrast to earlier periods, by 2000 there was a political/administrative/professional cluster of agencies supporting youth and school sport that made youth sport a 'crowded policy space' (Houlihan, 2000: 73). Sue Campbell advised both the education and sport ministries to develop a coordinated scheme, the PE, School Sport and Club Links Programme (PESSCL, DfES, 2003), to be delivered through secondary school sport coordinators, some in specialist Sports Colleges, working with their 'family' of primary feeders and linking with governing bodies, clubs and local authorities, and soon working at the next geographical scale through 49 Sport England-promoted County Sport Partnerships (Collins, 2010). New Labour decided that all secondary schools should be rebuilt in Building Schools for the Future, which sometimes included new sports provision. This totally changed the architecture of youth sport. GCSE and 'A' level PE developed fitness and sports science elements, which raised its status relative to 'academic' subjects, and grew in recruitment until 2009, and sports science, management and, lately, coaching and event management degrees proliferated. Step into Sport and other volunteering programmes developed.

In 2008 PESSCL was extended (Department for Children, Schools and Families (DCSF), 2008) to become the Physical Education, School Sport and Young People (PESSYP) strategy, with new strands for gifted and talented children. It seemed like the future was assured, but party political views can (and do) change rapidly. It was, therefore, both surprising and disappointing to the PE profession that, on non-substantiated evidence of excessive costs via County and School Sport Partnerships, new Coalition Secretary of State for Education, Michael Gove, should propose to cut all the programme as part of public sector shrinkage, relenting slightly after many protests including from (now) Baroness Campbell, to allow School Sport Coordinators to remain until May 2011, after which time individual schools had to decide whether to pay for them. This has left a patchwork quilt of provision full of local holes, even with the YST continuing to provide underpinning support. It remains to be seen whether or how well the sets of networks formed in this decade will survive (Houlihan and Lindsey, 2008). Scarcely credibly in this light, one right-wing think-tank (Centre for Social Justice (CSJ), 2011) suggested that sport should now come totally under the aegis of the DfE.

Elite sport continued to strengthen, with government and UK Sport support, in successfully bidding for major events, including the 2012 summer Olympics in London and 2014 Commonwealth Games in Glasgow. Despite concern about obesity and fitness, the links with health have been temporary and sporadic compared to many countries like Finland. The Chief Medical Officer (2004, 2011) did evidence the high social and economic cost of inactivity and made proposals for adult and child exercise regimes, though for both sport and physical activity there has never been a proper social marketing campaign powerful enough to attack the combination of sloth and gluttony that grips many citizens in a sedentary society (Collins, 2011). I now turn to contemporary events.

The Coalition and the short-term future

The Coalition government was a partnership of convenience to overcome the accumulated public debt and the effect of world-wide injudicious bank lending; but it cannot be said that the thinking is particularly well joined up: Why cut spending on higher education and research when the rest of the advanced world is not? Why cut the investment in school buildings so abruptly and unfairly? Why go back to competitive sport, when clearly sedentary youth and many girls are wholly disinterested in it? Other aspects affecting youth sport concern children's play, and gender equality.

Longitudinal research suggests that adequate provision for children's play is the basis of healthy, fulfilled growing up (Lester and Russell, 2008), but Coalition policies neglect such provision. Despite previously highlighting childrens' play as a major theme in their 2008 child policy review, once they were part of the Coalition the Conservatives abandoned the England Play Strategy and closed the related unit in the DfE, having already cut local Playbuilder grants. This was, moreover, despite evaluating the health and social net benefits of every staffed adventure playground at £2.8m, and of every after-school club staffed by qualified workers at £1.19m (Matrix Evaluation, 2010), and came over and above more general cuts in local government leisure spending, estimated at 30 per cent (Collins, 2012).

Under New Labour total childcare places had almost doubled in 2001–2005 to nearly 1.3m, especially in deprived areas, but both nursery and out-of-school club places started to decline in 2006 (Stewart, 2009), and this is likely to accelerate as poorer people's ability to pay reduces. The Coalition has also pondered cutting childcare allowances for some 250,000 part-time workers, many of whom would be forced to give up work and seek Income Support instead. So, these actions risk countermanding the intentions of local child poverty partnerships and of the Child Poverty Act 2010 (Nelson *et al.*,

2011); and the DCSF's (2008: 3) aspiration to make England 'the best place in the world to grow up' is certainly postponed.

Moving towards greater gender equality in PE and youth sport requires explicit support policies, women-friendly facilities and appointing role models, namely:

- national and international sports organisations to have explicit policies and plans to promote it, as in France (Ministry of Youth and Sport as part of a 2003 national policy *France, Committing to Equality between Men and Women*, with a national resource hub for sport at Aix-en-Provence) and a change in ideologies and attitudes;
- women-friendly facilities (Campbell, 1999) involving appropriate time and space programming for housewives, workers and retired women, crèches for parents and safe, private and encouraging settings for body-sensitive groups who doubt their competency; and
- appointing role-model women as leaders (like Sue Campbell and Dame Tanni Grey-Thompson, wheelchair Olympic athlete, as Chair of the Women's Sport and Fitness Foundation's (WSFF) Commission on the future of women's sport) is important.

As Deem (1986) noted, in the end this is a matter of empowerment: in the UK an international conference at Brighton backed by the IOC produced a declaration, *Women, Sport and the Challenge of Change* (Sports Council, 1994), soon after which the WSFF became a spearhead agency. But there are wider social issues affecting children regarding poverty and education.

Children and poverty

Save the Children (2011a) calculated that there was a 'poverty premium' of £1,280 a year for low-income families, arising from more expensive utilities, more expensive car and home contents insurance (from living in higher crime-risk areas) and not having access to bank overdrafts (because of not having bank accounts or a poor credit history and being driven to high-interest doorstep lenders, pawnbrokers or cheque-cashing agencies).

Moreover, Save the Children (2011b) also showed that still 13 per cent (1.6m) of the UK's children lived in severe poverty, rising to 14 per cent in Wales, 15 per cent in the West Midlands and over 24 per cent in Leicester, Newham, Westminster, Manchester and Tower Hamlets. Worklessness was the largest correlate (for 43 per cent of children, compared to 6 per cent where one parent worked), yet 680,000 severely poor children were in households with at least one low-paid worker. Other concentrations were: a quarter of children in single-parent households; a third in social housing; and 21 per cent in a household with a disabled adult. The charity expected increases after 2010 because of job losses, the freeze in child benefits and other welfare cuts. Moreover, these figures were confirmed by the Millennium Cohort study, showing a fifth of seven-year-olds in severe poverty (with household income of £254 a week, compared to the £563 UK average (Hansen, *et al.*, 2010)).

Local Futures (2009) found strong correlation with low child well-being and worklessness, and poorest overall scores in London, Birmingham, West Yorkshire/East Lancashire and the North East. Bradshaw (2011), a specialist in child poverty, characterised New Labour's policy as 'the right treatment but the dose inadequate', but saw the Coalition's package as overwhelmingly negative.

Children and education generally

The number of 16–24 year-olds Not in Education, Employment or Training (NEETS) hit a new high of 938,000 (15.6 per cent) in 2011. The government abolished Educational Maintenance Allowance of £10–30 a week per pupil, costing £560m and £36m per year to administer, with the Prime Minister expecting it to have little 'effect' despite evidence that its benefits outweighed its costs (Chowdry and Emmerson, 2010). Child poverty charities accused the government of failing a legal commitment in the Child Poverty Act to publish a strategy, whereas most local authorities had done so. All of this makes the context for children's work much tighter, with reduced human financial and organisational resources, and reduces hope for those children who need it most. It also cuts the likelihood of the UK climbing from its lowly place in the international ranking of childcare (UNICEF, 2008).

Flexibility in such times is important, and the YST provides an informative case study. The loss of PESSYP and its core government funding required the YST to reduce its staff and make major changes to funding, notably in bringing in corporate patrons/sponsors. It had already latched onto the NHS Change 4Life programme to fund out-of-school clubs, and the Department of Transport's Bikeability programme via School Sports Partnerships, and attracted the interest of retailers Matalan and Sainsburys. Lloyds TSB bank had been supporting county/national sports games and Sainsburys picked this up for 2012, together with major Lottery and Legacy funding; other programmes are supported by Sky Sports and the football Premier League. The YST still runs a range of ambitious programmes. Sadly, many local authorities and small companies do not have the status, track record, charismatic leadership or programmes of the YST for attracting hard-to-get sponsorship in a depressed financial market.

In 2002 Kirk's somewhat harsh judgment was that 'fifty years of sport-based PE is long enough an experiment ... and [we] must accept that [it] has failed spectacularly ... to meet its own goal of facilitating lifelong participation in physical activity' (Kirk, 2002: 5–6). The PESSCL/YP phase did counteract this, but it may be sinking back into a revised form of private-school-style, competition-led sport – a secular form of muscularity.

Youth sport, as a small policy sector, cannot but help reflect the pattern of society generally. Jarvie (2012: 59) agreed that in Britain the 'extremes of privilege and poverty remain sharply drawn'. Green *et al.* (2005: 27) surely overestimated things when saying 'it is apparent that sport and physical activity has become part of present-day youth cultures; once they leave school only the cocoon-wrapped and well-subsidised full-time higher education students do not show a substantial drop in participation'.

Conclusions

Taking Part 2010–11 (DCMS, 2011) clearly showed the deprivation gap – only 46.1 per cent taking part in sport including walking and cycling for recreation in the most deprived areas, compared to 59.6 per cent in the least deprived. So, despite its policy cluster, British youth sport, it seems, is in for a tough time: one of the sad likely outcomes of the growing social gap and the effects of any prolonged recession. The current situation echoes back from the Bukodi and Goldthorpe (2011) mobility study: their 1958 cohort went into a depressed job market and never achieved the increases in income or status of the other cohorts, and this could happen to our current young adults, on top of repaying higher student debts, working more years and having lower or more expensive pension provision. Once the spectacle and razzmatazz of London 2012 are over, maybe the elephant in the room and the moral panic about obesity will give the sector a new opening, certainly via its royal-Chartered Institute for the Management of Sport and Physical Activity. Otherwise, it will have to preserve the best and hold on.

References

Audit Commission (2009). *Tired of hanging around: Using sport and leisure activities to prevent anti-social activities by young people.* London: Audit Commission.

Azzarito, L. (2012). 'I've lost my football.' Rethinking gender, the hidden curriculum and sport in the global market, in Dagkas, S. and Armour, K. (eds) *Inclusion and exclusion through youth sport.* London: Routledge, pp. 73–86.

Bradshaw, J. (2011). *Child poverty in the UK.* Presentation to Scottish Assembly for Tackling Poverty, Glasgow, 17 February.

Bruner, M., Strachan, L. and Côté, J. (2011). Developmental transitions in sport in Stafford, I. (ed.) *Coaching children in sport.* London: Routledge, pp. 227–239.

Bukodi, E. and Goldthorpe, J. (2011). Class origins, education and occupational attainment in Britain: Secular trends or cohort effects? *European Societies* 13 (3): 347–376.

Burrows, L. and McCormack, J. (2012). Sporting fat: Youth sport and the 'obesity epidemic', in Dagkas, S. and Armour, K. (eds) *Inclusion and exclusion through youth sport.* London: Routledge, pp. 125–137.

Campbell, K. (1999). *Women-friendly sports facilities.* Facilities Factfile 1, Recreation Management. London: Sports Council.

Centre for Social Justice (CSJ) (2011). *More than a game.* London: CSJ.

Chief Medical Officer (2004). *At least five a week: Evidence of the impact of physical activity and its relationship to health.* London: HMSO.

——(2011) *Start active, stay active: A report on physical activity for health from the home countries Chief Medical Officers.* London: HMSO.

Chowdry, H. and Emmerson, C. (2010). *An efficient maintenance allowance?* London: Institute of Fiscal Studies

Coalter, F. (2007). *A wider social role for sport? Who's keeping the score?* London: Routledge.

Collins, M.F. (2003). *Sport and social exclusion.* London: Routledge.

——(2010). The development of sports development, in Collins, M.F. (ed.) *Examining sports development.* London: Routledge, pp. 14–42.

——(2011). Leisure cards in England – an unusual combination of commercial and social marketing? *Social Marketing Quarterly* 17 (2): 20–47.

——(2013). 2nd edn (forthcoming). *Sport and social exclusion.* Routledge: London.

Côté, J., Coakley, C. and Bruner, M. (2012). Children's talent development in sport: Effectiveness or efficiency?, in Dagkas, S. and Armour, K. (eds) *Inclusion and exclusion through youth sport.* London: Routledge, pp. 172–185.

Dagkas, S. and Benn, T. (2012). The embodiment of religious culture and exclusionary practices in youth sport, in Dagkas, S. and Armour, K. (eds) *Inclusion and exclusion through youth sport.* London: Routledge, pp. 113–125.

De Bosscher, V., Bingham, J., Shibli, S., van Bottenburg, M. and De Knop, P. (2008). *The global sporting arms race: An international study on sports factors leading to international sporting success.* Oxford: Meyer and Meyer Sport.

Deem, R. (1986). *All work and no play. The sociology of women and leisure.* Milton Keynes: Open University Press.

Department for Children, Schools and Families (DCSF) (2008). *PESSYP: Creating a world class system for PE and Sport.* London: DCSF.

Department for Culture, Media and Sport (DCMS) (2000). *A Sporting Future for All.* London: DCMS.

Department for Culture, Media and Sport (DCMS) (2008a). *Creating a Sporting Habit for Life: A new youth sport strategy.* London: DCMS.

Department for Culture, Media and Sport (DCMS) (2008b). *Playing to Win: A new era for sport.* London: DCMS.

Department for Culture, Media and Sport (DCMS) (2002). *Game plan: A strategy for delivering the government's sport and physical activity objectives.* London: DCMS.

——(2011). *The cultural and sporting life: The Taking Part 2010–11 Adult and Child report.* London: DCMS.

Department for Education (DfE) (1965). *A chance to share.* London: DfE.

Department for Education and Skills (DfES) (2003). *Learning through PE and sport: A guide to the PESSCL strategy.* London: DFES.

Department of National Heritage (DNH) (1995). *Sport: Raising the game.* London: DNH.

Dismore, H. (2007). The attitudes of children and young people towards PE and youth sport, with particular reference to transition from Key Stage 2 to Key Stage 3. Unpublished PhD. Christ Church Canterbury University.

Downward, P. and Rasciute, S. (2012). Sport and social exclusion: An economic perspective, in Dagkas, S. and Armour, K. (eds) *Inclusion and exclusion through youth sport.* London: Routledge, pp. 44–56.

English Sports Council (ESC) (1998). *The development of sporting talent.* London: ESC.

Farooq, S. and Parker, A. (2009). Sport, physical education and Islam: Muslim independent schooling and the social construction of masculinities. *Sociology of Sport Journal* 26 (2): 277–295.

Flintoff, A. (2008). *Black and ethnic minority trainees' experiences of PE initial teacher training.* Report to Training and Development Agency. Leeds: Leeds Metropolitan University.

Goodwin, D. and Peers, D. (2012). Disability, sport and inclusion, in Dagkas, S. and Armour, K. (eds) *Inclusion and exclusion through youth sport.* London: Routledge, pp. 186–202.

Green, K., Smith, A. and Roberts, K. (2005). Young people and lifelong participation in sport and physical activity: A sociological perspective on contemporary PE programmes in England and Wales. *Leisure Studies* 24 (1): 27–43.

Hansen, K., Jones, E., Joshi, H., and Budge, D. (eds) (2010). *Millennium Cohort Study 4th Survey: Users guide to initial findings.* London: Centre for Longitudinal Studies.

Hay, P.J. (2012). Ability as an exclusionary concept in youth sport, in Dagkas, S. and Armour, K. (eds) *Inclusion and exclusion through youth sport.* London: Routledge, pp. 87–99.

Henry, I. and Robinson, L. (eds) (2010). *Gender equality and leadership in Olympic bodies.* Loughborough: Institute of Sport and Leisure Policy.

Houlihan, B. (2000). Sporting excellence, school and sports development: The politics of crowded policy spaces. *European Physical Education Review* 6: 73–92.

Houlihan, B. and Green, M. (2006). The changing status of school sport and PE: Explaining policy change. *Sport, Education and Society* 11 (1): 3–92.

Houlihan, B. and Lindsey, I. (2008). Networks and partnerships in sports development, in Girginov, V. (ed.) *Management of sports development.* Oxford: Butterworth-Heinemann, pp. 225–242.

Houlihan, B. and White, A. (2002). *The Politics of Sports Development.* London: Routledge.

Jarvie, G. (2012). Sport, social divisions and social inequality, in Dagkas, S. and Armour, K. (eds) *Inclusion and exclusion through youth sport.* London: Routledge, pp. 57–71.

Jawad, H., Benn, T., and Dagkas, S. (2012). Facilitating positive experiences of PE and school sport for Muslim girls, in Dagkas, S. and Armour, K. (eds) *Inclusion and exclusion through youth sport.* London: Routledge, pp. 203–17.

Kirk, D. (2002). *Quality PE through partnerships. A response to Karel J. van Deventer.* Paper to 12th Commonwealth International Sport conference, Manchester, July.

Lester, S. and Russell, W. (2008). *Play for a change: Play, policy and practice – A review of contemporary perspectives.* London: National Children's Bureau.

Macdonald, D., Pang, B., Knez, K., Nelson, A. and McCuaig, L. (2012). The will for inclusion: Bothering the inclusion/exclusion discourses, in Dagkas, S. and Armour, K. (eds) *Inclusion and exclusion through youth sport.* London: Routledge, pp. 9–23.

Matrix Evaluation (2010). *An economic evaluation of play provision.* London: Play England.

Nelson, J., O'Donnell, L. and Filmer-Sankey, C. (2011). *Local authority progress in tackling child poverty.* Slough: National Foundation for Educational Research.

Nichols, G. (2007). *Sport and crime reduction: The role of sports in tackling youth crime.* London: Routledge.

North, J. (2009). *The Coaching workforce 2009–16.* Leeds: Sports Coach UK.

Ottesen, L., Skirstad, B., Pfister, G. and Habermann, U. (2010). Gender relations in Scandinavian sports organizations: A comparison of the structures and policies in Denmark, Norway and Sweden. *Sport in Society* 13 (4): 657–675.

Peters, R. S. (1966). *Ethics in education.* London: Allen & Unwin.

Rowe, N., Adams, R., and Beasley, N. (2004). Driving up participation in sport: The social context, the trends, the prospects and the challenges, in *Driving up participation in sport*. London: Sport England, pp. 4–11.

Save the Children (2011a). *The UK poverty rip-off: The poverty premium 2010*. London: Save the Children.

——(2011b). *Severe child poverty: Nationally and locally*. London: Save the Children.

Spaaij, R. (2011). *Sport and social mobility: Crossing boundaries*. London: Routledge.

Sport England (2000). *Young people and sport in England, 1999*. London: MORI, for Sport England.

——(2001). *Young people with a disability and sport: Headline findings*. London: Sport England.

——(2008). *Grow sustain excel: A strategy for 2008–11*. London: Sport England.

Sports Coach UK (2008). *The UK coaching framework*. Leeds: Sports Coach UK.

Sports Council (1994). *Women, sport and the challenge of change*. London: Sports Council.

Stewart, K. (2009). 'A scar on the soul of Britain': Child poverty and disadvantage under New Labour, in Hills, J., Sefton, T. and Stewart, K. (eds) *Towards a more equal society? Poverty inequality and policy since 1997*. Bristol: Policy Press, pp. 47–69.

Thomas, N. and Smith, A. (2009). *Disability, sport and society*. London: Routledge.

UNICEF (2008). *Child poverty in perspective: An overview of child well-being in rich countries*. Report Card 7. Florence: Innocenti Centre.

Wellard, I. (2012). Sexuality and youth sport, in Dagkas, S. and Armour, K. (eds) *Inclusion and exclusion through youth sport*. London: Routledge, pp. 100–112.

Wilkinson, R. and Pickett, K. (2009). *The spirit level: Why more equal societies almost always do better*. London: Allen Lane.

Wolfenden, J. (Sir, later Lord) (1960). *Sport and the community*. London: Central Council for Physical Recreation.

2 Sport, physical activity and play: A European perspective

Nic Matthews

Introduction

The Treaty on European Union (1992) established the political and social prerequisites for an economic union across Europe. Subsequent Treaties and Declarations between 1997 and 2009 have resulted in a developing dialogue between representatives of the European Union (EU), sporting bodies and others interested in provision for physical activity (PA) and play. The lobbying of EU institutions in the late 1990s by some sporting organisations focused on seeking the addition of sport as one of the EU's areas of responsibility and debating the implications of having a European perspective on sport. This chapter examines the nature of that debate and considers how a European dimension has come to exist in sport and cognate fields of policy.

The idea of Europeanisation: towards a European union

Decisions made in Brussels have provided many tabloid headlines in recent years, but the reality of what the EU does and what it represents can appear remote from the lives of European citizens. The metaphorical distance between those governing the EU and the 502.4 million people who reside within its geographical boundaries is epitomised by concerns over the mechanisms through which the Union operates. The European Commission is often criticised for being an anonymous bureaucracy responsible for the policy and legislative agenda for the EU despite being headed up by 27 unelected Commissioners. The European Parliament has only been an elected institution since 1979 and critics question the value for money provided by an institution that sits in two countries (Belgium and France), suggesting this commuting of the machinery of European governance symbolises the financial burden, rather than the added value, of being a Member State. Furthermore, crises in the Eurozone highlight the challenges of reconciling differences in the economies of the member countries. These discussion points are amongst many which illustrate why the idea of a European union divides political and public opinion.

In an era of global social networks, multinational corporations and international financial and political institutions, the pro-European lobby argue that the EU represents a necessary 'regional' bloc that protects the collective interests of (part of) Europe. For those opposed to supranational co-operation, any iteration of a European union is indicative of an encroachment on the autonomy and sovereignty of Member States. By unpacking the EU's founding principles, its political objectives and its policy intentions, it is possible to see how and why this model of supranational governance provokes so much interest and debate.

The areas of sport, physical activity and play offer insight into some of the challenges and opportunities presented by EU-level action. All are recognised in some way outside the EU. Examples include the Council of Europe's European Sports Charter 1992, revised in 2001 (Council of Europe, 2011); the Toronto Charter for Physical Activity (GAPA, 2010); and the United Nations Convention on the Rights of the Child (United Nations, 1989). This suggests that sport, PA and play have an importance which resonates with individuals and organisations on a global scale. However, despite such global appeal, difficulties emerge when attempts are made to develop policies to harmonise practices across borders. Sport is often viewed as the epitome of a national activity; it is relatively easy, for example, to find associations between sports and national identity (Bairner, 2007; Jarvie, 2003). Furthermore, international competition engenders European sporting rivalry rather than encouraging co-operation (Brown, 2000; Maguire and Poulton, 1999). The British Olympic Association's announcement on 21 June 2011 regarding the 'historic agreement' reached on a 'Team GB' Football team for the 2012 Olympic Games is a case in point (BBC, 2011; BOA, 2011). It is against this backdrop that the institutions of the EU are developing policies. To explain the Europeanisation of sports, PA and play-related issues it is necessary to examine the idea of a European 'project'. To this end, this chapter will: (i) outline what 'Europeanisation' is; (ii) chart the expansion of the EU; and (iii) examine how these developments translate into European perspectives on the aforementioned domains.

The principles of Europeanisation

Europeanisation refers to the links between governmental and non-governmental agencies at the supranational level (Featherstone, 2003). It is characterised by the 'deepening' and 'widening' of competences (responsibilities) at the level of the EU. The former represents greater levels of interdependency between Member States (i.e. more joint decisions); the latter suggests a broadening of the areas covered by supranational agreements (i.e. co-operation across more areas of policy). This means that Member States are less able to separate national interests from those of the Union, which means a greater role for EU institutions in defining the policy environment.

Europeanisation is typified by: the elevation of some powers to supranational institutions (i.e. the European Commission); some devolving of responsibilities to regional authorities (i.e. the *Länder* in Germany or the *Comunidades Autonoma* in Spain); a subsequent 'hollowing out' of the responsibilities of the nation state; and increases in direct communication between sub-national and supranational bodies. This adds to the complexity of governance, as lobbyists can align to groups traversing national boundaries. For example, it could be argued that rural communities across the EU might have a shared understanding of how best to facilitate their economic development. Parallels can be drawn with professional communities (i.e. play-workers, or health promotion specialists). Individuals in these networks are likely to gain as much from connections across borders as they are from links across professional groupings within their national contexts.

Whilst supranational co-operation was not intended to impact on sport, PA or play, these sectors have been influenced by European-level action. The institutions of the EU have come particularly to recognise the political, economic and socio-cultural importance of sport. The areas of PA and play are less well developed at the European level but they are also recognised as warranting action. When explaining the relationship between the EU and these fields, consideration needs to be given to the extent to which each area is impacted upon by the competences of the EU. To address this point, it is important to appreciate the drivers for a European union.

The development of a European community

The origins of the current EU are rooted in the aftermath of the Second World War and the subsequent dialogue between political leaders, but the original European Economic Communities, founded between 1951 and 1957, were not just a reaction to the devastation witnessed across Europe at that time. The Communities were merely the most contemporary interpretations of a European 'project' which was conceived in the thirteenth century, with the term 'Europe' then coming into use during the fourteenth century. Each project has been defined by three characteristics: (i) free trade; (ii) Europe-wide political representation; and (iii) associated rights of citizenship. Where each model differed was in relation to what was to constitute the political system and to whom the citizens would have allegiance. Post-1945 a united Europe has come to embody the aspiration (for some) of a continent unified by a single economic system and one parliamentary body.

Progress towards such a model of European relations has not been straightforward nor always welcomed. However, there is evidence of a maturing European project with more competences being gained. This reflects the promotion of responsibilities to the supranational level which occurs when countries seek collective action and common terms of reference. There have been eight Acts or Treaties which have defined the scope of European-level policy. In 1951 six countries (the Benelux countries, Italy, France and Germany) signed the Treaty of Paris creating the European Coal and Steel Community (ECSC). The Treaties of Rome (1957) formed the European Economic Community (EEC), creating the framework for economic co-operation and reducing trade barriers between countries through a Common Market.

An increase in competences has been achieved with successive Treaties, illustrating the 'widening' and 'deepening' of European interdependencies.

The Single European Act (1986) included measures that facilitated the completion of an internal market and provision for common foreign and security policy. The Treaty of European Union (1992 – The Maastricht Treaty) signified a key phase of integration, introducing European citizenship, co-operation in justice and home affairs, and articulating the goal of a social dimension to the Community. The Treaties of Amsterdam (1997), Nice (2001) and Lisbon (2009) have all sought to make the Union more efficient by reforming its mechanisms of governance.

The membership of the EEC has also grown, initially from six to nine countries in the 1970s when the UK, Ireland and Denmark joined. It expanded again during the 1980s when Greece, Spain and Portugal also gained membership. During the 1990s Austria, Finland and Sweden joined and a significant fourth wave of enlargement took place in 2004 when ten countries from Central and Eastern Europe gained entry. For the pro-European lobby this geographical expansion of the EU and the range of competences acquired offers opportunities to promote Europe-wide interests. For those opposed to the transfer of powers to the supranational level, it symbolises the erosion of the political, legal and economic autonomy of nation states. These polarised views on the EU are important to its progress as it is overseen by the 'checks and balances' offered by the sceptics and pro-integrationists. It is also these shifts in legal, economic, political and social 'borders' which have laid the foundations for European involvement in sport and related fields.

The social dimension of the European Union

In light of the hostilities that characterised early twentieth-century European history, advocates of a union were sensitive to the need for the continent's future to be founded on tolerance. They wanted to foster an understanding of diversity in order to promote continent-wide security and prosperity. The principle of promoting diversity is important, as the case for a role for European institutions in areas such as sport, PA and play is founded on the idea that European citizens share a social history and that these activities form part of that heritage.

What has provoked debate amongst those operating in sport and other sectors is the extent to which EU competences should be reflected in the rules that govern their activities. Equally, there are discussions regarding the gains to be made from recognition at a supranational level. For example, increasingly there are budgets for social and cultural programmes (i.e. *Eurathlon*, a sports programme started in 1994 and the European Capital of Culture programme, introduced in 1985). Ultimately, the sustainability of the EU depends on the will of politicians and the engagement of citizens. Sporting and other cultural events and interventions are one means of promoting the value of European integration.

The importance of preserving cultural diversity within the Union was given recognition in 1992, when The Maastricht Treaty included an Article on

Culture (Article 128). Subsequently, the Union has encouraged the audio-visual industries and promoted awareness of European history through programmes such as *MEDIA*, *Kaleidoscope* and *Culture*; however, these programmes have retained a narrow interpretation of 'culture'. The focus on film, broadcasting and the arts was justifiable but perhaps a missed opportunity to recognise sport and other activities. Despite this, policy 'space' has been created for areas such as sport, PA and play.

The European Union, sport, PA and play

Encapsulating the character of the EU and articulating the reach of its powers is a challenge. However, it is important to recognise the dynamics which drive its existence. The European project started by six founding Member States and confined to coal and steel is now a sophisticated bureaucracy of 27 Member States, five Candidate Countries and four Potential Candidate Countries. It is inevitable that, as the institutions at the EU level have grown in prominence, so more domains are drawn into their policy-making remit.

A number of rationales can be used to justify European-level interventions in sport, PA and play. First, there are policy drivers that reflect the need to ensure that these activities are managed in line with the principles of the Single European Market (these relate largely to the 'four freedoms': the freedom of goods, services, people and capital). In each of these instances the case is made that all activities undertaken within the Union should take place in line with EU Regulations and Directives (Parrish and McArdle, 2004), the argument being that all such activities should be treated equally in accordance with these agreed terms of 'membership' – done in part through harmonisation. Harmonisation recognises that whilst standardisation across 27 countries is impossible, it should be possible to set out requirements which Member States can accommodate within legislation or frameworks for provision (i.e. mutual recognition of qualifications to facilitate free movement).

The second set of rationales are characterised by the desire of pro-Europeans to create a social dimension to what is fundamentally an economic and political union. Interpreting the Union only within the terms of the Articles of the Treaties fails to recognise the complexity of European life and the ways in which some activities exist outside the market. Whilst it is appropriate to view issues associated with professional athletes, ticketing and sports merchandising as operating within markets, it is also reasonable to argue that grass-roots participation, volunteering and community programmes characterise the experience of many.

Sport: a European perspective

Sports provision, in particular, highlights the tensions between the economic agenda of the EU and the aspiration for a socio-cultural dimension to integration. Parrish (2003) argues that the EU sports policy sub-system involves two advocacy coalitions. Those with an interest in the application of the regulatory principles of the Single Market to sport comprise one grouping and the advocates of a socio-cultural Europe comprise the other. The efforts of both coalitions resulted in the Commission's *White Paper on Sport* (European Commission, 2007a). The 'Foreword' to this Paper suggests that it is the first document of its kind to address sports-related issues at the EU level. Of course, by the time of its publication such a statement was long overdue, given that the Treaties had always had the potential to influence sporting matters.

The relationship between sport and politics is well rehearsed (Green, 2004; Henry, 2001); however, sports bodies have enjoyed significant freedom to self-regulate. Such autonomy has resulted in governing bodies devising rules that control areas such as ticketing, the sale of broadcasting rights and transfer markets. These idiosyncrasies went largely uncontested in national contexts, but the development of a European economic space and efforts to harmonise practices across borders highlighted disparities between sporting regulations and European legislation. The extent of market activity associated with sport has therefore led to a reassessment of what it means to have a European perspective on such activities and how this should be represented in sporting practices.

The tensions between the 'four freedoms' and the governance of European sport was epitomised by a ruling of the European Court of Justice (ECJ) in 1995. The Belgian footballer Jean-Marc Bosman challenged the way that the Union of European Football Associations (UEFA) set up its international transfer system and applied nationality restrictions to the composition of club sides. Bosman asserted that UEFA's regulations limited players' freedom of movement, restricting their personal and professional rights as European citizens. In response UEFA argued for the 'special character' of sport and how it must be protected against being reduced to an economic activity. Talent identification, youth development and the longer term interests of football were the cornerstone of UEFA's counter-argument, with weight given to the socio-cultural significance of sport. Parrish (2003) describes the decision of the ECJ to rule in favour of Bosman as 'seismic' in terms of its wider implications, and there have been knock-on effects across a range of sports, with subsequent challenges to player restriction in, for example, handball (Kolpak), basketball (Malaja) and football (Balog) and further debate in other sports, such as cricket (Boyes, 2005).

The market for sports broadcasting rights has also seen changes as result of European-level intervention. Whilst the ECJ ruling placed the institutions of the EU in conflict with their sporting counterparts, the Commission has recognised the cultural value of sport, as illustrated by the 1997 revision of the *Television without Frontiers Directive* (EEC 1989). The Directive included measures associated with the audio-visual industries, amongst which were provisions to control the sale of sports rights. In revisiting the Directive, the EU institutions were reassessing the balance between two of the Union's key interests: market liberalism and the fostering of cultural diversity. As part of the consultation on the revisions a European Parliament report (*The Future of Public Sector Television in a Multi-Channel Digital Age*) argued for retaining restrictions to the number of major events offered on the free market (Tongue, 1996). The report argued that major sporting events were part of the EU's common cultural heritage. It is perhaps somewhat ironic, therefore, that this recognition of the social significance of sport in Europe was not welcomed by sporting bodies.

These events stimulated the European sports movement to review its own procedures for distributing rights. In the UK the Central Council for Physical Recreation (now the Sport and Recreation Alliance) issued a Voluntary Code of Conduct (CCPR, 1996), which was reviewed again in 2010. The original Code covered the sale of sports rights for 11 governing bodies, including the Football Association, the Lawn Tennis Association and the R&A (Royal and Ancient Golf Club). It did not stipulate how sports rights were to be divided between terrestrial and non-terrestrial broadcasters, nor did it list events. The onus was on the National Governing Bodies (NGBs) to assess what was in their interests: financial gain or broadest coverage. NGBs wanted the freedom to sell broadcasting rights in order to secure funds to invest in the development of their sport. For the federations the success of the European Parliament's submission on the revision of the Directive, which led to the protection of terrestrial broadcasting access to major sporting events, was an unwelcome challenge to their autonomy.

Whilst these examples differ in their focus the sense of an uneasy relationship between supranational political institutions and sporting organisations is evident. The potential for benefits to be accrued as a result of EU interest in sporting matters is also apparent. The wholesale elevation of sport-specific policy-making powers to the level of the EU, in the form of a competence for sport, has not happened; rather, there are a range of rationales originating from other EU competences (see Henry and Matthews, 1998). These include: sport as trade and as an economic activity; sport as a vehicle for urban and regional development (see Matthews and Henry, 2001); sport as a means of addressing social exclusion (i.e. *Eurathlon* and *Youth for Europe*); sport as an ideological tool (i.e. promoting the work of the Union itself); and sport as part of EU development aid programmes.

Until the mid-1990s this approach appeared sufficient for the Commission's purpose; however, decisions like the Bosman ruling suggested that a new approach to European sporting matters was necessary. Sports administrators began to question whether the existing arrangements offered effective mechanisms through which they might lobby their EU counterparts. The Treaty on European Union (1992) introduced Article 128 on culture and also recognised a role for the EU in tourism, and yet there was no evident move to provide a mandate for action in the field of sport. However, since then there have been two annexes to European Treaties which have gone some way to acknowledging sport formally. The Declaration on Sport added to the

Treaty of Amsterdam (1997) recognised the non-economic aspects of sport and the Nice Declaration (2000) set out that the EU institutions would check that their decisions and policies were 'sport-friendly' (European Commission, 2010a). Furthermore, in 2008 the European Council issued a Declaration recognising 'the importance of the values attached to sport, which are essential to European society', stressing the 'specific characteristics of sport, over and above its economic dimension' (The Council of the European Union, 2008: 21). However, in these instances the outcomes were not legally binding.

The Declarations were then supplemented by sport's inclusion in Article 165 of the Lisbon Reform Treaty (2009). Aquilina and Henry (2010) describe this as a 'soft' competence under Title XII – Education, Vocational Training, Youth and Sport. The wording suggested that the Union shall 'develop the European dimension in sport, by promoting fairness and openness in sporting competitions and co-operation between bodies responsible for sports, and by protecting the physical and moral integrity of sportsmen and sportswomen, especially the youngest sportsmen and sportswomen' (European Commission, 2010b, online). This language reflects aspects of sport's character, though not offering explicit grounds for action.

The Commission and the Parliament have also increased their policy and communication outputs. Parrish (2001) highlights the Parliament's role in critiquing the persistence of the Commission in adopting a regulatory approach to sport. In response the Commission might draw attention to its social programmes and initiatives: for example, the 2004 *European Year of Education through Sport*. This initiative promoted the educational merits of participation in sport (i.e. fair play, teamwork and tolerance), the contribution that volunteering might make to young people's informal education and the need to recognise the challenges of educating young athletes involved in competitive sport (European Commission, 2005). The initiative was the forerunner to the *European Year of Volunteering* (European Commission, 2011b), which also considered the contribution that sports volunteers make to communities.

Bringing these events full circle, the White Paper (European Commission, 2007) represented the culmination of years of dialogue as politicians, administrators and athletes grappled with the challenge of applying European law to sport whilst recognising its social dimension. The latest Communication adopted by the Commission, entitled, *Developing the European Dimension in Sport* (18 January 2011), is the first statement since the Lisbon Reform Treaty and aims to 'encourage debate among stakeholders, address challenges in sport and help the sector develop' (European Commission, 2011a, online). However, the Communication also reinforces the principle that the role of the EU is to 'support, co-ordinate and supplement sport policy measures taken by Member States' (European Commission, 2011c, online). The basis of the *EU Sports Programme 2014–2020* will therefore still be to mediate between the regulatory and the developmental interests of sports bodies (European Commission, 2010c).

Physical activity: a European perspective

The pro-integration lobby highlight the value of collective action where interests transcend national borders. Lower birth rates, an ageing population and a need to address health issues related to unhealthy lifestyles are global issues and the EU recognises its role in responding to these challenges (Europa, 2008). The European Commission White Paper, *Together for Health: A Strategic Approach for the EU 2008–2013* (European Commission, 2007b) and the *European Year for Active Ageing* (European Commission, 2012) are indicative of the Commission's efforts to address these issues. Recent World Health Organization figures suggest that chronic non-communicable diseases accounted for 86 per cent of all deaths in the European Region, one of the causal factors behind this figure being the lack of physical activity (EPHA, 2011); only 29 per cent of the EU population is sufficiently active to meet the recommendations of current guidelines (EUPHIX, 2009). Alongside the EU's health strategies there are also efforts to bring together organisations with an interest in health matters. For example, the EU Platform on Diet, Physical Activity and Health includes groups representing the food industry, consumers, advertisers and the fitness sector.

The health imperative makes a European perspective on PA understandable and (perhaps) more palatable for interested national parties. Whilst the documentation from the Commission and other networks reflects the tenor of the publications on sport (i.e. citing the benefits of participation), there is less obvious tension between the aspirations of the Member States and the EU. There is consensus on the extent of the health problems caused by inactivity and there are sufficient data on activity levels to monitor trends in participation. The EU argues that national and local government, the health and education sectors, and sport and PA providers are amongst those groups that should ensure that policies to promote accessible PA are developed, reflecting the necessity for collective action (European Commission, 2008).

An EU Working Group, Sport and Health, was given a mandate in 2006 to prepare guidance on PA levels. In keeping with work in sport, this Group met informally as there is no treaty-base for such work. The trigger was five European Council Resolutions between 2002 and 2006 which called for EU-level action to combat obesity, through nutrition and PA (European Commission, 2008). Whilst PA experts were appointed to the Working Group, it is telling that the title included reference to sport. It is also the case that PA and sport are both seen to be capable of enhancing the social dimension of the EU and contributing to other policy objectives. The *Pierre de Coubertin Action Plan* is a case in point. The Plan accompanied the *White Paper on Sport* (European Commission, 2007) and endorsed the role that sport and PA could play in improving public health. In order to deliver on this, however, it is important that the EU brings together expertise which can enhance national approaches to PA policy.

There is evidence that, since the 1990s, some progress has been made in this area, but the current policy agenda for sport and PA requires this to be sustainable in the longer term. The *European Network for the Promotion of Health-Enhancing Physical Activity* was funded by the EU in 1996–2001, but further funding was not secured. Subsequently the *European Network for the Promotion of Health-enhancing Physical Activity* (HEPA Europe) was founded in 2005. This network extends beyond the EU and seeks to disseminate information on evidence-based policies and strategies designed to 'improve the conditions favourable to healthy lifestyle' (Martin *et al.*, 2006: 53). Whilst this network is advantageous to the promotion of PA, the Sport and Health Working Group also made recommendations for an EU HEPA Network. It was suggested that this should not supplant existing co-ordinated activity in this area, but rather that it should identify ways to develop a series of common goals; however, the reality of co-existing networks may not match this hope. Again, longer-term sustainability needs to be the central focus.

Play: a European perspective

In line with sport and PA, play also attracts international interest. The *United Nations Convention on the Rights of the Child* (UNCRC) (UN, 1989) sets out a range of rights for every child and is seen as a 'universally agreed set of non-negotiable standards and obligations' (UNICEF, 2011, online). Although being a signatory is not a guarantee of a country's adherence to the Convention, those countries which have signed up are stating an intent to protect those rights. Play is covered under Article 31 (leisure, play and culture), which states that children have the right to rest and play and engage in a variety of recreational activities, as deemed appropriate to the age of the child. In 2004 *Sport, Recreation and Play* encouraged governments to develop 'comprehensive strategies to ensure that the right of every child to play is realised' (UNICEF, 2004: 5). Furthermore, the International Play Association has campaigned for the publication of a General Comment on Article 31, these materials offer guidance to State Parties on particular themes within the Convention. To this end, a Working Paper was commissioned to demonstrate the worldwide salience of play to children's lives (see Lester and Russell, 2010).

Its global reach means that the UNCRC supersedes any EU measures. Indeed, the institutions of the EU have no competence for children and young people, whilst it is acknowledged that they will be implicated in EU Regulations and Directives. Therefore much of the EU work regarding young people centres on supporting the activities of Member States on issues such as: immigration; education; media; and well-being, alongside children's rights. Play is rarely articulated explicitly in EU activity. By way of illustrating the minimal role of the institutions of the EU in this respect, it is worth setting out its approach to a specific area of policy: broadcasting. This in keeping with previous discussions on the balance between the economic and the social dimensions of the Union.

The *Television without Frontiers Directive* (EEC, 1989), which had implications for the sale of sports broadcasting rights, also had a role to play in defining aspects of policy which affect children and young people. This Directive was superseded by the *Audiovisual Media Services Directive* (2007), which included a number of provisions concerning children and young people (e.g. stricter advertising rules on unhealthy foods and measures to protect children from adult content). The amendments in the Directive resulted from the EU Communication *Towards an EU Strategy on the Rights of the Child* (European Commission, 2006), which also established a European Forum for the Rights of the Child. The issues identified by the Commission were diverse and inclusive of: education, initiatives for immigrant children, human trafficking, digital technologies (internet and gaming), sex tourism, health (obesity, drug abuse and smoking, in addition to PA) and violence against children. This work has been developed into *An EU Agenda for the Rights of the Child* which reiterates that EU policies are guided by the UNCRC, which reaffirms the EU's commitment to 'promoting, protecting and fulfilling' the rights of the child (European Commission, 2011c: 3). Again, the focus here is on the development of a broad set of rights, rather than addressing explicitly the role of play in children's lives.

Conclusions: final thoughts on a European perspective

The EU has changed the interdependencies between the Member States; altered the dynamics between quangos and governing bodies; conferred new rights and freedoms on citizens; and changed the way in which policy agendas are framed. In sport this has manifested itself through the contesting of NGB regulations, a recognition that there are characteristics of sport that do warrant protection at the European level and increasing budget lines for sporting initiatives when it is deemed that the nature of the issue 'exceeds the capacity of action of each individual Member State' (European Commission, 2010c: 3). The health imperative underpinning PA initiatives exemplifies the necessity and benefits of collective action where there are common challenges. Equally, access to play can be promoted as part of a package of measures to enhance and protect the rights of young Europeans. Whilst sceptics debate the merits of EU membership, the pro-Europeans would highlight such gains as evidence of the value of taking a European perspective.

References

Aquilina, D. and Henry, I. (2010). Elite athletes and university education in Europe: A review of policy and practice in higher education in the European Union Member States, *International Journal of Sport Policy*, Vol. 2 (1), pp. 25–47.

Bairner, A. (2007). From Sands to Sanchez: The making of a national sports stadium for Northern Ireland, *Entertainment and Sport Law Journal*, Vol. 5 (1), available from http://go.warwick.ac.uk/eslj/issues/volume5/number1/bairner, accessed 5 April 2012.

BBC (2011). *Team GB Olympic football deal angers nations*, available from http://news.bbc.co.uk/sport1/hi/front_page/13854492.stm, accessed 1 August 2011.

BOA (2011). *Historic agreement reached to enable Team GB to return to the Olympic football pitch*, available from www.olympics.org.uk/News/4399a4-historic-agreement-reached-to-enable-team-gb-to-return-to-the-olympic-football-pitch, accessed 1 August 2011.

Boyes, S. (2005). Caught behind or following on? Cricket, the European Union and the 'Bosman effect', *Entertainment and Sport Law Journal*, Vol. 3 (1), available from http://go.warwick.ac.uk/eslj/issues/volume3/number1/bairner, accessed 5 April 2012.

Brown, A. (2000). European football and the European Union: Governance, participation and social cohesion – towards a policy research agenda, *Soccer and Society*, Vol. 1 (2), pp. 129–150.

CCPR (1996). *Saving the game: The benefits to sport of a free market for the sale of television rights*, London, CCPR.

Council of Europe (2011). *European sports charter*, available from www.coe.int/t/dg4/sport/sportineurope/charter_en.asp, accessed 30 July 2011.

Council of the European Union (2008). *Brussels European Council 11 and 12 December 2008: Presidency conclusions*, available from http://ec.europa.eu/sport/information-center/doc/timeline/european_council_12-12-2008_conclusions_en.pdf, accessed 1 August 2011.

EEC (1989). *Council Directive 89/552/EEC Television without Frontiers*, Brussels, EC.

EPHA (European Public Health Alliance) (2011). *WHO global recommendations on physical activity for health*, available from www.epha.org/a/4340, accessed 1 August 2011.

EUPHIX (2009). *Physical activity*, available from www.euphix.org/object_document/o5427n27422.html, accessed 1 August 2011.

Europa (2008). *A new strategic approach to health for the EU (2008–2013)*, available from http://europa.eu/legislation_summaries/public_health/european_health_strategy/c11579_en.htm, accessed 1 August 2011.

European Commission (2012). *Europaen Year for Active Ageing*, available from http://europa.eu/ey2012/ey2012.jsp?langId=en, accessed 18 February 2013.

European Commission (2011a). *Communication on Sport Adopted*, available from http://ec.europa.eu/sport/news/communication-on-sport-adopted_en.htm, accessed 18th February 2013.

European Commission (2011b). *European Year of Volunteering*, available from http://ec.europa.eu/citizenship, accessed 18 February 2013.

European Commission (2011c). *An EU agenda for the rights of the child*, available from http://eur-lex.europa.eu/LexUriServ/LexUriServ.do?uri=COM:2011:0060:FIN:EN:PDF, accessed 9 April 2012.

——(2010a). *Timeline*, available from http://ec.europa.eu/sport/information-center/information-center141_en.htm, accessed 1 August 2011.

——(2010b). Title XII: Education, Vocational Training, Youth and Sport, *Official Journal of the European Union*, Luxembourg, Office of Official Publications of the European Communities, available from http://ec.europa.eu/sport/document/library/article165_en.pdf, accessed 18 February 2013.

——(2010c). *EU sport programme 2014–2020*, available from http://ec.europa.eu/sport/library/doc/a/provisional_ia_roadmap_sport_2014_2020.pdf, accessed 9 April 2012.

——(2008). *EU physical activity guidelines: Recommended policy actions in support of health-enhancing physical activity*, available from http://ec.europa.eu/sport/library/doc/c1/pa_guidelines_4th_consolidated_draft_en.pdf, accessed 1 August 2011.

——(2007a). *White paper on sport*, Luxembourg, Office of Official Publications of the European Communities.

——(2007b). *Together for Health: A Strategic Approach for the EU 2008–2013*, available from http://ec.europa.eu/health-eu/doc/whitepaper_en.pdf, accessed 18th February 2013.

——(2006). *Towards an EU strategy on the rights of the child*, available from http://eur-lex.europa.eu/LexUriServ/LexUriServ.do?uri=COM:2006:0367:FIN:EN:PDF, accessed 9 April 2012.

——(2005). *European Year of Education through Sport 2004*, available from http://europa.eu/legislation_summaries/education_training_youth/sport/l35008_en.htm, accessed 27 June 2011.

Featherstone, K. (2003). Introduction: In the name of Europe, in K. Featherstone and C.M. Radaelli (Eds), *The politics of Europeanization*, Oxford, Oxford University Press, pp. 3–26.

GAPA (Global Advocacy for Physical Activity) (2010). *The Toronto Charter for Physical Activity*, available from www.globalpa.org.uk/charter, accessed 30 July 2011.

Green, M. (2004). Changing policy priorities for sport in England: The emergence of elite sport development as a key policy concern, *Leisure Studies*, Vol. 23 (4), pp. 365–385.

Henry, I.P. (2001). *The politics of leisure policy*, 2nd edition, Basingstoke, Macmillan Press.

Henry, I.P. and Matthews, N. (1998). Sport, policy and European Union: The post-Maastricht agenda, *Managing Leisure*, Vol. 3 (1), pp. 1–17.

Jarvie, G. (2003). Internationalism and sport in the making of nations, *Identities*, Vol. 10 (4), pp. 537–551.

Lester, S. and Russell, W. (2010). *Children's right to play: An examination of the importance of play in the lives of children worldwide. Working Paper No. 57.* The Hague, The Netherlands, Bernard van Leer Foundation.

Maguire, J. and E.K. Poulton (1999). European identity politics in Euro 96: Invented traditions and national habitus codes, *International Review for the Sociology of Sport*, Vol. 34 (1), pp. 17–29.

Martin, B.W., Kahlmeier, S., Racioppi, F., Berggren, F., Miettinen, M., Oppert, J-M., Rutter, H., Šlachta, R., van Poppel, M., Zakotnik, J.M., Meusel, D., Pekka Oja, P. and Sjöström, M. (2006). Evidence-based physical activity promotion – HEPA Europe, the European Network for the Promotion of Health-Enhancing Physical Activity, *Journal of Public Health*, Vol. 14, pp. 53–57.

Matthews, N. and Henry, I.P. (2001). Sport, leisure and EU regional policy: A case study of Merseyside, in C. Gratton and I. Henry (Eds), *Sport in the city: The role of sport in economic and social regeneration*, London, Routledge, pp. 229–239.

Parrish, R. (2003). *Sports law and policy in the European Union*, Manchester, Manchester University Press.

——(2001). Sports regulation in the European Union: A new approach?, *Managing Leisure*, Vol. 6 (4), pp. 187–200.

Parrish, R. and McArdle, D. (2004). Beyond *Bosman*: The European Union's influence upon professional athletes' freedom of movement, *Sport in Society*, Vol. 7 (3), pp. 403–419.

Tongue, C. (1996). *The future of public sector television in a multi-channel digital age*, Brussels, European Parliament.

UNICEF (2011). *Convention on the Rights of the Child*, available from www.unicef.org/crc/, accessed 1 August 2011.

——(2004). *Sport, recreation and play*, New York, UNICEF.

United Nations (1989). *United Nations Convention on the Rights of the Child*, available from www2.ohchr.org/english/law/crc.htm, accessed 30 July 2011.

3 Utopian visions of childhood and play in English social policy

Stuart Lester and Wendy Russell

Introduction

This chapter explores the relationship between understandings of the nature and benefits of children's play within English social policy and within research into children's everyday expressions of playing in largely adult-produced and -regulated spaces. We suggest that policy constructs 'play' as an object that is defined, bounded and classified. This construction is then applied in a causal manner to the design of play provision to produce spaces that are also defined, bounded and purposeful. This ordering (placing) of children's play, and its associated productions of space, represents a narrow and instrumental value based upon a distant, future-focused utopian vision of the nature and purpose of childhood. The chapter critiques this modernist form of utopian vision through Bauman's (2003) two attributes of policy 'projects', namely fixity/finality and territoriality. This is then set alongside alternative perspectives in contemporary play scholarship that point to a broader value of play as a disposition that seeks to create time/spaces that disrupt and disturb the taken-for-granted ordering of the (adult) world. Such time/spaces afford moments of excitement and pleasure, representing an alternative present and near-utopian vision of being a child, and enabling life to simply 'go on' (resilience). This raises challenges both for policy makers and for practitioners within the play sector.

Hope, childhood and social policy

> Our aim is to make this the best place in the world for our children and young people to grow up.
>
> (Department for Children, Schools and Families (DCSF), 2007: 3)

This ambitious aspiration – couched in the language of opportunity, choice, liberty, achieving potential and futurity – embodies utopian ideas of hope invested both for and in children and implies that the actions of governments can realise this utopia. It was made in the 'Foreword' to *The Children's*

Plan: Building Brighter Futures, published in 2007 by the UK Labour Government (1997–2010) (DCSF, 2007). Despite a focus on addressing the national deficit through public spending cuts and replacing 'big government' with 'big society' through the localism agenda, the current Coalition Government retains this future hope perspective. It can be seen in documents that portray a particular vision of the purpose of childhood (see, for example, Department for Education (DfE), 2010; HM Government, 2011a), investing it with a version of hopefulness based on maintaining competitiveness in global markets and couching this both in the moral language of equality and the pragmatic language of economy:

> The failure to educate every child to the maximum of their abilities is not just a moral failure to accord every person equal worth, it is a piece of economic myopia which leaves us all poorer. For in a world rendered so much more competitive by globalisation, we can no longer afford to leave talents neglected. Every pair of idle hands, every mind left uncultivated, is a burden on all society as well as a weight on our conscience.
>
> (HM Government, 2011a: 4)

Hope is a defining feature of being human; it brings a sense of optimism and the belief that things can be better than they are now, meaning that we can carry on. We create visions of what a better life might look like (Bauman, 2003). Kraftl (2008: 83) shows how children are 'an important repository for hope in the diverse political agendas of human rights and well-being'. This elision of childhood and futurity decouples children's lives in the here and now. It also renders children the passive recipients of a form of paternalistic philanthropy based in a logic that assumes that investment in development is inevitably a force for good. Furthermore, Kraftl (2008: 82) suggests this form of 'affective logic' becomes, by definition, a universalising force, through statements proclaiming a single vision of the future for every child. Such a vision can be seen in the 'Foreword' to the 2010 *The Importance of Teaching: The Schools White Paper*:

> It is only through reforming education that we can allow every child the chance to take their full and equal share in citizenship, shaping their own destiny, and becoming masters of their own fate ... we believe in teaching as the means by which we liberate every child to become the adult they aspire to be.
>
> (DfE, 2010: 6–7)

That these forms of hope can be critiqued should not deny the good intentions and potentially beneficial consequences of policies and practices aimed at children and young people. However, their universalising nature eclipses other ways of conceptualising the hopes of children and young people, as Kraftl (2008) points out.

Drawing on Bauman's (2003) analysis of utopian projects, it is possible to identify two key attributes associated with recent and current social policy formulations for children. The first is that universal utopian ideas expressed in policy become totalising, with fixity and finality of vision producing a singular imagined perfect state. Deviance is not tolerated, and those children 'at risk of poor outcomes', a phrase used in both New Labour and Coalition government policy documents (see, for example, DCSF, 2008b: 38; HM Government, 2011b: 17; HM Treasury and DfES, 2007: 40, 66), become the objects of professional interventions aimed at normalisation. This is what Moss (2007) describes as a dominant paradigm that eclipses alternative understandings. It has its roots in modernity, claiming universal truths and certainties, valuing control and regulation. This is not achieved through force or coercion but by systems of control that encourage and promulgate self-regulation, what Deleuze and Guattari (1988) term a *plane of organisation*.

This pervasive and all-encompassing paradigm of childhood assumes the nature of common sense and is continuously reproduced through everyday practices, technologies, materials and symbols; it is engrained into daily habits, routines, and relationships and through this process assumes the mantle of rightness (Lester, 2010). Through this lens, childhood is seen as a preparatory period for adulthood, where each child passes through universal developmental stages, acquiring the necessary skills and attributes to take their place in the world, producing and consuming in the global marketplace. This fixity and finality of vision interconnects with Bauman's second attribute of utopian projects, namely that children are put in their place through territorialisation, and this is conceptualised in two ways in this chapter. First, as Rose (1999: 33) shows, in order to govern a particular aspect of social life, it is necessary to delineate it, to map 'a set of bounded processes and relations' in order to create an object, a site that is 'amenable to management'. Much of social policy territorialises childhood in this way, delineating and reifying it, rendering it a site for adult colonisation.

The second approach to discussing Bauman's idea of territorialisation is through the analysis of 'spaces of enclosure' (Rose, 1999: 35), the separated and bounded institutions of childhood such as the school, the club and the playground. These spaces are designed for a purpose and are produced and constantly reproduced through practices, making this seem like the natural order of things, so that other practices (and children and young people) are seen as out of place (Lester, 2010). This brief conceptual framing of ways in which childhood is understood, territorialised and colonised in social policy provides the foundations for considering how this extends to children's play.

Play and social policy

It is easy to see how something as irrational and apparently trivial and goalless as play might be sidelined or constrained unless it can be enlisted as a technical tool to be exploited by policy makers and professionals in the overall socialisation project. During the Labour administration (1997–2010), play featured increasingly as a social objective. Generally, policies aimed directly at children and young people adopted an instrumental understanding of play (Powell and Wellard, 2008), enlisting it as a means to realise aims such as: readiness for school, cognitive development, acquisition of social and emotional skills, or the reduction of obesity or crime. The Coalition Government distanced itself from Labour's Play Strategy, proclaiming provision for children's play to be a matter not for central government but for local communities (Clegg, 2010; Gove, 2011). Within the Coalition Government's Big Society project, encapsulated in the Localism Act (2011) and the *Open Public Services White Paper* (HM Government, 2011a), play's instrumental value becomes embedded in concepts such as 'community cohesion' and the development of 'social capital'. These ideas align fully with the neoliberal agenda that seeks to render citizens as self-regulating subjects and conduits for policy goals and targets.

Such utilitarianism is not a new phenomenon. Although not often occupying a central position in social policy, children's play has consistently been harnessed as a driver for meeting policy agendas. Since the restrictions on child labour through the Factories Act of 1833, social campaigners and governments alike have sought to address social ills and to create a better future through harnessing the perceived qualities and benefits of play (Brehony, 2003; Cranwell, 2003). Of particular relevance to key themes raised in this chapter is the development of adventure playgrounds, which were first introduced in the late 1940s by Lady Allen of Hurtwood after her visit to the junk playground in Emdrup, Copenhagen. These facilities sprung up in the spaces left by wartime bombs, using waste materials, tools and the permissive supervision of a playleader to create spaces where children could build play structures, make dens and engage in outdoor play. Largely developed and run by voluntary organisations, such spaces were welcomed by the authorities as an effective response to the rise in delinquency amongst working-class boys (Cranwell, 2007). In his analysis of adventure playgrounds, Kozlovsky (2008: 172) argues that:

> Enlightened societies take up the obligation to provide children with the means of play, yet children do not possess play as their right, as it is subjected, just like education, to the social and political designs of others.

According to Kozlovsky, adventure playgrounds sought to offer a place where children's subjective play desires could be expressed, but this very permissiveness was aimed ultimately at meeting policy's instrumental goals more effectively. Out of anarchy and freedom would come an understanding of democracy and citizenship. Adventure playgrounds, or their contemporary equivalents, were also an element of the English Play Strategy (DCSF, 2008a). This form of provision, although having undergone significant changes since its introduction in the years following World War II in England, is often regarded by the playwork sector as particularly authentic and effective (see for example, Hughes, 2001; Sturrock and Else, 1998). We argue that the founding principles underpinning the adventure playground movement can help navigate the worst excesses of the territorialisation of children's play within social policy. In order to arrive at our conclusion, it is first necessary to consider understandings of play from academic research beyond that used to inform social policy.

Constructions of play and playing

Adult representations of play are inevitably situated in particular paradigms, perspectives and contexts and, as such, often say more about adults themselves than they do about children's own subjective experiences of playing. In their review of contemporary research on children's play, Lester and Russell (2008) found that the relationships between research, policy and practice were far from neatly aligned. Academic research highlights the intrinsic and immediate value of play; policy sees its usefulness in terms of the acquisition of skills needed in later life, with practitioners having to find ways of navigating these tensions.

In the territorialisation of play for social and political purposes, it is necessary for it to become something classified and bounded, a thing that can be 'delivered' by adults to children who then consume it as a part of the diet of welfare provisions aimed at producing healthy bodies and minds for the future of the nation. Inevitably, in the grand utopian project, some forms of play become more desirable than others, causing conceptual problems for playwork practitioners who espouse the officially endorsed (and rationalised) understanding of play as 'a process that is freely chosen, personally directed and intrinsically motivated' (PPSG, 2005). The fixity and territorialisation of the utopian project require that:

> [p]lay becomes an 'activity', subsumed into the plane of organisation, ordered, structured, and situated in dedicated time/spaces and for specific purposes ... children's freedom to discover is strictly monitored and controlled as it is essential that children are discovering the right things.
>
> (Lester, 2010: 1)

This reification of play as a concrete 'thing' to be planned, provided and manipulated is predicated on an assumption that play represents the rehearsal of nascent skills or behavioural traits to be used in adulthood, thereby providing the rationale for adult direction of play. There is a focus on the content of playing, the observable behaviour, which is interpreted literally. This is reflected, for example, in discussions on rough-and-tumble play, often interpreted as practising aggression, whereas the research evidence suggests it is more to do with social competence and bonding, particularly in early and middle childhood (Panksepp, 2007; Pellegrini, 2002). Given the modern tendency to see play as a tool for skill development, it follows that forms of play seen as developing the 'wrong' skills attract sanctions from many adults. Taunts, pranks, initiations, bullying, obscenities, toilet humour, cruel rhymes and songs, and games of power and resistance against adults often provoke disapproval and prohibition. All of these are a part of children's play repertoires and have been described in textbooks as 'bad' play (for example, Scarlett *et al.*, 2005: 17). What the evidence demonstrates is that 'much of what play entails may not be as it seems' (Burghardt, 2005: xiii). Indeed, it is our contention that, whilst play is neither inherently morally good nor bad (Henricks, 2008), the very non-literal, emotional, emergent and irrational characteristics of play form the basis of its value.

This reification of play through policy initiatives achieves territorialisation through the adult planning and management of both supervised and unsupervised play provision. Purposeful design encompasses the idea of 'activities' and of planned space. In supervised projects much attention is paid to planning activities, or to the zoning and naming of spaces that presumes particular activities will take place in each designated area (for example, the den-building area, the quiet corner or the arts and crafts table). This is encouraged through directives and guidance on the implementation and inspection of policy initiatives, producing and reproducing causal and utilitarian understandings of the adult role in supporting children's play until they become understood as common sense. For example, Ofsted (2009) talks of settings that '*provide* freely chosen, self-directed play for children' (p.1) or '*arrange* [a] type of play and experience for children' (p.6) (emphasis added).

A second manifestation of the territorialisation of children's play through social policy initiatives can be seen in the development of fixed, bounded and named spaces for play as another element of the institutionalisation and colonisation of childhood (Rasmussen, 2004; Thomas and Hocking, 2003). The designation of segregated and specific spaces has been the focus of policy relating to children's play over the last 150 years and was a significant aspect of the previous Labour Government's Play Strategy (DCSF, 2008a). This has come about through two key and interconnected discourses reproduced in both the media and policy: one of prevailing fears for and of children if they are left to roam independently, which often assumes a meaning of 'aimlessly', and the other of the importance of educational achievement (Ginsberg, 2007), which promotes purposeful use of free time. Much of the research cited in Lester and Russell (2008) shows significant reduction in children's independent mobility (for example, Hillman, 2006; Karsten and van Vliet, 2006; Kytta, 2004), although there is also research that demonstrates the continuation of playing out as a defining feature of childhood (Armitage, 2004; Burke, 2005; Ross, 2004; Thompson and Philo, 2004), with variations across social divisions such as class, gender, ethnicity, age and disability, demonstrating that these issues are perhaps more complex than headline concerns would suggest.

In designing unsupervised play spaces, inevitably the focus is on material content, with particular physical design of spaces expected to produce specific forms of playing. Technical devices such as planning diagrams, maps and the naming and categorising of equipment or zones in catalogues become 'inscription' devices (Latour, 1986). What is essentially a subjective conceptualisation becomes fixed and named and thus given authority through these devices, which Rose (1999: 37) describes as 'little machine[s] for producing conviction in others'. One effect of this is that a discourse develops that sees these 'play spaces' both as spaces that meet children's 'play needs' (DCSF, 2008a) and as the rightful place where children should play: children and young people playing elsewhere in the public realm may be seen as being 'out of place', as evidenced through the restriction of independent mobility and the use of age-based curfews, 'mosquito' devices and other exclusion techniques (Beunderman et al., 2007; Lee and Motzkau, 2011).

Playing and producing space: the everydayness of moments of disordering

Having shown how policy constructs both play and space as a noun, a 'thing' to be designed and directed towards specific distant utopian ends, we now turn to an alternative construction of children's playful relationship with space. Our starting point here is to put forward a reconceptualisation of play, or more accurately 'playing', as a disposition that is not time and space bound but which surfaces whenever and wherever conditions allow, interwoven into the fabric of everyday life. This is nothing new, in the sense that it is a point made by several play scholars (for example, Bruner, 1977; Huizinga, 1950; Sutton-Smith, 1997). However, it is something that is frequently overlooked, given the dominance of discussing play as a 'thing'.

Despite disagreements over common definitions within play scholarship (Burghardt, 2005; Sutton-Smith, 1997), there is broad consensus that play is largely voluntary (notwithstanding the need for interdependence and compromise in group play and ever-present environmental and individual constraints); it tends to be intrinsically motivated and autotelic (although within this, external reward may play a part); it is not directed immediately at survival, standing alongside the real world, yet having some simulated or symbolic relation to it; it is usually associated with positive affect, being enjoyable and giving rise to positive emotions. Other unique features of play are that it is self-organising, emergent, unpredictable, spontaneous and flexible. Although behaviour that looks like imitation and experimentation sometimes occurs, it is the very playfulness, the non-literal, *as if* nature of playing that sets it apart from these behaviours. In many forms of play, the limits of the real world no longer apply; children plot flights away from the plane of organisation to create a space in which their desires can find expression, or a *plane of immanence* (Deleuze and Guattari, 1988) or *lived space* (Lefebvre, 1991). Playing creates positive affect and with it a sense that life is worth living *for the time of playing* – a utopian moment of hope in the here and now rather than an adult-imagined and distant future. Play simply enlivens everyday time/space and through this creates a sense that life can go on.

Descriptions of play and playful dispositions make much use of spatial metaphors. Children's lives are inherently spatial and their relationships with their local environments are intimate (Hart, 1997). Yet space is not an inert, fixed or exclusively physical entity, it is produced and reproduced by social practices; the design and organisation of space is a social, cultural, economic and political production (Lefebvre, 1991). Massey (2005: 9) suggests that space is produced through the passing encounters of heterogeneous bodies each with its own 'story-so-far'; as such, spaces are always under construction. This construction of space is a representation of power structures; common-sense productions of space seek to establish a true meaning and associated practices by creating fields of promoted and constrained action (Kytta, 2004), encouraging and inscribing the right way to behave in space and reinforcing this through the threat of sanctions against misuse.

Yet children see, feel and act in and on the world differently from adults. A playful disposition offers the chance to create an alternative production, a more clandestine use that counters and disturbs dominant productions, while at the same time emerging from the very presence of these adult structures and patterns; playing in this sense may be seen as a field of free action (Kytta, 2004) that arises from children's momentary appropriation of time/space for their own desires.

Why play is important in the lives of children as children

Such moments of everyday playfulness offer space and time for *ordinary magic*, a phrase coined by Masten (2001) to describe the properties of resilience. Lester and Russell (2008) adopt this phrase to consider the relationship between playing and the enhancement of key adaptive dispositions and systems that can be associated with resilience: pleasure and enjoyment; emotion regulation; stress response systems; attachment to people and places; creativity and openness to learning. This resilience perspective allows for an alternative way of understanding the nature and value of playing to the dominant *progress rhetoric* (Sutton-Smith, 1997) that sees play as a mechanism for learning and preparation for adulthood.

In their play, children can experience strong emotions such as anger, fear or disgust in relative safety because the frame is playful rather than 'real'; in order for the frame to hold and the game to continue, the expression of these emotions needs to be understood as playful by all players (Sutton-Smith, 1999). Spinka *et al.* (2001) found that juveniles deliberately seek out both physical and emotional uncertainty in their play. Rehearsing a range of responses promotes emotional flexibility, supporting the acquisition of repertoires for avoiding emotional over-reaction to threats. Play becomes a means of creating novel and exciting situations that are not constrained by the limits of the 'real' world. It generates possibilities of feeling, acting and thinking in non-literal and non-linear forms, maintaining flexibility and openness to environmental interaction rather than fixed and stereotypical responses. Lester and Russell (2008) suggest that this unique way of placing oneself in such situations is likely to prime mind/body stress response systems that enable children to simply cope with uncertainty in the 'real' world: what Haglund *et al.* (2007: 890) refer to as 'stress inoculation'.

Resilience, play and policy formulation

We suggest that it is important that a broader and deeper understanding of play informs the guiding principles of policy formulation and planning for play. The notion of play as *ordinary magic* acknowledges its unique properties as a common feature of children's everyday lives that contains the power to transform children's relationships with each other and their environments. A resilience perspective suggests the need for a fundamental paradigm shift in understandings of the nature and purpose of childhood, play, services and outcomes, and particularly of the role of adults within services. So, rather than seeing childhood as a universal set of decontextualised stages requiring technical interventions based on 'developmentally appropriate practice' (Woodhead, 2006) in order to guide each child towards a single and totalising utopian future, a resilience approach foregrounds the ways in which children's playful engagement with a range of social, cultural and physical environments and artefacts enables them to build a repertoire of flexible responses, culturally contextual competencies and identities for the here and now. In developing this approach, the focus shifts from deficit, need and risk to a strength-based approach that recognises competence, capacity, possibility and hope. Commentators have long articulated that children need to claim space for themselves (Abbot-Chapman and Robertson, 2009; Hart, 1979; Moore 1986; Sobel, 2002). In a prevailing climate of zero tolerance, control, surveillance, accountability and instant justice, children's social space for determining how they wish to be and act is highly constrained. Play, with the ability to create uncertainty and disorder, appears irrational to adults and therefore does not fit easily into the ordered logic of the adult world (Aitken, 2001).

Conclusions: re-visioning hope through lessons from playwork and history

Having considered understandings of play within English social policy and set these alongside contemporary research into children's everyday experiences of playing, we close this chapter with a brief examination of what playwork, and particularly adventure playgrounds, might offer to the process of shifting from the dominant paradigm to one that respects children's otherness, their competence as children, the value of playing with uncertainty and disorderliness, and the complex interrelationship between children and their physical, social and cultural environments. This shift represents a move away from a distant totalising utopian vision for the future towards a more everyday, near-future sense of hope that children create in their own play.

The change in perception and understanding advocated in this chapter, based on the evidence from contemporary research, echoes the intuitive exhortations of the early pioneers of adventure playgrounds (Danish landscape architect Carl Theodore Sorensen and, in the UK, Lady Allen of Hurtwood). They recognised the need to conceive of adventure playgrounds as fields of free action for children, as disorderly, unfinished *terrains vagues*, chaotic places where children can manipulate materials and the elements to create their own spaces for play; they emphasised the need to intervene as little as possible and have confidence in children's capacity to develop their own ideas of play (Allen, 1968). Yet, even then, playworkers struggled to maintain this ethos in the face of adults' need to control children and to bring order to public spaces: the very first junk playground leader resigned his post when his committee wanted him to control and organise activities (Cranwell, 2003). Playworkers have struggled to defend the original ethos against *adulteration* (Sturrock *et al.*, 2004; Sturrock and Else, 1998), a term used to describe the persistent and increasing incursions of adult rationality and control into spaces where children play.

Given the evidence from contemporary literature on the importance of play in the lives of children, it may be that today's policy makers and planners need to revisit and reapply this ethos and widen it out to children's use of general public space. This has particular relevance for the Coalition Government's concept of a Big Society of which children and young people are members. In considering how this may be done, alternatives to Bauman's (2003) two attributes of utopian projects, fixity/finality and territorialisation, need to be considered in order to imagine a better life in more modest, multiple and mundane ways that embrace the 'otherness' of children. Rather than the adult project of child socialisation being one that seeks to control, rationalise and homogenise children's otherness by seeing them as proto-adults, it might perhaps be more ethical to look beyond grand universal and universalising narratives towards a multiverse that allows for different orderings of space and time (Jones, 2008). Children's disturbance of adult order through their play might suggest that things are not fixed and final, that space or territory is not rigid and closed and that a distant utopian project is not destiny, but that many possibilities can exist alongside this. From this perspective, the gaze shifts from surveillance of children towards us as adults and our responsibility to appreciate and accept our state of not-knowingness alongside our response-ability to make space and time for children to play. This requires paying attention not simply to the external manifestations of children's play but to the conditions in which playfulness thrives (Lester and Russell, 2010). Such a reconfiguration not only offers hope for children but for adults also – a new form of social and political engagement that accepts the right of children to playfully contest dominant productions of space and, through this, enables adults and children to be 'thrown together' and by this very process to get on together (Massey, 2005: 49).

References

Abbot-Chapman, J. and Robertson, M. (2009) Adolescents' Favourite Places: Redefining the Boundaries between Private and Public Space. *Space and Culture*, 12(4): 419–434.

Aitken, S. (2001) *Geographies of Young People*, London: Routledge.

Allen, M. (1968) *Planning for Play*, London: Thames and Hudson.

Armitage, M. (2004) Hide and Seek – Where do children spend their time after school? Paper presented to the *Child in the City* Conference, London.

Bauman, Z. (2003) Utopia with No Topos. *History of the Human Sciences*, 16(1): 11–25.

Beunderman, J., Hannon, C. and Bradwell, P. (2007) *Seen and Heard: Reclaiming the Public Realm with Children and Young People*, London: Demos.

Brehony, K. (2003) A 'Socially Civilizing Influence'? Play and the Urban 'Degenerate'. *Paedagogica Historia*, 39(1): 87–106.

Bruner, J.S. (1977) Introduction. In Tizard, B. and Harvey, D. (Eds) *The Biology of Play*, London: Spastics International Medical Publications.

Burghardt, G.M. (2005) *The Genesis of Animal Play: Testing the Limits*, Cambridge, MA: The MIT Press.

Burke, C. (2005) 'Play in Focus': Children Researching Their Own Spaces and Places for Play. *Children, Youth and Environments*, 15(1): 27–53.

Clegg, N. (2010) *Deputy Prime Minister Highlights the Government's Commitment to Children and Families*, London: Cabinet Office.

Cranwell, K. (2003) Towards Playwork: An Historical Introduction to Children's Out-of-school Play Organisations in London (1860–1940). In Brown, F. (Ed.) *Playwork Theory and Practice*, Buckingham: Open University Press.

——(2007) Adventure Playgrounds and the Community in London (1948–70). In Russell, W., Handscomb, B. and Fitzpatrick, J. (Eds) *Playwork Voices: In Celebration of Bob Hughes and Gordon Sturrock*, London: London Centre for Playwork Education and Training.

Deleuze, G. and Guattari, F. (1988) *A Thousand Plateaus*, London: Continuum.

Department for Children, Schools and Families (DCSF) (2007) *The Children's Plan: Building Brighter Futures*. Norwich: The Stationery Office.

——(2008a) *The Play Strategy*, Nottingham: DCSF Publications.

——(2008b) *2020 Children and Young People's Workforce Strategy*, Nottingham: DCSF Publications.

Department for Education (DfE) (2010) *The Importance of Teaching: The Schools White Paper*, Norwich: The Stationery Office.

Ginsberg, K. (2007) The Importance of Play in Promoting Healthy Child Development and Maintaining Strong Parent Bonds. *American Academy of Pediatrics*, 119(1): 182–191.

Gove, M. (2011) *Hansard*, HC, 23 May, c628.

Haglund, M., Nestadt, P., Cooper, N., Southwick, S. and Charney, D. (2007) Psychobiological Mechanisms of Resilience: Relevance to Prevention of Treatment of Stress-related Psychopathology. *Development and Psychopathology*, 19(3): 889–920.

Hart, R. (1979) *Children's Experience of Place*, London: Irvington Press.

——(1997) *Children's Participation*, New York: Earthscan.

Henricks, T.S. (2008) The Nature of Play: An Overview. *The American Journal of Play*, 1(2): 157–180.

Hillman, M. (2006) Children's Rights and Adults' Wrongs. *Children's Geographies*, 4(1): 61–67.

HM Government (2011a) *Open Public Services White Paper*, Norwich: The Stationery Office.

——(2011b) *A New Approach to Child Poverty: Tackling the Causes of Disadvantage and Transforming Families' Lives*, Norwich: The Stationery Office.

HM Treasury and DfES (2007) *Aiming High for Children: Supporting Families*, London: The Stationery Office.

Hughes, B. (2001) *Evolutionary Playwork and Reflective Analytic Practice*, London: Routledge.

Huizinga, J. (1950) *Homo Ludens: A Study of the Play Element in Culture*, London: Beacon Press.

Jones, O. (2008) 'True Geography ... Quickly Forgotten, Giving Away to an Adult-imagined Universe'. Approaching the Otherness of Childhood. *Children's Geographies*, 6(2): 195–212.

Karsten, L. and van Vliet, W. (2006) Increasing Children's Freedom of Movement: Introduction. *Children, Youth and Environments*, 1(1): 69–73.

Kozlovsky, R. (2008) Adventure Playgrounds and Postwar Reconstruction. In Gutman, M. and de Coninck-Smith, N. (Eds) *Designing Modern Childhoods: History, Space and the Material Culture of Children*, Piscataway, NJ: Rutgers University Press.

Kraftl, P. (2008) Young People, Hope, and Childhood-Hope. *Space and Culture*, 11(2): 81–92.

Kytta, M. (2004) The Extent of Children's Independent Mobility and the Number of Actualized Affordances as Criteria for Child-Friendly Environments. *Journal of Environmental Psychology*, 24(2): 179–198.

Latour, B. (1986) Visualisation and Cognition: Thinking with Eyes and Hands. In Kuklick, H. and Long, E., (Eds) *Knowledge and Society, Studies in the Sociology of Culture Past and Present*, Vol. 6, Greenwich, CT: JAI Press, pp.1–40.

Lee, N. and Motzkau, J. (2011) Navigating the Bio-politics of Childhood. *Childhood*, 18(1): 7–19.

Lefebvre, H. (1991) *The Production of Space*, London: Blackwell.

Lester, S. (2010) Play and Ordinary Magic: The Everydayness of Play, paper presented at Playwork Voices conference, London: Playwork London, June.

Lester, S. and Russell, W. (2008) *Play For A Change: Play, Policy and Practice – A Review of Contemporary Perspectives*, London: National Children's Bureau.

——(2010) *Children's Right to Play: An Examination of the Importance of Play in the Lives of Children Worldwide, Working Paper No. 57*, The Hague: Bernard Van Leer Foundation.

Massey, D. (2005) *For Space*, London: Sage.

Masten, A. (2001) Ordinary Magic: Resilience Processes in Development. *American Psychologist*, 56(3): 227–238.

Moore, R. (1986) *Childhood's Domain*, London: Croom Helm.

Moss, P. (2007) Meetings Across the Paradigmatic Divide. *Educational Philosophy and Theory*, 39(3): 229–245.

Ofsted (2009) *Regulating Play-based Provision*, Ofsted: Manchester.

Panksepp, J. (2007) Neuroevolutionary Sources of Laughter and Social Joy: Modelling Primal Human Laughter in Laboratory Rats. *Behavioral Brain Research*, 182(2): 231–244.

Pellegrini, A.D. (2002) Perceptions of Playfighting and Real Fighting: Effects of Sex and Participant Status. In Roopnarine, J.L. (Ed.) *Conceptual, Social-cognitive and Contextual Issues in the Fields of Play*, Play and Culture Studies, Vol. 4, Westport, CN: Ablex Publishing.

Playwork Principles Scrutiny Group (PPSG) (2005) *The Playwork Principles*, Cardiff: Play Wales.

Powell, S. and Wellard, I. (2008) *Policies and Play: The Impact of National Policies on Children's Opportunities for Play*, London: National Children's Bureau.

Rasmussen, K. (2004) Places for Children – Children's Places. *Childhood*, 11(2): 155–173.

Rose, N. (1999) *Powers of Freedom: Reframing Political Thought*, Cambridge: Cambridge University Press.

Ross, N. (2004) 'That tree used to be everything to us': The Importance of Natural and Unkempt Environments to Children. Paper presented to *Open Space, People Space* Conference, Edinburgh, Scotland: 27–29 October, 2004.

Scarlett, W.G., Naudeau, S., Salonius-Pasternak, D. and Ponte, I. (2005) *Children's Play*, Thousand Oaks, CA: Sage Publications.

Sobel, D. (2002) *Children's Special Places*, Detroit, IL: Wayne State University Press.

Spinka, M., Newberry, R. and Bekoff, M. (2001) Mammalian Play: Training for the Unexpected. *The Quarterly Review of Biology*, 76(2): 141–168.

Sturrock, G., and Else, P. (1998) *The Playground as Therapeutic Space: Playwork as Healing*. 'The Colorado Paper', Sheffield: Ludemos Associates.

Sturrock, G., Russell, W. and Else, P. (2004) *Towards Ludogogy Parts I, II and III: The Art of Being and Becoming Through Play* 'The Birmingham Paper', Sheffield: Ludemos Associates.

Sutton-Smith, B. (1997) *The Ambiguity of Play*, Cambridge, MA: Harvard University Press.

——(1999) Evolving a Consilience of Play Definitions: Playfully. In Reifel, S. (Ed.) *Play Contexts Revisited, Play and Culture Studies*, Vol. 2, Stamford, CA: Ablex.

Thomas, G. and Hocking, G. (2003) *Other People's Children: Why Their Quality of Life is Our Concern*, London: Demos.

Thompson, J. and Philo, C. (2004) Playful Spaces? A Social Geography of Children's Play in Livingston, Scotland. *Children's Geographies*, 2(1), p. 111–130.

Woodhead, M. (2006) Changing Perspectives on Early Childhood: Theory, Research and Policy. Paper commissioned for the EFA Global Monitoring Report 2007, *Strong Foundations: Early Childhood Care and Education*, UNESCO, Woodhead: Paris.

Part II
Intervention

4 Sport, intervention and self-esteem: Promoting physical activity with disengaged adolescents

Denise M. Hill, Nic Matthews, Lindsey Kilgour, Tom Davenport and Kara Wilcox

Introduction

Various forms of physical activity (PA) are known to enhance physical health (see Bouchard *et al.*, 2012), with evidence suggesting that PA may also influence mental health (Ahn and Fedewa, 2011). Yet, such evidence has been generated from studies which have been primarily small scale, cross-sectional in nature and lacking measurement consistency. Moreover, as a consequence of the fact that the literature in this area has predominantly focused on adult populations, the influence of PA on adolescent[1] mental health remains equivocal (Biddle and Asare, 2011). This is somewhat surprising given that adolescence represents a life-stage in which cognitive and biological changes are often seen to detrimentally affect psychological health (see Adams, 2005), with mood disturbance, anxiety, depression and low self-esteem being cited as commonplace (Paus *et al.*, 2008). Of the limited amount of research that does exist in relation to adolescents, it is suggested that PA may have a positive influence on mental health primarily through the enhancement of self-esteem (Biddle and Asare, 2011).

Despite the potential benefits of PA, a significant percentage of adolescents fail to engage in school-based physical education (PE) and sporting/exercise behaviour (Department of Health (DoH), 2006). Numerous perceived barriers to PA have been identified within this population including: the demands of schoolwork, a lack of interest, limited social support, perceptions of incompetence, past negative experiences and self-presentational concerns (see Biddle and Mutrie, 2008). Hence, many adolescents do not accrue the psychological benefits associated with PA. Accordingly, measures need to be taken to encourage more young people to adopt an active lifestyle. The Qualifications and Curriculum Authority (2007), the PE and School Sport Strategy for Young People (2009), Healthy Weight, Healthy Lives (DoH, 2008), the National Institute for Health and Clinical Excellence (NICE, 2009) guidelines on PA for children, Start Active, Stay Active (DoH, 2011), the Healthy Schools Toolkit (Department for Education (DfE), 2011) and Changing the Game for Girls (Women's Sport and Fitness Foundation (WSSF), 2012) are indicative of recent efforts to promote PA and address the level of inactivity within the adolescent population.

This chapter reports on a longitudinal research project that involved the delivery of a targeted programme of PA designed to increase pupil engagement and, in turn, raise their levels of self-esteem. The pupils concerned were drawn from the Year 10 (aged 13–14 years) cohort of a state secondary school in the South West of England, UK. All participants had disengaged from PA and demonstrated low levels of self-esteem.

Sport, physical activity and self-esteem

Defining self-esteem

Self-esteem is the degree to which individuals value themselves (Debate *et al.*, 2009) and is derived from the holding of positive self-evaluations. Hence, those who evaluate themselves favourably will experience high global self-esteem, whereas those who perceive themselves negatively will suffer from low global self-esteem (Biddle and Mutrie, 2008). Global self-esteem is a multi-dimensional construct influenced through a range of life-domains that include the physical, academic and social. Each domain can affect global self-esteem independently, depending on how much value the individual places upon them. For example, a positive self-evaluation of physical competence will enhance the individual's global self-esteem if they consider the physical domain as important to them (Ekeland *et al.*, 2005).

The impact of self-esteem on psychological health

It is argued that self-esteem underpins every aspect of human life (Baumeister *et al.*, 2003) and provides, 'the single most important measure of psychological well-being' (Biddle and Mutrie, 2008, p. 181). It provides an indicator of mental and social adjustment throughout the life course (Boden *et al.*, 2007) and has been associated with subjective well-being, emotional stability, a resilience to stress, confidence, positive emotions (e.g. happiness) and increased life satisfaction amongst young people (see Mruk, 2006). Furthermore, high self-esteem can lead to adolescents exhibiting positive behaviours such as undertaking exercise, persistence, autonomy and pro-social conduct (e.g. Kristjánsson *et al.*, 2010). Conversely, low self-esteem is linked with poor psychological health including anxiety, low confidence, reduced life satisfaction, depression (e.g. Brausch and Gutierrez, 2010) and unhealthy or deviant behaviour (see Barry *et al.*, 2007). However, because much of this research has been cross-sectional, it has not been conclusively ascertained whether high self-esteem is a cause of such positive outcomes or a consequence of them (Biddle and Asare, 2011). Therefore, there is a need for further exploration of the relationship between self-esteem and adolescent mental health through longitudinal and/or intervention research design.

The mechanism by which self-esteem develops

The level of self-esteem experienced across the lifespan is thought to follow a similar pattern for most individuals. That is, it remains high during childhood, drops during adolescence, rises through adulthood and then declines sharply in old age (Robins and Trzesniewski, 2005). It is notable that individuals with high self-esteem during adolescence tend to maintain comparatively higher levels throughout their life (e.g. Orth *et al.*, 2010). The challenge, therefore, is to increase or maintain the self-esteem of adolescents at a time when they are experiencing rapid biological, cognitive and psycho-social changes that often influence self-esteem negatively (Orth *et al.*, 2008). This is particularly pertinent for females who tend to experience a greater decrease in their self-esteem in comparison to their male counterparts (Orth, *et al.*, 2010).

It has been suggested that adolescents are able to maintain or even increase their self-esteem through acceptance and positive experiences (Mruk, 2006). Acceptance occurs as a result of the individual perceiving that they are valued by significant others. Thus, being respected, admired and cared for can lead to acceptance and enhanced self-esteem (e.g., Blackhart *et al.*, 2009). In contrast, being ignored, devalued and mistreated will often lower self-esteem (Bean and Northrup, 2009). Exposing individuals to success within activities which are of value to them, often increases feelings of autonomy and mastery that, in turn, increase self-esteem (see Mruk, 2006), whereas individuals subjected to negative experiences and a continual sense of failure within activities of value, tend to experience lowered self-esteem (Robins and Trzesniewski, 2005).

It is also important to note that self-esteem can be self-perpetuating. Thus, because individuals with high self-esteem are more likely to engage and persist with new activities, they tend to experience success and gain further rises in self-esteem. Those with low self-esteem are more likely to avoid challenging tasks, withdraw effort when experiencing failure, externalise success (Lane *et al.*, 2002) and suffer a downward spiral of lowered self-esteem. Consequently, a priority for practitioners working with adolescents is to encourage perceptions of success, autonomy and mastery, and to enable positive reflections of failure and success. PA has been identified as an activity that can provide adolescents with such experiences and influence appreciably self-esteem.

The relationship between physical activity and self-esteem

Regular PA is generally considered to have a positive influence on self-esteem (see Ahn and Fedewa, 2011; Biddle and Asare, 2011) and this perceived link is commonly offered as a rationale for promoting sport and exercise both in the community and in schools (Ekeland *et al.*, 2005). In fact, although a number of researchers have offered support for this relationship, it is considered to be moderate (see Lubans *et al.*, 2012), with several studies failing to find any correlation (e.g. Moksnes *et al.*, 2010). Such equivocal findings have been attributed in the main to limitations of research design, including inappropriate measures of self-esteem, a failure to include control groups, the adoption of differing intensities/frequencies of PA and an over-reliance on cross-sectional and/or short-term projects (see Biddle and Asure, 2011).

Recent systematic reviews of related literature (e.g. Ahn and Fedewa, 2011; Biddle and Asure, 2011) have concluded that PA is likely to enhance the self-esteem of adolescents if the activities concerned are targeted to meet their needs, facilitate an increase in perceptions of physical competence/body attractiveness and encourage a sense of success, mastery, autonomy and acceptance. Furthermore, through the recent growth of longitudinal studies, there is evidence to suggest that PA may have the potential to exert a durable impact on self-esteem (Schmalz et al., 2007).

The policy landscape

The potential benefits of PA for young people have resulted in a number of policy developments and related initiatives targeting this population. Whilst such progress is welcomed, it has been argued that this has created a crowded policy space for schools with health, welfare, education and sports performance all being part of their agenda (Houlihan, 2000; Cale and Harris, 2006). The National Curriculum for Physical Education (NCPE) formed part of a series of wider educational reforms in England and Wales, brought about by the Education Reform Act (1988). The inception of the NCPE in 1991 established PE as a core element of primary and secondary education, but subsequent revisions to the Curriculum (1995, 1999, 2000 and 2008) indicate that the nature of this provision has changed. The NCPE focused originally on traditional team games and sports (i.e. football, rugby and netball) and, whilst the Curriculum has evolved to include a wider set of activities (e.g. karate), it fails to acknowledge the breadth of activities that engage adolescents (Smith et al., 2009). Indeed, it has been argued that school-based opportunities need to reflect provision outside of the school system, which may encourage lifelong participation in PA (e.g. Lubans and Morgan, 2008). Whilst it is not necessarily the place of the school to reflect the full range of activities undertaken by adolescents, by retaining a strong link to traditional sports, PE continues to present barriers to participation.

Alongside developments in the NCPE, broader policy initiatives have encouraged schools to work in partnership with other local providers to offer adolescents an array of opportunities for sport and PA. Following the promotion of elite and competitive sport within schools during the 1990s by both Conservative and Labour governments (see Department of National Heritage (DNH), 1995; Labour Party, 1996; Department for Culture, Media and Sport (DCMS) (2000, 2002), attempts were then made to use sport and PA to address 'broader social policy objectives' (Houlihan and Green, 2006, p. 77). This included policies such as PE, School Sport and Club Links (PESSCL, 2002) (see DCSF/DCMS, 2003), Learning through PE and Sport

(DfES/DCMS, 2003) and, more recently, the PE and Sport Strategy for Young People (PESSYP, 2008) (Youth Sport Trust and Sport England, 2009). However, it remains unclear whether an aspiration to develop competitive sport complements or contradicts the need to encourage lifelong PA participation.

Against this backdrop, the present study aimed to investigate the perceptions and attitudes of a group of adolescents towards PA and to explore their experiences of a targeted programme of activities that was designed to enhance their levels of engagement and self-esteem.

Methods and methodology

The methodological framework adopted within this study was action research, an approach which seeks to facilitate the investigation of 'real-life' problems with the aim of developing new understandings and practices (McNiff and Whitehead, 2006). A key element of action research is the action-reflection cycle which entails observation, reflection, action and modification of an intervention (Elliot, 1991). Within this study a targeted programme of PA was introduced to a group of adolescents who had disengaged from PA and who demonstrated low levels of self-esteem. The PA intervention aimed to attract the interest of participants and to increase their levels of perceived success, mastery, autonomy and self-esteem. Throughout the study, the intervention was reflected upon both by the participants themselves and by the research team and, where necessary, amendments and modifications were made.

Participants

A cohort of Year 10 pupils (n = 90; aged 13–14 years) from a selected secondary school in the South West region of England (UK), completed the Physical Activity Questionnaire for Adolescents (PAQ-A; Kowalski *et al.*, 1997) and the Rosenberg Self-Esteem Scale (Rosenberg, 1965) in order that their levels of PA and self-esteem could be assessed. The 12 pupils with the lowest combined scores for both PA and self-esteem were invited to take part in the study. Of the 12 pupils recruited, five were male and seven were female; all were 13 years old.

Intervention

To ensure the programme of PA was targeted towards the specific needs and interests of the participant group, its content was designed through consultation with the participants themselves. This was achieved via two focus groups (six participants in each) which were led by one member of the research team (a different member for each focus group). Based on the resultant discussions, and in accordance with the financial and time constraints placed on the study, a seven-week programme of PA was constructed (see Figure 4.1).

Initial intervention proposal			*Delivered intervention*		
Week	*Time*	*Activity*	*Week*	*Time*	*Activity*
Half Term	Monday 09.30–12.30 13.30–16.30	Canoeing Climbing	Half Term	Monday 9.30–12.30 13.30–16.30	Canoeing Climbing
Week 1	Monday 08.40–09.40 Thursday 13.00–13.40 Weekend	Tag rugby Dance Walking	Week 1	Monday 08.40–09.40 Thursday 13.00–13.40 Weekend	Tag rugby Dance Walking
Week 2	Monday 08.40–09.40 Thursday 13.00–13.40 Weekend	Body combat Dance Walking	Week 2	Monday 08.40–09.40 Thursday 13.00–13.40 Weekend	Body combat Dance Walking
Week 3	Monday 08.40–09.40 Thursday 13.00–13.40 Weekend	Walking Dance Walking	Week 3	Monday 08.40–09.40 Thursday 13.00–13.40 Weekend	Circus skills Snowed off Walking
Week 4	Monday 08.40–09.40 Thursday 13.00–13.40 Weekend	Body combat Dance Walking	Week 4	Monday 08.40–09.40 Thursday 13.00–13.40 Weekend	Snowed off Dance Walking
Week 5	Monday 08.40–09.40 Thursday 13.00–13.40 Weekend	Trampolining Dance Walking	Week 5	Monday 08.40–09.40 Thursday 13.00–13.40 Weekend	Boxing Dance Walking
Week 6	Monday 08.40–09.40 Thursday 13.00–13.40 Weekend	Badminton Dance Walking	Week 6	Monday 08.40–09.40 Thursday 13.00–13.40 Weekend	Boxing Dance Walking

Figure 4.1 Targeted programme of physical activity

The PA intervention was implemented during the spring (i.e. January–February) of 2010 and included both in-school and out-of-school activities. In terms of the former, a weekly hour-long exercise session replaced the timetabled Physical Education lesson in which the participants normally took part. This was accompanied by an additional 40-minute (weekly) lunchtime session. In terms of out-of-school activities, each participant was provided with a pedometer and asked to achieve 10,000 steps during each weekend (aligned closely with public health recommendations relating to walking; NHS, 2009).

An outdoor activity day was also arranged during the school holiday period. Initially, the in-school activities were to include tag rugby, body combat (i.e. aerobic activity based on martial arts), trampolining, badminton and dance. However, based on the participant feedback received after a number of the activity sessions, the research team arranged for circus skills and boxing to replace trampolining, badminton and one session of dance. Two in-school activities that were due to take place during weeks three and four were cancelled due to inclement weather.

Procedure

This study followed the University of Gloucestershire's ethical protocols for researching children and young people. Informed consent was gained from the school's Headteacher in order to recruit the 90 pupils for the initial stage of the study. Parental and participant informed consent was received before the PA intervention began. The PA activities were delivered by coaches who were approved to work with young people. Risk assessments were completed prior to all elements of the intervention taking place and the Outdoor Education Centre utilised was licensed by the Adventure Activities Licensing Regulations (Health and Safety Executive, 2012).

Data collection

Participants completed a reflective logbook after each PA session. They were required to record their perceptions of the activity completed, level of enjoyment and reasons for engagement/disengagement. Participants also used the logbook to reflect upon their attitudes towards PA and to record whether or not the intervention had influenced their self-esteem. A member of the research team also completed an informal focus group discussion after each session to ascertain the group's response to the activity. This primarily concentrated on whether or not the delivered activity had been enjoyable and/or facilitated perceptions of mastery/competence. The outcomes of these discussions were used to inform modification to the intervention programme. At the end of the intervention, participants took part in one-to-one semi-structured interviews which explored their attitudes towards PA and the impact of the programme on their self-esteem. Data collection and analysis was ongoing and cyclical throughout the study (McNiff and Whitehead, 2006). Data were analysed via open, axial and selective coding, allowing experiential themes to emerge.

Discussion

The results of the study indicate the positive impact of the targeted programme regarding participant attitudes towards PA, with specific reference to notions of opportunity, enjoyment, autonomy and integration. Moreover, participants' perceived levels of self-esteem were enhanced through participation.

Opportunity

It was noted by participants that the programme had introduced them to new PA opportunities which, for some, were 'surprisingly' enjoyable and which they intended to pursue post-intervention. Additionally, the experience of taking part in novel activities led several participants to state that they were more inclined to attempt other PA opportunities before dismissing them. As explained by Adam:

> The school offers different activities ... but I don't go 'cos I think they will be boring ... I would have dismissed tag rugby, but found it brilliant ... it's definitely given me more opportunities ... 'cos I'll at least go and try something, before saying ... it'll be rubbish.

Enjoyment

Participants experienced increased enjoyment of PA as a result of the targeted programme because the outcome of their participation was positive. That is, they gained an immediate sense of competence as a consequence of coaches offering positive reinforcement regarding their initial attempts at the various tasks and their subsequent progress. Such perceptions of competence increased participant engagement which, in turn, increased levels of perceived success. Anna articulated such feelings in more detail:

> When I started the boxing, I wasn't sure ... I was about to give up. But the instructor walked me through it, told me what to do, and I caught on quick .... He said I had a lot of potential ... . He told me about this local [boxing] club ... I have been going [ever] since ... I've got better and [am] really enjoying it.

Such sentiments reinforce the assertion that enjoyment is a key determinant of PA participation (see Sallis *et al.*, 2000) and that perceived competence is a significant influencing factor of enjoyment, engagement and motivation in PA (Elliot and Dweck, 2005). These findings also highlight the critical role of the practitioner in developing perceived competence through the use of positive reinforcement (see Hein and Croker, 2007) and emphasise the need to ensure that individuals with low self-esteem experience perceived success during the initial stages of a new PA activity, for they are less likely to persist without such reassurance.

Autonomy

All participants acknowledged how their involvement in the design, and subsequent modification, of the programme led to a sense of autonomy which increased their motivation to attend and engage with PA. Ben suggested that, 'Even though there was some stuff I didn't like ... I still wanted to take part as there was loads of things I wanted to do, and knew I liked.' He went on:

> I am sick of being told what sport I have to play ... To be able to say ... I want to do this ... and then actually doing just that ... being asked after each session what we thought about it ... and then what we thought actually mattered ... meant I really wanted to do it [PA].

Consequently, these findings offer further support for the suggested relationship between perceived autonomy and increased motivation towards PA during adolescence (e.g., Roemmich *et al.*, 2012). Thus, PA practitioners working with adolescents should remain mindful of the need to maintain levels of autonomy through methods such as encouraging choice, fostering a mastery-involved motivational climate, avoiding competition and providing external references for success, and informational and competence-related feedback (see Hagger *et al.*, 2005).

Integration of physical activity

The findings of the study also demonstrate how pedometers are a useful means of changing participant attitudes towards PA, enabling a number of the respondent group to recognise the ease with which they could integrate PA into their lives. As a result, the majority experienced enhanced levels of perceived competence. As observed elsewhere in the related literature (Biddle and Mutrie, 2008), an increase in perceived competence encouraged a number of participants to set challenging, self-referenced goals which raised their activity levels further. Carol explained this cyclical relationship in more detail:

> I used the pedometer on the first weekend and easily made the 10,000 steps ... I was surprised at how well I had done ... so then I tried to beat that the next weekend ... . Then, when I had achieved that, I thought I could do more ... so I did. I found myself wanting to walk more and more, and really enjoyed it.

Attitude and physical activity behaviour

It was evident that a change in attitude towards PA had altered participant behaviours, with a number identifying engagement in additional activities beyond those offered within the programme. For example, Dave discussed

how he had adopted a new approach to exercise: 'I go on my Wii Fit much more now ... I do jogging and yoga and stuff.' Esther reported similar changes: 'I've started walking home after school ... me and my mum have started walking round our block twice every day. It [the PA programme] has made us realise that we need to do more.' Thus, it seems that influencing an individual's attitude towards PA can lead to behavioural change (e.g. Hagger and Chatzisarantis, 2009), particularly if the activity is integrated into a daily routine (Pate *et al.*, 2011).

Physical activity and self-esteem

All participants reported low levels of self-esteem prior to the intervention and also attested to negative self-perceptions. However, the data indicated that the programme had positively influenced participants' perceived levels of self-esteem. For example, Graham stated, 'I feel good about myself, for the first time in a long time.' Correspondingly Esther suggested that she was 'happier' in herself and that she felt a 'real sense of achievement' at the completion of the programme. Ben also identified that the intervention had made him, 'feel proud of [himself] ... more positive about what I can achieve', with Carol specifically identifying that the programme had influenced her self-perceptions positively, especially regarding notions of body image:

> I think at our age we rely on our image so much, and I just felt ugly and fat all the time ... taking part in this programme has really helped that [body image] ... I know I have lost weight from the walking, and it has made me feel much better about myself.

Several participants noted that the supportive 'climate' of the targeted PA programme differed from their PE lessons and that this had also positively impacted their self-perceptions. They perceived PE lessons as 'competitive', 'less supportive' and, at times, a place where they felt 'embarrassed'. Through encouraging a sense of mastery and acceptance, the intervention engendered a more task-orientated climate which enabled participants to feel more comfortable in their PA environment. Jenny explained how this had encouraged her to engage with PA and how it had also enhanced her self-esteem:

> I just got stuck in. I didn't worry about being fat or what I was wearing, cos everyone was so positive ... we just had to have a go ... even though I was nowhere near as good as the rest ... I got better and still enjoyed it ... that was the biggest difference between this [the intervention] and my PE lessons. I tend to feel like a failure in PE.

Evidence of this nature supports the need for a predominantly task-orientated PA environment to encourage engagement and positive self-perception that may, in turn, enhance self-esteem (see Mruk, 2006). These findings also confirm that the intervention encouraged a sense of mastery which influenced effectively the participants' sense of perceived competence and which appeared to enhance levels of self-esteem. For example, Graham identified that, 'when we did the circus skills ... and I managed to do it ... it made me feel proud ... like I had achieved something. This made me feel good about myself ... I know I can do things I didn't think I could, if I put my mind to it.' Such perceived competence also increased the participants' motivation to engage with other PA activities, as Ben concluded:

> I hated PE ... I didn't think I can do any of it, and I felt that I looked stupid. But ... this [the intervention] has shown me that I can do some things ... I look at myself differently now ... I used to think I was useless ... but I am better than I thought ... . So, I will at least try and have a go in my PE lessons now.

Conclusions

The aim of this chapter has been to examine the impact of a PA intervention on adolescents with low self-esteem. The findings indicate that PA may positively influence levels of self-esteem providing that the activities concerned are targeted towards the interests of participants and that they encourage perceptions of competence and mastery through a supportive and task-orientated motivational climate. It must be noted that the duration of the present intervention was only seven weeks in total and that a number of PA sessions were cancelled due to inclement weather. Thus, further longitudinal research is required to ascertain the long-term impact of PA on self-esteem.

The interest in, and provision of sport and PA opportunities for adolescents has been enhanced by the efforts of successive Labour governments (1997–2010). Future policy, however, will be influenced by the priorities of the Coalition government. It is too early to anticipate the implications of this change in administration, but cuts in public spending and a contrasting ideological position on the role of providers from different sectors may well have an impact on how sporting opportunities are packaged and delivered. The funding cuts announced for School Sport Partnerships in October 2010 by the Secretary of Education Michael Gove (and the subsequent, if partial, U-turn in December of that year) are indicative of the flux in school-based PA and physical education. Coalition policy has since emerged, proffering 'a more rigorous, targeted and results-oriented way of thinking about grass roots sport' (DCMS, 2012, p. 1): the emphasis being on competitive sport (i.e. the School Games), enhancing links between schools and clubs and rewarding governing bodies which have a focus on youth. Of particular interest here is the embedding and incentivising of structured, intra- and inter-school competition which appears contrary to many of the issues and themes considered in this chapter. On the basis of the findings presented, identifying what adolescents want to do, understanding why these activities engage them and articulating what they gain from their participation will help providers design effective initiatives for those marginalised by mainstream provision.

Note

1 Although there is no singularly accepted definition of adolescence (see Adams, 2005), we adopt the traditional view that this particular life-stage comprises the period between the onset of puberty and adulthood (i.e. between the ages of 12 and 18 years).

References

Adams, G.R. (2005). Adolescent development. In T.P. Gullotta and G.R. Adams (Eds), *Handbook of adolescent behavioural problems: Evidenced-based approaches to prevention and treatment* (pp. 3–16). New York: Springer.

Ahn, S. and Fedewa, A.L. (2011). A meta-analysis of the relationship between children's PA and mental health. *Journal of Pediatric Psychology*, 36(4), 385–397.

Barry, C.T., Grafeman, S.J., Adler, K.K. and Pickard, J.D. (2007). The relations among narcissism, self-esteem, and delinquency in a sample of at-risk adolescents. *Journal of Adolescence*, 30, 933–942.

Baumeister, R.F., Campbell, J.D., Krueger, J.I. and Vohs, K.D. (2003). Does high self-esteem cause better performance, interpersonal success, happiness, or healthier lifestyles? *Psychological Science in the Public Interest*, 4(1), 1–44.

Bean, R.A. and Northrup J.C. (2009). Parental psychological control, psychological autonomy, and acceptance as predictors of self-esteem in Latino adolescents. *Journal of Family Issues*, 30(11), 1486–504.

Biddle, S.J.H. and Asare, M. (2011). PA and mental health in children and adolescents: A review of reviews. *British Journal of Sports Medicine*, 45(11), 886–895.

Biddle, S.J.H. and Mutrie, N. (2008). *Psychology of PA: Determinants, well-being and interventions* (2nd ed.). Oxon: Routledge.

Blackhart, G.C., Nelson, B.C., Knowles, M.L. and Baumeister, R.F. (2009). Rejection elicits emotional reactions but neither causes immediate distress nor lowers self-esteem: A meta-analytic review of 192 studies on social exclusion. *Personality and Social Psychology Review*, 13(4), 269–309.

Boden, J.M., Fergusson, D.M. and Horwood, L.J. (2007). Self-esteem and violence: Testing links between adolescent self-esteem and later hostility and violent behavior. *Social Psychiatry and Psychiatric Epidemiology*, 42(11), 881–891.

Bouchard, C., Blair, S.N. and Haskell, W.L. (2012). *PA and health* (2nd ed.). Champaign, IL: Human Kinetics.

Brausch, A.M. and Gutierrez, P.M. (2010). Differences in non-suicidal self-injury and suicide attempts in adolescents. *Journal of Youth and Adolescence*, 39(3), 233–242.

Cale, L. and Harris, J. (2006). School-based PA interventions: Effectiveness, trends, issues, implications and recommendations for practice. *Sport, Education and Society,* 11, 401–420.

Debate, R.D., Gabriel, P.K., Zwald, M., Huberty, J. and Zhang, Y. (2009). Changes in psychosocial factors and PA frequency among third- to eighth-grade girls who participated in a developmentally focused youth sport program: A preliminary study. *Journal of School Health,* 79(10), 474–484.

Department for Culture, Media and Sport (DCMS) (2000). *A sporting future for all.* London: DCMS.

——(2002). *Game plan: A strategy for delivering government's sport and PA objectives.* London: DCMS/Strategy Unit.

——(2012). *Creating a sporting habit for life: A new youth sport strategy.* London: DCMS.

Department for Education (DfE) (2011). *Healthy schools toolkit,* available from www.education.gov.uk/schools/pupilsupport/pastoralcare/a0075278/healthy-schools, 23 May 2012.

Department for Education and Skills and Department for Culture, Media and Sport (DfES/DCMS) (2003). *Learning through PE and sport.* London: DfES/DCMS.

Department of Communities and Local Government (2007). *The new performance framework for local authorities and local authority partnerships.* London: DCLG.

Department of Health (DoH) (2006). *Health challenge England – next steps for choosing health.* London: HMSO.

——(2008). *Healthy weight, healthy lives: A cross-government strategy for England.* London: HMSO.

——(2011). *Start active, stay active.* London: HMSO.

Department of National Heritage (DNH) (1995). *Sport: Raising the game.* London: DNH.

Ekeland, E., Heian, F. and Hagan, K.B. (2005). Can exercise improve self-esteem in children and young people? A systematic review of randomised control trials. *British Journal of Sports Medicine,* 39(1), 792–798.

Elliot, J. (1991). *Action research for educational change.* Milton Keynes: Open University Press.

Elliot, A.J. and Dweck, C.S. (2005). *Handbook of competence and motivation.* Guildford Press: New York.

Hagger, M.S. and Chatzisarantis, N.L.D (2009). Integrating the theory of planned behavior and self-determination theory in health behavior: A meta-analysis. *British Journal of Health Psychology,* 14(2), 275–302.

Hagger, M.S., Chatzisarantis, N.L.D., Barkoukis, V., Wang, C.K.J. and Baranowski, J. (2005). Perceived autonomy support in physical education and leisure-time PA: A cross-cultural evaluation of the trans-contextual model. *Journal of Educational Psychology,* 97(3), 287–301.

Health and Safety Executive (2012). *Information about adventure activities licensing,* available from http://www.hse.gov.uk/aala/about-activities-licensing.htm, accessed 16th February 2013.

Hein, V. and Crocker, M.S. (2007). Global self-esteem, goal achievement orientations, and self-determined behavioural regulations in a physical education setting. *Journal of Sports Sciences,* 25(2), 149–159.

Houlihan, B. (2000). Sport Excellence, schools and sports development: The politics of crowded policy spaces. *European Physical Education Review,* 6(2), 171–193.

Houlihan, B. and Green, M. (2006). The changing status of school sport and physical education: Explaining policy change. *Sport, Education and Society*, 11(1), 73–92.

Kowalski, K.C., Crocker, P.R.E. and Kowalski, N.P. (1997). Convergent validity of the PA Questionnaire for Adolescents. *Pediatric Exercise Science*, 9(4), 342–352.

Kristjánsson, A.L., Sigfúsdóttirand, I.D. and Allegrante, J.P. (2010). Health behavior and academic achievement among adolescents: The relative contribution of dietary habits, PA, body mass index, and self-esteem. *Health Education & Behavior*, 37(1), 61–64.

Labour Party (1996). *Labour's sporting nation*. London: The Labour Party.

Lane, A.M., Jones, L., and Stevens, M.J. (2002). Coping with failure: The effects of self-esteem and coping on changes in self-efficacy. *Journal of Sport Behavior*, 25(4), 331–345.

Lubans, D., and Morgan, P. (2008). Evaluation of an extra-curricular school sport programme promoting lifestyle and lifetime activity for adolescents. *Journal of Sports Sciences*, 26(5), 519–529.

Lubans, D.R., Plotnikoff, R.C. and Lubans, N.J. (2012). Review: A systematic review of the impact of PA programmes on social and emotional well-being in at-risk youth. *Child and Adolescent Mental Health*, 17(1), 2–13.

McNiff, J. and Whitehead (2006). *All you need to know about action research*. London: Sage publications.

Moksnes, U.K., Moljord, I.E.O., Espnes, G.A. and Byrne, D.G. (2010). The association between stress and emotional states in adolescents: The role of gender and self-esteem. *Personality and Individual Differences*, 49(5), 430–435.

Mruk, C.J. (2006). *Self-esteem research, theory and practice: Toward a positive psychology of self-esteem*. New York: Springer Publishing Company.

National Institute for Health and Clinical Excellence (NICE) (2009). *Promoting PA, active play and sport for pre-school and school-age children and young people in family, pre-school, school and community settings*. London: NICE.

NHS (2009). *The 10,000 steps challenge*, available from www.nhs.uk/Livewell/lose-weight/Pages/10000stepschallenge.aspx, accessed 21 April 2010.

Orth, U., Robins, R.W. and Roberts, B.W. (2008). Low self-esteem prospectively predicts depression in adolescence and young adulthood. *Journal of Personality and Social Psychology*, 95, 695–708.

Orth, U., Trzesniewski, K.H. and Robins, R.W. (2010). Self-esteem development from young adulthood to old age: A cohort-sequential longitudinal study. *Journal of Personality and Social Psychology*, 98(4), 645–658.

Pate, R., Saunders, R.P., O'Neill, J.R. and Dowda, M. (2011). Overcoming barriers to PA: Helping youth be more active. *ACSM's Health and Fitness Journal*, 15(1), 7–12.

Paus, T., Keshavan, M. and Giedd, J.N. (2008). Why do many psychiatric disorders emerge during adolescence? *Nature Reviews Neuroscience*, 9(12), 947–957.

Qualifications and Curriculum Authority (2007) *Physical Education Programme of study for Key Stage 4*, London, DfE.

Robins, R.W. and Trzesniewski, K.H. (2005). Self-esteem development across the lifespan. *Current Directions in Psychological Science*, 14(3), 158–162.

Roemmich, J.N., Lambiase, M.J., McCarthy, T.F., Feda, D.M. and Kozlowski, K.F. (2012). Autonomy supportive environments and mastery as basic factors to motivate PA in children: A controlled laboratory study. *International Journal of Behavioural Nutrition and PA*, 9(16), 1–16.

Rosenberg, M. (1965). *Society and adolescent self-image.* Princeton, NJ: Princeton University.

Sallis, J.F., Prochaska, J.J. and Taylor, W.C. (2000). A review of correlates of PA of children and adolescents. *Medicine and Science in Sport and Exercise*, 32(5), 963–975.

Schmalz, D.L., Deane, G.D., Birch, L.L. and Davison, K.K. (2007). A longitudinal assessment of the links between PA and self-esteem in early adolescent non-Hispanic females. *Journal of Adolescent Health*, 41(6), 559–565.

Smith, A., Green, K. and Thurston, M. (2009). 'Activity choice' and physical education in England and Wales. *Sport, Education and Society*, 14(2), 203–222.

Women's Sport and Fitness Foundation (WSFF) (2012). *Changing the game for girls.* London: WSSF.

Youth Sport Trust and Sport England (2009) *The PE and Sport Strategy for Young People: A guide to delivering the five hour offer*, Loughborough, Youth Sport Trust.

5 Sport, physical activity and youth imprisonment

Andrew Parker and Rosie Meek

Introduction

Delinquency and anti-social behaviour amongst young males has long been regarded as a problem in UK society. The transition from child to adulthood has proved to be one of considerable tension and frustration, especially for those at risk of offending (Hendry *et al.*, 1993; Barry, 2010). One response to this has been for the state to structure the activities of such groups via employment training packages and sport and leisure opportunities (Hollands, 1990; Mizen, 2003). In recent years youth offending has become an issue of serious concern for politicians and policy makers alike. Criminal statistics suggest that recorded crime rose by 900 per cent from 1950 to 1991, from around 1,100 to just over 10,000 per 100,000 (Home Office, 1992). Official figures indicate that crime rates have decreased of late, yet rates of reoffending among young people in prison remain stubbornly high, with three out of four committing further crime within a year of release (Ministry of Justice (MoJ), 2010). Indeed, criminal and anti-social behaviour among young people remains a primary societal concern, especially in relation to offences such as assault, theft, criminal damage, illegal drugs and knife possession, with offending rates peaking in the late teens (Roe and Ashe, 2008). Offenders aged 18–24 years commit a third of all crime, comprise a third of prisoners (at a unit sum of *c.*£50,000 p.a.) and cost the UK taxpayer £16.8–20bn per year (T2A, 2009).

Strategies to curb youth imprisonment and reoffending have adopted a range of methods and guises, one of which is sport and physical activity. The aim of this chapter is to consider how sport might be used as a way to discourage (or even reduce) offending behaviours and as a means by which to engage young people in custody in relation to their broader lifestyle choices. Focusing on the work of one particular sport-based initiative, the chapter demonstrates how physical activity has the potential to impact on the decisions that young people make in terms of their attitudes and approaches to life both within and beyond custodial settings.

Youth, marginalisation and sport

Since the 1960s, sport has been increasingly viewed as a suitable intervention in youth delinquency both in the UK and elsewhere. Indeed, there is a plethora of academic research concerning the re-engagement of marginalised young people in and through sporting locales, the majority of which surrounds community-based initiatives and programmes (see, for example, Bailey, 2005; Coalter, 2007; Nichols and Taylor, 1996; Nichols, 2007). The overwhelming consensus from studies of this nature is that: (i) physical activity and sport can be an effective means through which to engage young people in activities that they dislike and/or fail in at school (see Sharpe *et al.*, 2004); (ii) most sport and physical activity is beneficial to young people's health: in physical terms (improving fitness, diet and reducing smoking and drug taking) and in psychological terms (improving mood and self-esteem and reducing self-destructive behaviour, i.e. self-harming/suicidal tendencies) (Coalter, 2004; Collins, 2009); and (iii) in a social sense sport can improve interpersonal and communication skills (amongst peer groups and adults) and increase levels of self-confidence. Indeed, sport has traditonally been associated with a whole series of positive impacts on a range of personal conditions and characteristics, including active citizenship (Muncie, 2009; Theeboom *et al.*, 2010; Waring and Mason, 2010). Collectively, such research findings highlight the extent to which both the personal and social aspects of sporting involvement can positively impact individuals and communities.

Meanwhile the deployment of sport specifically within the context of custodial settings has received relatively little attention, save for a small number of academic and evaluative studies (see Andrews and Andrews, 2003; Frey and Delaney, 1996; Martos-Garcia *et al.*, 2009) and the monitoring and accountability measures of government agencies. Findings from Her Majesty's Inspectorate of Prisons and the Youth Justice Board suggest that overall physical activity levels in male Young Offender Institutions (YOIs) are inconsistent and relatively low (see Lewis and Meek, 2012; Parke, 2009). For example, in six out of the 18 institutions (and of the 1,159 respondents) surveyed by Parke (2009), less than one in ten young men said that they were allowed to take daily exercise. Certain kinds of physical activity remain high in such settings with 77 per cent reporting that they visit 'the gym' at least once per week. Surveys of juveniles coordinated by the Inspectorate of Prisons have revealed that the number of young people attending gym sessions at least five times per week and exercising outside everyday has increased consistently in recent years (Cripps, 2010; Tye, 2009).

Summarising the findings of research in this field, Meek (2012) concludes that, whilst sport alone should not be seen as a panacea to youth crime, it is useful in providing an initial point of engagement for those within custodial settings. In so doing, Meek goes on, sport can also serve to increase levels of motivation amongst those within custody whilst facilitating positive relationships both between offenders themselves and between offenders and the professionals with whom they interact. In terms of the impact of sporting intervention on the lives of the participants featured within her study, Meek reports that, of the 50 (representative) individuals released, only nine reoffended or were recalled to custody (within one year), representing an 18 per cent reconviction rate overall (compared to an institutional average of 48 per cent). Meek further reports statistically significant improvements amongst her participants in established measures of conflict resolution, aggression, impulsivity and attitudes towards offending. Moreover, members of the research cohort confirmed that participation in sport had led to improvements in their physical health, sleeping patterns and attitudes to healthy eating and that regular physical activity had proved an effective means of managing stress and anxiety. Meek's (2012) findings are based upon an evaluation of one particular sporting initiative, the 2nd Chance Project,[1] and its implementation with male young offenders within HMP and YOI Portland, UK.[2] Building upon these foundations, this chapter aims to demonstrate how the replication of such initiatives may prove fruitful across custodial settings by presenting qualitative data findings from 2nd Chance Project participants within an alternative secure environment.

Context and method

The empirical data presented here derive from research carried out during the spring (January–April) of 2012 at Holroyd Young Offender Institution (HMP and YOI).[3] Holroyd is located in the South of England and caters for up to 400 male juveniles (aged 15–18) at any one time. As well as operational prison staff, personnel include teachers, caseworkers, psychologists and healthcare professionals. The prison seeks to provide a high-quality learning environment, with all residents receiving at least 27 hours of education per week, including mathematics, English, IT, music, art, physical education and life skills. Holroyd also hosts various resettlement and employability programmes.

The study utilised those methods of sociological enquiry traditionally associated with qualitative research (i.e. participant observation, semi-structured interviews and documentary analysis) in order to explore the everyday lives of the respondent sample. A fieldwork journal was used to record observational events, and all interviews were recorded and transcribed in full.[4] Observations were carried out during educational activities either in classroom or physical education settings, i.e. on the prison's outdoor astro-turf pitch or in and around the gym and sports hall. Alongside interviews with residents, discussions also took place with mentors, caseworkers and Physical Education (PE) Department staff. The data analysis process revealed a series of key themes relating to the way in which respondents perceived the benefits of sporting involvement. Here we discuss two of these, namely 'personal motivations for sport' and 'sport and social skills'. Before considering these themes in more detail we take a closer look at the broader institutional factors impacting on day-to-day life at Holroyd.

Holroyd residents are encouraged to engage in a range of sporting activities. Through the creation of a series of community partnerships, a number of in-house programmes have been devised which offer residents the opportunity to take part in physical activity during their time in custody; such opportunities are linked to various education, training and employment pathways. Against this backdrop (and in partnership with the 2nd Chance Project) the Holroyd 'Sports Academy' has been established facilitating a 12-week programme of activities, including physical education/sport-based tuition, coaching awards, community placements and mentoring roles. The respondents featured in this research were either currently serving prisoners (at Holroyd) or had been released from the prison during the previous 12 months. The participant sample comprised ten young men aged between 15 and 17 years. A further two participants were interviewed, both of whom had been released from custody on licence[5] during 2011. Whilst it is the norm for each 12-week sports academy to be designed around a specific activity (i.e. football, boxing, rugby or cricket), a wide variety of sporting interests were present amongst the respondent group (including weight training, rugby, boxing and football) and, for this reason, the programme of events under consideration was designated a 'multi-sports' academy.

Inside Holroyd physical activity is delivered in accordance with the highly structured educational regime in place, with sports academies only being open to those who have a consistently positive institutional profile.[6] Academies are advertised and promoted around the prison and residents are able to express an interest in taking part via initial referral forms. These expressions of interest/applications are processed by the Holroyd Physical Education Department and subsequently screened by the prison's Education and Security staff in order to ascertain the suitability of applicants for academy involvement. Once enrolled, academy candidates attend six classroom sessions per week (of 1.5 hours' duration) where they study the 'theoretical' aspects of sport; they also take part in six 'practical' sessions per week (also 1.5 hours in duration) where they participate in their chosen sporting activity. All academy programmes operate in line with a partnership model which sees Third Sector and statutory organisations come together to provide a comprehensive package of multi-agency support for the young people concerned. To this end, academies include: sports coaching; sport education qualifications (such as Sports Leaders awards); life-skills mentoring (one hour per week); community/industry-related guest events; and pre-release resettlement support, the latter providing assistance to residents in their negotiations with case workers, Youth Offending Teams (YOTs) and Parole and Review Boards, and in relation to issues surrounding family re-engagement. Depending on length of sentence, residents may complete as many different academy programmes (and associated qualifications) as they wish.

Holroyd residents bring with them a wide variety of offences (ranging from assault to manslaughter) and sentence histories. In terms of the overall profile of the academy group featured in this research, a number were considered 'at risk' either as a consequence of a lack of parental support or because of their previous offences. Five of the group emanated from the Greater London area and were affiliated with gangs. In terms of the length of sentences being served, these ranged from 10 months to 4.5 years, with most falling between 18 and 24 months. Offences included burglary, aggravated burglary, robbery, wounding with intent, possession with intent to supply Class A and Class B drugs and money laundering. All participants identified as being male; individual profiles indicated that 65 per cent had few or no formal educational qualifications.

Personal motivations for sport

As is the case within wider social spheres, sport does not appeal to everyone in custody, neither are all custodial settings in a position to facilitate a wide range of sporting opportunities. However, by encouraging residents to pursue some form of sporting interest, Holroyd HMP and YOI (in partnership with the 2nd Chance Project) has found a significant measure of success. One of the features of the work at Holyroyd is that, as well as attracting young men who have an existing interest in (and passion for) sport, many participants have little, if any, previous sporting exposure, as Majid pointed out during interview:

> AP: Tell me about how you got involved with 2nd Chance.
> Majid: Well, basically I chose the Academy to do some sport and educational qualifications ...
> AP: So, when you came here [to Holroyd], were you a sports person anyway ... like at school?
> Majid: Definitely not. When I was in school an' that I was quite lazy. But ever since I've come in here I've been doing lots of sport an' stuff. It gives me a real buzz, running about an' that. An', y' know, sports really push you to the limit an' I really enjoy that ... . Boxing is the main thing that made me do it ... instead of just doin' weights ... 'cos they all [other residents] wanna do weights and just get big, but it's about stayin' fit on the inside; your lungs an' everything. That's what I really wanna do as well. All that running and training. It's just pushin' me to the limit.

Neither had the post-school experience been particularly productive for Majid. During his time at Holroyd, however, sport had come to provide a means by which he could focus his thoughts and energies and start to think about life in an altogether more positive way:

> It [sport] takes my mind off other things, y' know, stress an' stuff, family problems, stuff that goes on in the world. It just takes my mind off it. 'Cos it's like a motivation for me, y' know. Before I couldn't

think about anything; fuck school, fuck education, I can't be arsed with any of it, y' know … people aren't teaching me stuff that I'm gonna need in the future. But ever since I've come in here I've been doing my studies, been doing my boxing as well …. Instead of smoking drugs I do boxing and that makes me think more about my future to be honest.

AP: So, do you think that you get the buzz out of boxing that you used to get out of smoking?

Majid: Yeah. Y' see, when you smoke weed you get the buzz at the time … but in the morning you wake up an' it's just like the headache an' like … if you don't smoke a spliff then you're just gonna constantly keep having this headache. But when I'm doing boxing it helps to release endorphins which keeps me happy all the time but then afterwards I feel healthy about myself y' know. So, in the mornings I jump out of bed and I get on with the day. But before I'd get up and I was like: 'Fuck it, I'll just go back to sleep.'

Evident amongst Majid's comments are vestiges of previous research findings concerning the psychological benefits of sporting involvement and the motivational stimulus (and release from anxiety/stress) which this can provide, especially within custodial environments (see, for example, Meek, 2012). For other residents, too, sport was something which had passed them by during their days in school (and in the community) and only on entering prison had it become an activity with which they had chosen to engage. Granted, there were various reasons and motives in play here. Some chose to do sport simply because they saw it as 'better than other lessons' but who 'looked forward to it anyway'. For Dean (like Majid), sport provided an avenue of emotional release, 'if you're angry and you go to the gym, hit the weights, do a bit of boxing … [it] takes your mind off certain things'. Dean was conscious of the broader benefits of doing 'every qualification that you can … while you're in prison'. Either way, and for whatever reason, through the presence of the 2nd Chance Project sport was presented as a possible point of engagement for academy members and one through which a whole host of further life skills and learning opportunities had opened up for them.

Indeed, for some, sport had provided not only a way of re-directing their thoughts and energies but, for the first time in their lives, a sense of achievement. In Gavin's case his relationship with the Project had played out far beyond his initial intentions or expectations. Gavin had been introduced to sport prior to entering the prison system, albeit as a consequence of previous exposure to the Courts, but, once in Holroyd, 2nd Chance had served as an opportunity for re-engagement:

AP: So, what made you get interested in sport in here [Holroyd]?

Gavin: I'd been here a couple of weeks and the Gym lads (PE Department staff) said 'Do you wanna play football?', and I said I'd give it a go ... . And then they said 'Do you wanna have a go on the [foot-ball] team', and so they got me on the team. And then every other sport they said 'Do you wanna have a go at this, do you wanna have a go at that ... ?' and so I had a go ...

AP: And you're keen on the boxing. How did that happen?

Gavin: Well, when I was out [prior to prison] I got arrested for ABH [Actual Bodily Harm] and they put me on a Community Order. And part of that was that I went boxing at a gym round my area and I went there for about four months and I got into it. And then I came here and found out that they do a boxing club here, so I joined in ...

Gavin's engagement with sport as a consequence of his experiences within the criminal justice system bears testament to the way in which such programmes can (and do) act as useful avenues of intervention (see Nichols and Taylor, 1996; Nichols, 2007). So successful had the process of sporting re-engagement been for Gavin that he had progressed through the various levels, ranks and stages of the 2nd Chance Academy to earn himself a position as a Gym Orderly, working alongside full-time staff in Holroyd's Physical Education Department. Like most other services within the prison, 2nd Chance operated in line with a clear punishment/reward ethos: if young men were deemed suitable (by the relevant internal authorities) to take part in one of the sports academies, then they were eligible for initial recruitment. If their behaviour (both on the Academy and within the prison itself) remained positive during the designated 12-week period, then they were allowed to stay on the programme. If, as a consequence of engagement, their general behaviour demonstrated significant improvement, then more opportunities opened up for them within the context of the academy structure. Such opportunities might include progression to Gym Orderly or Project Mentor and, ultimately, work placements in the community.[7] Gavin was one such individual who had responded positively to his academy experiences and had made the most of all the opportunities presented to him. In turn, his everyday life inside prison had become much more focused and purposeful:[8]

Gavin: When I first come here I was on the [prison] wing an' I used to mouth off at staff and have fights an' all that. But on social time, if I'm off the wing doing sport, I'm not getting into trouble ... You've got to behave to keep coming [to academy sessions]. And so I kept coming and started to enjoy it. ... So, it taught me how to behave really; just started behaving ...

AP: So, can you now train each day?

Gavin: There's two [Gym] Orderlies ... and we take it in turns; one lesson one person refs the football while the other's training. So, we just take it in turns really and help each other out ... . After the lessons people go back to the wings and are banged up in their cells for half an hour but because I'm here [in the Gym] I've got the option to stay over here and do a bit of cleaning an' that, or do a quick training session.

Just as Gavin's involvement in sport had resulted in increased benefits in terms of his everyday lifestyle, it had also offered him a sense of individual progress and development:

> Gavin: Yeah ... [before] I came in [to prison] I used to smoke weed an' that and I never used to talk to no one really. But I started to do sport an' you get to know people an' you get more confident talking to them an' that .... I talk to the family, I talk to the 'missus' [girlfriend] an' that. Sport's definitely kept me out of trouble while I've been in prison ...
> AP: And do you feel better about yourself?
> Gavin: Yeah, definitely. You can see a difference as well. Like, I'm much fitter ... more confident with people, more confident when I play the sport. 'Cos when I first come in I'd get the ball and just pass it to someone else but now I get the ball and take people on an' that ...

What Gavin provides here is clear evidence of the kind of personal benefits which academic commentators have, for some time, associated with sporting engagement (see Coalter, 2004; Collins, 2009; Muncie, 2009). Yet, a further advantage of Gavin's position as Gym Orderly was that he was able to come into contact with (and get to know) a range of other residents who, under normal circumstances, he would not have had the opportunity to interact with. In this sense, sport was a means by which he was able to develop socially as well as personally, a scenario common to a range of other academy members.

Sport and social skills

For some years politicians, social commentators and academics alike have proclaimed the social benefits of sport; leadership, teamwork and self-sacrifice are words and concepts which are commonly used in association with sporting endeavour (Collins, 2009). What then of sport in custody? In a world where social interaction is often a risky and sensitive business, how might sport oil the wheels of relationship building?

It would be fair to say that, for many academy members, custody had been an isolating experience and a place where 'keeping your head down' and 'staying out of trouble' was their main objective. Despite all this, sport had come to be seen by project participants as a way that relational interaction might be promoted and through which their own social skills might develop, as both Dean and Majid described:

> AP: Do you think sport helps your relationships with other people?
> Dean: Yeah, it's like, in prison you meet different people in the gym sessions an' that. You're in there doin' a bit of 'shoulders' an' they're givin'

you hints on how to get bigger an' that. An' while you're workin' out you're talkin' with them ...

AP: And these are people that you don't know?

Dean: Yeah, you see them round the prison but you don't really talk to them. But when you see them in the gym an' stuff and they're doin' the same work-out as you're doin', then you get to talk to them. You just start communicating with them, y'know what I'm sayin' ...

Majid: Yeah, yeah. It helps you gain friends as well. You get to meet new people from other areas [of the prison] an' everything. You think that everyone's from London and are just gangsters an' everything, but it's not like that ... . When you get to know them they're not actually people that are like that, they're totally different.

Gavin talked of similar experiences with regard to the way in which, as a consequence of his Gym Orderly role, he had begun to build relationships with people who he came into regular contact with: 'you get people from different [accommodation] blocks mixing together so when they come in [to the Gym] ... I do their [physical] assessments, so you meet people every-day really.' Having attended a number of sports academies during his time at Holroyd, Brett (now living in the community 'on licence') reflected on how rugby, in particular, had brought home to him the ways in which sport has the potential to develop social relationahips and how important this kind of developmental process is:

Brett: From looking at [the] rugby academy and from the way that people didn't like each other [at first] ... when it came to [playing] a match, when one of those guys went down, the other one was there to support him ... . It's like ... competition, competitiveness; get us all out on the rugby field, smash your way through 15 blokes, y' know, but have fun and pass the ball round. Matey boy gets tackled, three of us run in, get everyone off him, look after him, y' know, protect him, while someone gets the ball out again. Scrums as well, like ... cos you have to communicate with each other, hold it tight, squeeze and press together, y' know ...

AP: So, does sport force you to do that, to talk to each other?

Brett: Well, you have to or else you'll get hurt. If you're not communicating with your teammates you're gonna end up paying for it. You're gonna end up losing the ball for the team and you don't wanna be the odd one out ... . If you're the only one who's not committing to the team you'll soon be noticed, y' know what I mean, you won't get passed the ball or anythin'. I mean, who's gonna give the ball to someone who's not gonna listen to anyone ...

For Brett, the transformations which had taken place during the 12 weeks of the rugby academy which he had attended had been something that he would never have imagined beforehand:

Brett: I think if someone could have video'd at the end of the rugby academy that team that we had ... 'cos there was a lot of conflicts in the team between people at first verging on fighting an' that comin' from the wings and outside [in the community] and previous stuff an' that. But we all come together as a team. And we were doin' stuff in the classroom and on the pitch ... [and] after a few weeks ... the team gelled so well [that] we never lost .... Two people that were arguing at the start of it, they might have an argument in the classroom, but as soon as we got out on the pitch they'd support each other on the field ... . Y' know, you never used to speak to each other on the wings but now it [was] different.

Respondents frequently spoke of the volatility of prison life and the potential for tempers to fray amidst the vortex of sporting endeavour. Yet, testimonies of this nature bear witness to the potential benefits of sporting involvement for those in custody and reinforce the findings of previous research which has attested to the development of mutual respect among offenders and, indeed, between offenders and the professional staff with whom they interact (see Meek, 2012). In turn, they provide exemplary narratives of the functional role of sport: individual catharsis, social cohesion, character formation, inclusive practice – sport transforming people's lives, for the better, for the social good. For sure, the practical sporting activities of the 2nd Chance Project proved beneficial to those taking part, so much so that participants recognised the personal and social transformations taking shape. What Brett was also clear about was the way in which such transformations had been facilitated by the Project and the importance of the wide-ranging networks, connections and avenues of referral which 2nd Chance staff had at their disposal.

For the majority of the young people concerned, there was a feeling that the work that they did within the academy context did not simply represent a series of false hopes and hollow promises, but rather a sense of possibility and opportunity: a way out of the crime–custody cycle. For Majid this meant a change in attitude towards his lifestyle choices and towards his future:

Majid: Well, hopefully, Justin [2nd Chance case worker] is going to help me join a project called 'Fight for Change'. I'll join up with that ... . And I'm thankful to Justin for trying to help me get into that.
AP: And will you do things at college as well?
Majid: Well, my dad's an electrician and he wanted me to follow in his footsteps and become an electrician as well and so I might do electronic engineering, or I might do Public Services ...

What such sentiments indicate is the kind of benefits on offer when interventions and initiatives operate within a coordinated network of joined-up thinking; hence the ability of Majid to progress from the sports academy within Holroyd to a community-based project on release. For him, and for others, part of the role of the 2nd Chance Project was to make these connections: to hand over young people to wider (trusted) partners and support agencies and to ensure that the specific needs and interests of those concerned were appropriately and adequately met during the post-custody transition. Amidst such tailored provision there was at least the possibility that sporting hope would become an everyday reality on the outside.

Conclusions

> Freedom man, I can't wait. Freedom ... do my licence ... and then go back to college ... . I'm looking to work with my Dad in the future, get my own business. Everyone deserves a '2nd Chance', init. Y've got to learn from your mistakes.
>
> (Dean, Holroyd Sports Academy member)

Building upon the findings of previous research, the aim of this chapter has been to highlight the potential of sporting activity as a means of engagement for young people in custodial settings. In turn, our intention has been to demonstrate the value of replicating a particular sporting initiative across similar custodial settings. Focusing on the experiences of the young people concerned, we have attempted to show how taking part in sport within such settings may have various physical, social and psychological benefits which can impact both participants and those with whom they interact.

A common criticism of the criminal justice system in the UK is that, despite the provision of structured programmes of support within custody and the provision of multi-agency assistance within the community, there remains insufficient integration of the two. Amidst a whole raft of new responsibilities (and from a position of vulnerability and risk), too often, on release from prison, young people find themselves without the personal or social skills to engage with the agencies which are designed to support them. For these young people the easiest way to survive is to return to the life that they know best and around which they feel most secure: a life of crime. The 2nd Chance Project aims to act as some form of corrective in this respect, by creating a climate in which marginalised and vulnerable young people can develop a sense of confidence and belief in themselves, trust in others and hope for the future. At a practical level this means empowering young people to think positively about life, to develop coherent self-advocacy, to interact with multi-agency support and, where appropriate, to re-establish familial connections and relationships. All of this is designed to enable 2nd Chance participants to (re)gain a sense of active citizenship, to access a better quality of life and to give 'voice' to those who, for one reason or another, may have never before been heard. With such skills and attributes in place, it is hoped that project participants will be better equipped to articulate their needs, which, in turn, increases their chances of receiving appropriate help and support to make the transition back into society.

Notes

1 The 2nd Chance Project is a social enterprise which provides a wide range of opportunities and services for marginalised young people. Such provision includes custodial programmes designed to engage offenders through sport and physical activity in order to impact their behaviours, achievements, skills and attitudes. See: http://2ndchanceproject.co.uk/view/1/home.
2 For further insight into the role of sport in custodial settings, see Meek *et al.* (2012).
3 To preserve anonymity, pseudonyms have been used throughout.
4 Prior to the onset of the study, ethical approval was gained from the NHS Research Ethics Committee (REC) for Wales, Holroyd HMP and YOI, and the University of Gloucestershire Research Ethics Sub-Committee (RESC).
5 The term 'on licence' refers to the fact that individuals may be released from custody in order to serve the remainder of their sentence within the community.
6 In order to remain as a sports academy participant, residents must maintain certain behavioural standards across the institution, i.e. in their relationships with other residents and their daily interactions with prison staff. Changes to this behavioural profile can lead to individuals being denied further access to sports academy programmes and/or to the forfeiture of privileges in relation to sport/ physical activity sessions.
7 Work placement opportunities are only available to those residents eligible for release on temporary licence (ROTL).
8 For similar findings (within the context of Portland YOI) see Meek (2012).

References

Andrews, J.P. and Andrews, G.J. (2003), 'Life in a secure unit: The rehabilitation of young people through the use of sport', *Social Science and Medicine*, 56 (3): 531–550.

Bailey, R. (2005), 'Evaluating the relationship between physical education, sport and social inclusion', *Educational Review*, 57 (1): 71–90.

Barry, M. (2010), 'Youth transitions: From offending to desistance', *Journal of Youth Studies*, 13 (1): 121–136.

Coalter, F. (2004), *The social benefits of sport: An overview to inform the community planning process.* Edinburgh: Sport Scotland.

——(2007), *A wider social role for sport: Who's keeping the score?* London: Routledge.

Collins, M. (ed.) (2009), *Examining sports development.* London: Routledge.

Cripps, H. (2010), *Children and young people in custody 2009–2010. An analysis of the experiences of 15–18 year olds in prison.* HM inspectorate of Prisons/Youth Justice Board. London: The Stationery Office.

Frey, J. and Delaney, T. (1996), 'The role of leisure participation in prison: A report from consumers', *Journal of Offender Rehabilitation*, 23: 79–90.

Hendry, L.B., Shucksmith, J., Love, J.G. and Gledinning, A. (1993), *Young people's leisure and lifestyles.* London: Routledge.

Hollands, R.G. (1990), *The long transition.* London: Macmillan.

Home Office (1992), *Criminal statistics.* London: Home Office.

Lewis, G. and Meek, R. (2012), 'The role of sport in reducing offending among young men in prison: Assessing the evidence base', *Forensic Update*, 107: 12–18.

Martos-Garcia, D., Devis-Devis, J. and Sparkes, A.C. (2009), 'Sport and physical activity in a high security Spanish prison: An ethnographic study of multiple meanings', *Sport, Education and Society*, 14 (1): 77–96.

Meek, R. (2012), *The role of sport in promoting desistance from crime: An evaluation of the 2nd Chance Project rugby and football academies at Portland Young Offender Institution*. Southampton: University of Southampton/2nd Chance Project.

Meek, R., Champion, N. and Klier, S. (2012), *Fit for release: How sport-based learning can help prisoners engage in education, gain employment and desist from crime*. Mitcham, Surrey: Prisoners Education Trust.

Ministry of Justice (MoJ) (2010), *Population in custody: Monthly tables August 2010 England and Wales*. Statistics bulletin. London: Ministry of Justice.

Mizen, P. (2003), *The changing state of youth*. London: Macmillan.

Muncie, J. (2009), *Youth and crime*. London: Sage.

Nichols, G. (2007), *Sport and crime reduction*. London: Routledge.

Nichols, G. and Taylor, P. (1996), *West Yorkshire sports counselling: Final evaluation report*. Sheffield: University of Sheffield Management Unit.

Parke, S. (2009), *Children and young people in custody 2006–2008: An analysis of the experiences of 15–18-year-olds in prison*. HM Inspectorate of Prisons/Youth Justice Board. London: The Stationery Office.

Roe, S. and Ashe, J. (2008), *Young people and crime: Findings from the 2006 offending, crime and justice survey*. Statistical Bulletin 08/09. London: Home Office.

Sharpe, C., Schagen, I. and Scott, E. (2004), *Playing for success: The longer term impact*. London: Department for Education and Science/National Foundation for Educational Research.

Theeboom, M., Haudenhuyse, R. and De Knop, P. (2010), 'Community sports development for socially deprived groups: A wider role for the commercial sports sector? A look at the Flemish situation', *Sport in Society*, 13 (9): 1392–1410.

Transition to Adulthood Alliance (T2A) (2009), *A new start: Young adults in the criminal justice system*. London: T2A.

Tye, D. (2009), *Children and young people in custody 2008–2009. An analysis of the experiences of 15–18-year-olds in prison*. HM inspectorate of Prisons/Youth Justice Board. London: The Stationery Office.

Waring, A. and Mason, C. (2010), 'Opening doors: Promoting social inclusion through increased sports opportunities', *Sport in Society*, 13 (3), 517–529.

6 Young people, football and 'respect'?

Mark Elliot, Andy Pitchford and Celia Brackenridge

Introduction

This chapter builds on a study of young people in football carried out by academics at the University of Gloucestershire, UK and Brunel University, UK during 2008–09. In particular, it focuses on the concept of 'respect' and its place in the sporting experiences of young people. The impetus for the study was initially generated by The Football Association (FA) and their desire to respond to previous research which pointed to the need to deal with perceptions of increasingly anti-social behaviour within professional and amateur football in the UK. The FA were especially interested to explore the interaction between players, spectators, coaches and referees. The grass-roots youth game appeared to have been especially badly affected by this problem, with aggressive parents creating intolerable situations for match officials. As a result, referees appeared to be leaving the sport in significant numbers.

In order to assess the position of young people in this context, we explore the contested concept of 'respect' before unpicking the background to the desire of the then Labour Government to intervene and to tackle the anti-social behaviour and the apparent incivility that permeated British society. While Prime Minister Tony Blair was building his Respect Taskforce, The FA was recognising that it too had social and behavioural issues to address. The aim of this chapter, therefore, is to examine the rationale for The FA's own Respect programme and to then draw upon qualitative research from two related evaluation projects in order to gauge the reaction of the key stakeholders (the young people themselves) to the series of interventions that were central to the programme. The chapter concludes by assessing the extent to which these interventions were successful, but also the extent to which more radical structural change might be possible, and whether such change might fundamentally impact on social relations in the game in a way that could recognise the needs of young people more effectively and, in so doing, secure a more respectful and civil sport long into the future.

Understanding 'respect'

The concept of 'respect' has considerable significance in everyday life. Traditionally children are taught to respect their parents, elders, people in positions of authority, the law, different cultures, other people's feelings and so on. Due to the apparent ubiquity of respect, moral and political philosophy has consistently shown an interest in the subject (Dillon, 1995). In particular, philosophers have debated what respect is and who, what or why someone or something deserves to be respected. Despite the acknowledged importance of the concept, no agreement has been reached on how to address such questions. Kant has been credited as the first important Western philosopher to place respect for other people at the heart of his work (Dillon, 1995). Kant argued that all people are worthy of respect unconditionally and irrespective of whether they have acted in an acutely disrespectful way towards others. This belief has become central to the modern ideal of humanism and political liberalism (Dillon, 1995).

Darwall's (1977) conception of respect has also been influential. He identified two kinds of respect, 'recognition respect' and 'appraisal respect'. The former 'consists ... in a disposition to weigh appropriately in one's deliberations some feature of the thing in question and to act accordingly' (Darwall, 1995: 183). People, the law and social institutions can all be the object of recognition respect. For Darwall, the central issue is that 'to conceive of all persons as entitled to respect is to have some conception of what sort of consideration the fact of being a person requires' (Darwall, 1995: 183). Appraisal respect involves the positive appraisal of a person or his or her qualities (Darwall, 1995) or, in other words, it is an assessment of character. Appraisal respect can exist to a greater or lesser degree depending upon the level of excellence being judged and it can co-exist alongside the negative appraisal of an individual's character. For example, it is possible to have respect for someone as excellent at their job yet still regard them as immoral (Dillon, 1995). American sociologist Richard Sennett devoted a chapter of his 2003 book *Respect: The Formation of Character in an Age of Inequality* to discussing what respect means, stating that, 'Respect seems so fundamental to our experience of social relations and self that we ought to define more clearly what it is' (Sennett, 2003: 49). Sennett concludes that 'what respect means is complicated socially and psychologically' identifying that 'an enormous gap exists between wanting to act well towards others and doing so' (Sennett, 2003: 59). In seeking to establish the meaning of respect Sennett considers a number of sociological concepts that could be interpreted as synonyms for respect. His analysis of 'status', 'prestige', 'recognition', 'honour' and 'dignity' leads him to suggest that none of these concepts are suitable and that 'respect' is something quite different.

Incivility and disrespectful behaviour

Sennett's work can be located in a body of literature pertaining to 'incivility' (Home Office, 2006: 5) in urban areas. Other scholars have also noted that related concepts have not been clearly defined. Fyfe *et al.* (2006) point out that the term 'incivilities' (Home Office, 2006: 1) has largely been replaced by the term 'anti-social behaviour' (Home Office, 2006: 3), but note, along with Burney (2005), that, although used interchangeably, these terms often have differing connotations. Incivilities are understood as something that is 'applied collectively to communities', whilst anti-social behaviour is 'something done by individuals who are thereby singled out and blamed for the harm they inflict upon communities. One is about outcomes: the other is about inputs' (Burney, 2005: 2).

Early sociological conceptions of incivility can be found in the micro-sociology of Erving Goffman. Goffman explains (1972: 258) that individuals will often deal with behaviour that is disrespectful with a series of 'accommodations', thus ensuring that minor altercations do not degenerate in to more serious confrontation. Burns (1992: 31) is in agreement with Goffman, further believing that 'there is a readiness on the part of most people to see order restored, whenever it has been disrupted'. Existing literature also claims that anti-social or disrespectful behaviour may be less of a problem than the public and politicians think. Research conducted by Phillips and Smith (2006) found that encounters with 'rude strangers', even in inner-city areas that were considered to be high risk, were infrequent and rarely escalated into more serious episodes. Findings also suggested that 'the personal intent to become more tolerant in the future far outnumbered the response of aversion and retreat' (Phillips and Smith, 2006: 899).

The Respect Action Plan

As we have seen, the word 'respect' became prominent in the UK as part of New Labour's law and order policy agenda during their three consecutive terms in government in 1997–2010. The oft quoted promise to be 'tough on crime, [and] tough on the causes of crime' was at the heart of a zero-tolerance policy which successive Labour administrations adopted towards anti-social behaviour. This approach was laid out specifically in the government's Respect Action Plan (The Home Office, 2006). Bannister *et al.* (2006: 921) note that the Plan aimed 'to enforce a culture of respect' and urged the majority to reclaim their communities from the grasp of an intimidating minority who engaged in disrespectful anti-social behaviour. This approach was similar to that of Bill Bratton who became Commissioner of the New York Police Department in 1994 and who introduced zero-tolerance policing (Fyfe *et al.*, 2006). Bratton believed that civility 'could be achieved through the exclusion of incivilities and the exclusion of the unrespectable' (Fyfe *et al.*, 2006: 854).

In the Respect Action Plan, respect is rather loosely defined as 'an expression of something that people intuitively understand'. Furthermore, respect is said to comprise 'values that almost everyone in this country [the UK] shares' and which 'the majority of people want'. Anti-social behaviour is defined as 'the most visible form of disrespect' (Bannister *et al.*, 2006: 921). New Labour's loose definition of respect allowed them scope to attempt to eradicate what they saw as anti-social behaviour through policy development and use of the criminal justice system. Amidst all of this Prime Minister Blair is believed to have been influenced by the work of Sennett (Jeffries, 2006).

However, the claim that Blair's Respect Action Plan was heavily influenced by Sennett appears somewhat strange. Whilst a zero-tolerance approach to anti-social behaviour was at the heart of the Plan, Sennett's work, alongside that of others (Bannister *et al.*, 2006; Fyfe *et al.*, 2006; Phillips and Smith, 2003; 2006), is critical of the notion that respect can be enforced through a zero-tolerance approach, in part, at least, because 'we become less tolerant, more fearful and increasingly prone to overreact to minor representations of difference' (Bannister *et al.*, 2006: 934). Furthermore, it may also be the case that an attempt to 'enforce respect could have the unintended effect of heightening anxiety about so-called disrespective behaviours' (Bannister *et al.*, 2006: 930), thus causing an unnecessary moral panic.

Several commentators observe that the conditions of modern-day life are different from the past (Phillips and Smith, 2003; Bauman, 2000; Sennett, 2003). For example, it can be argued that 'the experience of incivility is underpinned by the growth of freedom and movement in contemporary urban settings' (Phillips and Smith, 2003: 85), which has facilitated increased contact with strangers who we do not, and cannot, know personally, but with whom we are compelled to interact. In turn, this growth in freedom, has led to less security and less certainty in people's lives and a situation where the constant interaction with strangers causes anxiety (Bauman, 2000). Indeed, Bauman suggests that individuals have sought to protect themselves from such anxiety-ridden situations by retreating into social isolation (2000).

Historically, the dominant position towards disrespectful behaviour is that it is a detriment to society and should be controlled and eliminated from everyday life. The Respect Action Plan (The Home Office, 2006) is a recent example of this. Yet, Phillips and Smith (2003: 105) challenge this position by asking if 'a little incivility in everyday life can be a good thing?' In this sense they offer a more hopeful perspective by proposing that incivility could be seen as 'an irritant and stimulus for the growth of tolerance, moral awareness and everyday solidarity in a society increasingly marked by difference, and more importantly by indifference' (Phillips and Smith, 2003: 105). They agree with Bauman that any attempt to control and eradicate incivility might simply lead to an increasingly fragmented and isolated society. However, they conclude that 'what is needed is an active and creative way of managing ... encounters with incivility in our society' and that we may 'begin to understand incivility as like a tax: the price we each have to pay for the participation on a vital and expanding civil society' (Bauman, 2000: 105). Respect is not something to be enforced from above; it requires negotiation (Sennett, 2003). Such negotiation is contingent upon taking the needs of others seriously; '[i]t emerges from below and is based on a tolerance of difference' (Bannister *et al.*, 2006: 934).

Respect and the world of football

In 2008 The FA launched a pilot project within amateur football around the notion of respect in order to test a series of interventions. These related to new codes of conduct for participants and clubs; the use of spectator barriers at the sides of football pitches; and the introduction of a communication system during matches where only the Captain talks to the referee. In 2009, these interventions were modified and extended into the professional game. The FA's Respect programme was launched on this basis and was championed by the then Chief Executive of The FA, Brian Barwick. Alongside a series of high-profile promotional videos or 'virals' that were originally hosted on The FA's website, professional matches would now incorporate pre-match briefings where the referee would remind players of their responsibilities and of particular interpretations of the laws of the game. A 'Respect handshake' would take place between all opposing players and between all players and match officials before kick-off, and within the match itself referees would 'manage' the flow of the game while team captains would be expected to 'lead' on communication and interactive issues. In addition, The FA agreed to try to manage sideline technical areas[1] more effectively in order to minimise conflicts between managers, coaches and officials. Some of these emphases would be repeated in the open-age (adult) amateur sector, and in the grass-roots youth (predominantly under 16s) game, with codes of conduct and barriers representing a key element of the programme in this sector. Since 2009, the Respect programme has expanded with the launch of educational online videos for parents and carers, further promotional films, new reporting mechanisms and the appointment of a designated Lead Officer within The FA. This work is designed to complement existing standards promoted through The FA's Equality Policy, Safeguarding Policy and the Laws of the Game.[2]

Both The FA's own internal assessment of Respect and independent academic evaluations (e.g. Brackenridge *et al.*, 2011) suggest that some of these interventions are proving to be effective. However, the purpose of this chapter is to look specifically at youth football and ask whether there might be other ways of understanding respect in this context, and whether other structural, rather than predominantly cultural, possibilities might be considered (as possible remedies to existing and emerging respect issues) as the game develops. In order to do this we need to consider first the context of youth football, before asking what young players themselves feel about respect specifically and their experiences of the game.

Youth football in England

As with any sport, football is shaped by broader societal influences and concerns. The way the game is played, the size and scope of its physical and geographical parameters, the numbers and attitudes of participants and the role of coaches and educators are, for example, all factors that are inextricably linked to the ways in which society works, the ideas it values and the institutions that provide its foundations. Clearly, there are connections that could be explored between the rising concerns about parental behaviour in youth football, as expressed in relation to the Respect programme, and the changing nature of parenthood itself. We have argued elsewhere (Brackenridge *et al.*, 2007) that shifting family dynamics, relational fragmentation and distant parenting may place extra pressures on familial interactions and that challenges to traditional forms of masculinity may lead to sporting contexts being recognised as arenas in which more aggressive, physical or combative conceptions come to the fore. 'Pushy' parents – parents who confront referees when decisions go against their offspring or team, or parents who are not sufficiently engaged in the lives of their children in ways that will support their sporting pursuits – might well be located in such scenarios. However, there are also specific elements of the sport itself that may contribute to the problems alluded to thus far, or at least there are elements of the game that are not as fixed or historic as is often assumed.

To date, grass-roots youth football in England has been dominated by two forms of the sport; a 7-a-side version is played amongst children under the age of 11 and the majority of those above this age play an 11-a-side version of the game. The vast majority of games in both forms take place in highly regulated, commodified spaces in the sense that the pitches, goals, corner flags and other equipment are approved and effectively licensed by The FA or its local incarnations, the County FAs. Matches are supervised by a referee. Teams play in bespoke kit with regulation size 3 or size 4 footballs. The results of games are recorded by team managers and then normally appear on an FA branded website within two to three hours of the final whistle. Players can only play if they are registered with the league to which their team is allied and have provided proof of identity and age. The exponential growth of teams and clubs in the period since the 1990s has led to attempts by The FA to regulate teams and to incentivise best practice through a quality kite-marking model called The FA Charter Standard. The final characteristic of modern-day English youth football, and one which is often overlooked because of its 'obvious' and 'traditional' nature, is that the vast majority of competition is between clubs organised around immediate neighbourhoods or specific communities. This competition is inter-club and feeds off the rivalries that are associated with a professional club football, with 'derby games' and 'grudge matches'.

This particular way of organising youth football is peculiarly English and is a much more recent phenomenon than is often assumed. In fact, before the 1980s, there was little in the way of organised football for young people in England under the age of 16 outside school. Until this time, the English Schools Football Association (ESFA) had dominated the provision of coaching, leadership and organised competition. Children played for their school team and then had the opportunity to climb the representative ladders, through district to county teams, or to join the 'ground staff' of a professional club and eventually access an apprenticeship. The grass-roots, voluntary sector game existed in only very limited form. Children who participated in football outside school or Boys Clubs often did so in an unregulated, playful manner, in parks or on the streets, away from the watchful eye of coaches, referees or even parents. The growth of the game in the voluntary sector began at the same time as the apparent demise in teacher-led extra-curricular activity in the mid-1980s, and the gradual commodification of coaching and coach-led products (such as soccer schools and camps). The ease with which coaches, the majority of whom were parents, could organise a team and enter them into competition appears to have led to a spiralling growth in competing clubs and a rapid rise in the number of leagues facilitating organised matches and tournaments.

The FA has attempted to regulate this voluntary sporting landscape in a variety of ways. The FA's Charter for Quality (1997) led to proposals for young children to be restricted to small-sided games, rather than the full 11-a-side version; for the introduction of the Charter Standard; for enhanced coach education; and for the further development of a professional staffing infra-structure within the association. Whilst these changes have clearly had a positive impact on the voluntary sector, it is important to note that they do not address the fundamental structure of the sport, in the sense that it is organised in an essentially arbitrary way and has not been designed with the needs of the central participants in mind. In other words, the grass-roots youth game developed initially as a version of the adult game, with few modifications. Children were not consulted, in any meaningful way, about a version of the sport that might suit their needs or preferences. Instead, adults have created a sport on their terms and, while children may well enjoy this, it is also conceivable that heavily regulated, outcome-oriented adult sport is not ideally suited to the needs of young people. It is also possible that the essentially arbitrary design also contributes to interactions where anti-social actions, or incivility, are heightened due to the adult-centred and confrontational nature of the contest.

Such were the concerns of a number of pressure groups which attempted to influence FA policy on youth football during the mid- to late 2000s. *Give Us Back Our Game* and *Don't Cross the Line* were grass-roots campaigns which lobbied for either a greater focus on the needs and demands of children, or a diminution of adult influence and control.[3] Both raised concerns about the 'win at all costs' culture that appeared to be dominating youth football and about the behaviour of coaches and parents who allegedly applied too much pressure to children and referees and who seemed unable to deal with conflict aside from aggressive or violent means. To a certain extent, the Respect pro-gramme was a reaction to this pressure, but the fact that the essential struc-tures of the game remained the same meant that the situation was not entirely resolved.

Young people and Respect

With all of this in mind, the following section draws on data from two research projects commissioned by the FA in order to evaluate the success of the Respect pilot initiative and the first full year of the Respect programme itself. A range of stakeholders were tracked and interviewed in order to assess the impact of the programme's major interventions, specifically in the youth game's referee-captain relationship, the new Respect codes of conduct and the 'designated spectator areas' marked by the Respect barriers.[4] During the 2008–09 season (September–April) we conducted semi-structured interviews with over 100 young people under the age of ten who were active participants in affiliated football. The sample was drawn from a range of clubs across the UK in both urban and rural settings and included representatives from both the male and female versions of the sport. Participants offered views on the notion of respect, the need for specific interventions and the success of the tactics deployed in order to modify behaviour. These offerings provided interesting insight into the sporting experiences of young people, but also further evidence of how participants would like sport in general, and football in particular, to be organised. The data presented here are representative of the overall tenor of respondent opinion and are structured around the key conceptual themes which emerged during interview.[5]

Youth football and incivility

There was widespread acceptance amongst respondents that bad behaviour existed in and around football and that there was need for a cultural change programme. Most participants shared the view that some kind of intervention was necessary in order to deal with the levels of incivility which appeared to be a part of their experiences of the game. One of the participants commented, 'A lot of the time people do behave badly but if this [the Respect initiative] prevents it that's a good thing' whilst another young footballer stated: 'There's too many people out there just insulting the other team's supporters and the referee and the players. That's why they've started it [the initiative].'

Young people spoke of their experiences in relation to the specific interventions that formed part of the Respect initiative and the impact that these had had on their playing and matchday experiences. Most obvious to them was the changing relationship between players and referees, with the initial focus on team captains taking responsibility for communication with the official in the first instance. Most accepted the need for change in this area and also the need to understand the role of the official if the game was to be conducted in an appropriate manner. For example, one participant stated: 'I think it's good because it's trying to stop players from arguing with the ref and fighting, and trying to make football a better sport.' Another remarked: 'We have just been having one player [the team captain] go up to the referee if they think that something's happened and we've tried to behave a bit better.' There was also a clear acceptance of the need for pitch-side barriers to create more space for players and to generate a sense of distance between spectators, parents and the field of play, with one participant noting: 'You have to shake the hands of the opposition and, say there's a line of the pitch, the crowd have to stand six yards behind that to give the linesman space ... . It's good, it keeps the supporters off the pitch.'

Participant understandings of codes of conduct, and their requirements, were much more limited, although those who were aware of their presence were, again, generally supportive. For example, a participant observed: 'A few weeks ago, there was like people pushing me and fighting me and I was like shouting to the ref, but now I'm gonna stop that. I know it's not nice and that's all in the codes we had to sign.' A different participant was also in favour of this intervention, seeing it as 'part of a programme that helps people who get bullied in football and they're going to stop it. So people want to go out there and play football.'

With very few exceptions, the young people that we interviewed were supportive of The FA's Respect programme. They had an understanding of key elements of the programme and related these to their own experience. Many felt that more respect and more enjoyment was a necessary feature of an improving experience, and the vast majority welcomed the key interventions. This is clearly encouraging news for The FA and bodes well for the organisation's desire to instigate a cultural change programme that has the interests of young people at its core. Participants understood that, in order to be respectful themselves, they had to accept and tolerate the position of those in authority, namely the referee. The young people identified specific incivilities that, in their view, needed to be addressed, mostly on the part of spectators but also on the part of some opposing players and teammates. These incivilities were also measured against the implicit expectations of the sport, so it was important, for example, to 'shake hands at the end of a match' and to 'do the three cheers thing' and to recognise the contribution of opponents to any encounter. However, they also articulated more complex conceptions of respect that resonate with the academic conceptions presented earlier. Interestingly, respondents were willing to offer 'accommodations' (Goffman, 1972: 258) for adults who 'misbehaved' or 'crossed the line' in some instances in order to ensure that minor incidents did not escalate into something more serious. For example, one of the young people commented: 'The parents and coaches get a bit excited sometimes but it's only because they really care. I wish that they didn't do it but I guess they can't help themselves.' All of which indicated that it was not simply players that needed to be more respectful, but adults also.

Respectful adults?

A key strand within young participants' conceptions of respect that went beyond the common sense was the feeling that the needs of children were not always recognised or treated respectfully by adult stakeholders. So, while it may be argued (by adults) that it is respectful for players to recognise the needs and accept the authority of referees, coaches and other adults, how could those adult stakeholders be encouraged to act in mutually respectful ways? Sennett (2003) suggests that respect must be mutually negotiated, yet cannot be imposed. Some respondents considered this in relation to the current structures of football with comments such as: 'The way the referees talk to us sometimes. It doesn't exactly encourage us to be respectful to them. They can really talk down to people' and, 'I've seen the adults arguing sometimes and I just want to say, "What are you doing?" We just want to play football.' Other respondents pointed to versions of football where adults were less prominent: 'People say there would be loads of arguments if there was no referee, but I don't know. Sometimes I think they can cause as many problems.' Another participant made the observation: 'The best games are when you don't hear anything from the line and you don't notice the ref. You just enjoy the game.' Finally, one of the young footballers interviewed acknowledged: 'My Dad is the worst sometimes. But how do you tell your Dad that you don't want him to come? I can't do that!'

Implicit in these views is the possibility that the structure and format of the sport actually creates particular situations in which adult incivility is heightened. There is certainly potential for interaction with 'rude strangers' (Phillips and Smith, 2006: 899) in these settings, especially where the stakes are raised by the potential to gain status through team success. Crowds of spectators, whether they are behind barriers or not, will inevitably create pressure and expectancy for young people and, while it might be argued that this pressure is a necessary stimulus for heightened performance, it was clear that the young people interviewed preferred to put a sense of enjoyment first. More radically, the need for fully qualified, experienced referees to supervise competition in the primary school age groups can be questioned. Might greater mutuality and respect be achieved by the young people themselves taking responsibility for decision making or even by undertaking the role of official? Allowing children the freedom to experience and deal with incivilities during their experiences in football may allow them to develop 'tolerance, moral awareness and everyday solidarity in a society increasingly marked by difference, and more importantly by indifference' (Phillips and Smith, 2003: 105).

It became clear during the course of data collection that the Respect programme had had an impact on respondents' perceptions of sporting conduct. Whether this impact has been sustained in the second and third year of the programme is open to question, but early signs suggest that the interventions may well mitigate some of the incivilities that so concerned The FA at the outset. However, it is also clear that the versions of the game that have predominated for the past two decades are not the only possible alternatives and that other, more child-centred interpretations are possible and, perhaps, from the point of view of the participants, preferable. If such child-centred interpretations are to be successful, it would seem that respect needs to be at the heart of them. However, adults who are involved would do well to be cognisant that respect revolves around 'taking the needs of others seriously'

(Sennett, 2003: 52). Despite the higher social status of adults, within the development of children's football, children should be treated as collaborators and not unrepresented subordinates.

Conclusion: youth football – a new way forward?

For most of the first decade of the twenty-first century, it seemed unlikely that The FA would attempt to implement any radical changes to the format of youth football. Proponents of more child-centred approaches, and we would count ourselves among them, faced dogged opposition from clubs and leagues who, at so many levels, had proved to be successful, on the surface at least. The Respect programme itself has been based on modifications to existing provision rather than fundamental change. For example, there is now a heightened expectation of good behaviour towards referees, rather than any challenge to the purpose of officiating at different levels and in different formats of the game. Respect introduced barriers to contain spectators and to stimulate group 'norming' around more positive behaviour, but did not consider a version of the sport where adults had a reduced stake or where confrontations were minimised by the diminution of adult influence.

All of this makes the publication of The FA's (2011) *National Game Strategy* of particular interest. The Strategy sites The FA's Youth Development Review, the basis of which is the restructuring of the youth game in order to address the needs of young players, as expressed in a series of major consultations carried out by The FA during the previous two years.

The Review details a number of recommendations, the outcome of which could be the most radical restructuring of the youth game in England to date. Chief amongst these are:

- The development of more-flexible, child-centred competitions for primary school-aged children. This includes an end to published results and published league tables for these participants and the encouragement of more inclusive coaching and selection approaches.
- A new player pathway which moves children through 5 v. 5, 7 v. 7, 9 v. 9 and 11 v. 11 formats of the game as they get older, as opposed to the more rigid 7 v. 7 and 11 v. 11 formats currently in place.
- An intervention programme which aims to counter the relative age effect (RAE), which relates to the tendency for birth date to be a key factor in the selection and retention of footballers at all levels of the sport. In general, the historic position has been that footballers born between September and December are more likely to succeed and progress than those born at later stages of the academic year, due to their more advanced physical and psychological development.

As we write, these proposals are under review, with the potential for a phased introduction from the season 2013–14 onwards. They represent changes that focus on the expressed needs and demands of young people and have the potential to create sporting encounters that are quite different in character from those that have gone before. It is possible that these changes will lead to the development of more, and better, footballers and it is also possible that they may create more inclusive, enjoyable and sustainable footballing environments. Needless to say, how people experience respect and civility, and how The FA encourages these values in their new versions of the youth game, will be of considerable interest.

Notes

1 The technical area is a designated area for team managers, coaches, other technical and medical staff and substitutes. All personnel must remain within the confines of the technical area unless they are given permission to leave it by the referee. Only one person at a time is allowed to coach or give tactical instructions from the technical area.
2 See http://TheFA.com.
3 Details of these campaigns can be found at: http:www.giveusbackourgame.co.uk/ and http://www.dontxtheline.com respectively.
4 Referees were encouraged to work with team captains in order to manage the behaviour of players during the game. Captains were asked to take more responsibility for the behaviour of their players. Players, spectators, coaches/managers and referees were encouraged to sign up to Codes of Conduct. Branded 'Respect' barriers were introduced to keep spectators in a designated area and away from the side of the pitch.
5 It should be noted that 'Respect' is a long-term behavioural change programme. This research was carried out during the early stages of the initiative.

References

Bannister, J., Fyfe, N. and Kearns, A. (2006) Respectable or Respectful? (In)civility and the City. *Urban Studies*, 43(5/6), 919–937.
Bauman, Z. (2000) *Liquid Modernity*. Cambridge: Polity Press.
Brackenridge, C., Pitchford, A. and Wilson, M. (2011) Respect: Results of a Pilot Project Designed To Improve Behaviour in English Football. *Managing Leisure*, 16 (3), 175–191.
Brackenridge, C., Pitchford, A., Russell, K. and Nutt, G. (2007) *Child Welfare in Football: An Exploration of Children's Welfare in the Modern Game*. London: Routledge.
Burney, E. (2005) *Making People Behave: Anti-social Behaviour, Politics and Policy*. Collumpton: Willan.
Burns, T. (1992) *Irving Goffman*. London: Routledge.
Darwall, S. (1977) Two Kinds of Respect. *Ethics*, 88(1), 36–49.
——(1995) Two Kinds of Respect. In R.S. Dillon (ed.) *Dignity, Character, and Self-Respect*. New York: Routledge, 181–197.
Dillon, R.S. (ed.) (1995) Introduction. In *Dignity, Character, and Self-Respect*. New York: Routledge, 1–49.
Football Association (FA) (2011) *National Game Strategy 2011–15*. London: Football Association.

Fyfe, N., Bannister, J. and Kearns, A. (2006) (In)civility and the City. *Urban Studies*, 43(5/6), 919–938.

Home Office (2006) *The Respect Action Plan*. London: The Home Office.

Jeffries, S. (2006, 14 January) With Respect. *The Guardian*. Available at: www.guardian.co.uk/politics/2006/jan/14/politicsphilosophyandsociety.books

Phillips, T. and Smith, P. (2003) Everyday Incivility: Towards a Benchmark. *The Sociological Review*, 51 (1), 85–108.

——(2006) Rethinking Urban Incivility Research: Strangers, Bodies and Circulations. *Urban Studies*, 43(5/6), 879–901.

Sennett, R. (2003) *Respect: The Formation of Character in an Age of Inequality*. London: Penguin.

Wilkinson, H. (1997) *Football Education for Young Players: A Charter for Quality*. London: Football Association.

7 Sport, development and African culture

Elizabeth Annett and Samuel Mayuni

Introduction

The purpose of this chapter is two-fold. First, it seeks to provide an overview of how sport has come to be seen as a mechanism through which international development might be facilitated. Second, it presents empirical evidence from one particular sport-for-development programme in southern Africa, 'Sport Malawi', in order to illustrate the impact of African culture on programme delivery. The empirical findings under consideration were obtained during a series of collaborative data collection visits to the Malawian cities of Lilongwe, Blantyre and Mzuzu by the two authors in the summer of 2010. This fieldwork yielded qualitative data from a range of community sports providers about the ability of sport to bring 'development' to individuals and collectives within communities. Ensuing discussion brings to the fore the 'voices' of local people concerning their experiences of sport-for-development provision and raises a series of key questions about the nature of work in this substantive area. The recent expansion of research in the sport-for-development field has been closely accompanied by mandatory monitoring and evaluation obligations. This has resulted in many researchers 'trying their hand' at reporting the impact of such programmes in environments of social, cultural and political complexity. It is particularly difficult for Western researchers to grapple with these issues in non-Western cultures and it is for this reason that the chapter is co-authored by a researcher from the West (EA) and one from Malawi (SM). The hope is that this approach will bring added balance and insight to the issues under consideration.

The chapter is structured around three main themes. The first addresses the current state of sport-for-development and contemporary debates surrounding how research in this area should be conducted. The second then briefly outlines the scope and remit of the Sport Malawi programme. The third considers the key aspects of African culture that continue to shape Sport Malawi, namely how sport is perceived within government, school-based education and faith communities.

Sport-for-development: an overview

The increasing prominence of sport in the public policy agendas of advanced industrial societies is a characteristic of late twentieth-century politics. The concept of sport-for-development, originally linked to the domestic policy arena, has increasingly become part of wider debates concerning international development. A number of high-profile political statements (including the Sport and Development International Conference Magglingen Recommendations of 2003 and 2005, and United Nations (UN, 2003) Resolution 58/5) have further fuelled expectations surrounding the capacity of sport to deliver a range of development goals. The popularity and acceleration of sport-for-development initiatives over the last decade (Jeanes and Kay, 2010; Kay, 2009; Kidd, 2008; Levermore, 2011) has witnessed the onset of a range of projects from those that target specific social issues or 'problems' to broader ventures that have an altogether wider remit or geographical spread. Their forms are many and, perhaps somewhat inevitably, it is the grass-roots, community-initiated, sport-for-development programmes that are often 'invisible' to those who attempt to map (i.e. measure) this growing movement. Therefore, sport-for-development frameworks should not only consider those programmes that benefit from external funding, but also the variety of local projects resulting from what Kay (2011a: 282) refers to as the 'interaction of internal and external interests'.

The Sport for Development and Peace International Working Group (SDP IWG), a body hosted by the United Nations and charged with the task of promoting the integration of Sport for Development and Peace (SDP),[1] identifies eight areas in which sport contributes to development, namely: (i) individual development (health, social skills and organisational ability); (ii) health promotion and disease prevention; (iii) the promotion of gender equality; (iv) social integration and disease prevention; (v) peace building and conflict prevention or resolution; (vi) post-disaster trauma relief and normalisation of life; (vii) economic development; and (viii) communication and social mobilisation (SDPIWG, 2006). These areas were reflected in the perceived compatibility of sport to contribute towards the international development community's attainment of the United Nations (UN) Millennium Development Goals (MDGs).

Despite the enthusiastic promotion of sport-for-development by specialist development agencies such as the UN and the World Health Organization (WHO), the same kind of approach cannot be said to be evident among traditional development agencies. This lack of engagement is recognised by a range of commentators, including the International Labour Organization (Di Cola, 2005: 1) which has stated that, 'in most cases development leaders perceive sports as a recreational tool rather than a value-based engine of social changes'. Similarly, it is suspected that some non-governmental organisations (NGOs) view things in much the same manner, seeing sport-for-development projects as somewhat amateurish and as a potential distraction from other forms of intervention for which funding is required. Paradoxically, Levermore and Beacom (2009: 1) suggest that the expansion of sport-for-development in recent years is 'partially the result of the recognition that the orthodox polices of "development" have failed to deliver their objectives'. Reflecting these shortcomings, SDP faces the same challenge: that, despite the rhetoric and expansion, researchers are still unsure whether sport-for-development actually works (Kay, 2011a; Coalter 2007, 2009).

Sport-for-development: research, practice and praxis

The high expectations surrounding the capacity of sport to deliver development has not been matched by the level of critical analysis applied to the impact of sport-for-development programmes (Beacom and Levermore, 2008). Characterised by notions of programme justification, such research has primarily been descriptive in nature (Levermore and Beacom, 2009), leaving Coalter (2007, 2009) to call for more robust and sophisticated forms of analysis that disentangle the 'process' to better understand the 'outcomes', or lack of them. In turn, Kay (2009) has insightfully observed that, having been traditionally grounded in positivist, empirical epistemologies (prioritising 'hard' evidence), research within this field has overlooked the value of indigenous views and knowledge.

More recently, there has been a concerted effort from a network of academic scholars to engage in debates surrounding the decolonisation of methodology and knowledge, and to develop an understanding of sport-for-development impact that originates authentically from the communities in which projects are located (see Jeanes, 2010; Lindsay *et al.*, 2010; Magee, 2010; Mwaanga, 2010; Annett, 2011; Banda, 2011; Beacom and Read, 2011; Kay, 2011b). The emergence of such discussion is crucial to the work of both practitioners and researchers from the Global North in helping to contest uncritical social, cultural and political assumptions and to address the neocolonial relationships involved (Coalter, 2010; Darnell, 2010; Jarvie, 2011).

This growing literature extends beyond research to practice. For example, there is no lack of criticism from those who view sport-for-development through dependency and post-colonial perspectives (Darnell and Hayhurst, 2011). Indeed, a number of theoretical and empirical studies have highlighted how a series of political issues remain unresolved in this respect (Black, 2010; Darnell, 2010; Darnell and Hayhurst, 2011; Kay, 2009). In this sense, contemporary sport-for-development programmes remain implicated in the Northern hegemony of institutions and international relations. This reflects concerns that much of sport-for-development is driven by Northern aims, objectives and what is seen as feasible – therefore marginalising and excluding Southern alternative approaches (Bendell, 2005). Moreover, Southern sport-for-development NGOs are also criticised for being excessively influenced by the Northern partners who fund them. Of late, such concerns have culminated in calls for the adoption of a 'decolonising praxis' by way of approaches that question and challenge institutions, practices and ideas which serve to sustain (and promote) inequality and Northern power, as well as misrepresenting and ignoring the voices within localities (Darnell and Hayhurst, 2011). For some scholars, this is comparable to the historical utilisation of sport for the colonial purposes of strengthening empires, 'civilising' local populations and securing social hegemony (Mangan, 2006). Central to the decolonisation of sport-for-development is an acknowledgment of the 'decentred' approaches of many localities in the Global South that are primarily indigenous, and which operate with limited international input (Lindsay and Grattan, 2012). Such approaches contradict the neocolonial critique advocated by others (Darnell and Hayhurst, 2012) that sport-for-development can only be viewed as 'part of an external agenda with essentially no local design or input' (Akindes and Kirwan, 2009: 242).

Sport Malawi

Founded and co-ordinated by the present authors, Sport Malawi is a sport-for-development initiative centred around a partnership between the University of Gloucestershire (UoG), UK and significant local agencies within sport, education and outreach in Malawi, southern Africa.[2] The initiative has a strong sport-for-development agenda focussing both on sports development and development through sport. The emphasis is on training indigenous sports community workers (coaches, teachers and youth workers) and organisations (Sports Council, Football Association, schools and community groups) through workshops and coaching sessions; addressing the role of sport as a vehicle for change, with a particular focus on young people, inclusion and HIV prevention.

University communities have the potential to tackle social issues and lead practical change. The Sport Malawi programme aims to fulfil this ambition by training and educating organisations and individuals on how sport can fuel change for economic development, poverty alleviation, health improvement, community building and the promotion of equality and justice for all. Sport Malawi began in 2008 and has developed resilient partnerships with government ministries, the media, universities, schools, civil society and faith-based organisations in Malawi – all of which unite behind its 'sport for good' agenda. It is a long-term project which, to date, has involved 50 UoG students and staff working with nearly 1,500 Malawians, sharing skills and ideas on how to use sport to reach vulnerable groups, to attract young people into education, to communicate messages associated with the prevention of HIV and the promotion of good health, and to carry out development projects such as providing sports facilities in local communities.

Sport Malawi 'development' is two-way; UoG staff and students who visit Malawi inevitably shift their perspectives when faced with complex issues in new global settings. The University gains a wealth of energy and ideas from these visits which feed into curricular activities across its sport, exercise, health, social care and youth work courses. UoG students lead workshops in Malawi and experience being catalysts for social change, as well as gaining new skills to support their own futures. The underlying ethos of the programme is as follows:

- using workshops and coaching sessions to establish the role that sport can play as a vehicle for sustainability and social change and as an entry point for thinking about equality, education and development;
- placing responsibility on UoG students to 'train trainers' – namely sports community workers (i.e. coaches, teachers, and youth workers);
- sharing techniques and skills to show how development and education can be integrated within sports programmes with a focus on youth, inclusion, health and HIV prevention;
- providing Malawian participants with new skill sets which they can adapt to projects in their local area, thereby bringing change to communities.

The direct benefits 'on the ground' for Malawians do not simply manifest themselves in the tangible project legacies but also by way of community building in local societies, improving skills in local organisations, sharing ideas and best practice, coaching opportunities, the development of local athletes and opportunities to study at the UoG. It is to a closer analysis of the practical impacts of the initiative that we now turn.

Context and method

Malawi is a country that is relatively peaceful, stable, yet fearfully poor. The capital city, Lilongwe, is leafy, sleepy and ever sprawling into the surrounding countryside. By day, sunlight bounces off a million palm fronds. By night, the city is so dark one could almost imagine its non-existence. There are few working street lights, except in the Old and New Town areas. Lilongwe's grander buildings were largely paid for by the old South African regime, to reward the late Life President, Hastings Banda, for not supporting wider political sanctions. Banda was unusual among African leaders in that he demonstrated elements of flexibility within his leadership, yet in other respects he manifested characteristics of dictatorship. As he entered his nineties, he started to lose political control. In 1994, he succumbed to pressure to allow elections. Malawi is now more democratic, but none the richer.

The data presented here were gathered as part of a larger research project concerning the wider sustainability of the Sport Malawi initiative and were collected by way of three focus group interviews (16 participants in total) which were carried out in July–August 2010 (see Annett, 2011). Respondents comprised community sports providers (i.e. coaches, teachers and youth workers), government officials and church leaders,[3] all of whom had previously attended training led by Sport Malawi programme staff. Focus groups lasted 60–90 minutes and were transcribed verbatim. The subsequent analysis revealed a series of themes concerning the implementation and impact of the initiative. In what follows we provide a more in-depth exploration of three of these themes, namely: (i) sport and Malawian culture; (ii) sport, community and religion; and (iii) sport, church and spirituality.

Sport and Malawian culture

A particular challenge facing sport development and sport-for-development in Malawi is that of developing sport and physical activity in the education system. As things stand, there is an urgent need for improved training for teachers and for curriculum development. This situation was expounded by Luguno,[4] who worked in the regional Ministry of Education office in Lilongwe:

> Physical Education is not taught in most of the schools. Teachers take it just as a mere subject, they don't dare teach it ... they'll say you can't teach this [as] it's a non-examinable subject ... so that is a very big hindrance. But if these teachers can be fully trained to follow the career path, with a good curriculum, based on what we [Sport Malawi] are focussing, I'm sure we are going to achieve something.

Evident here are two key issues. First, Physical Education is denied equality with other curriculum subjects. The main reason for this is that, during the last two decades, there has been an overemphasis on the core examinable subjects in schools to the effect that non-examinable subjects such as Physical Education have received very little, if any, attention. In most schools Physical Education predominantly equates to a class of pupils being allowed to play football and netball on surrounding school land. Second, this situation is compounded by the fact that Malawi does not currently provide adequate teacher training (nor does it have the institutions to provide such training) to those seeking to specialise in Physical Education.

There are several educational institutions that train teachers in Malawi. Primary school teachers are trained in four public teacher training colleges in Blantyre, Karonga, Kasunga and Lilongwe. Some attend grant-aided and private colleges, namely St. Joseph, Development Aid from People to People (DAPP) and Emmanuel teacher training colleges. Secondary school teachers are trained in three public institutions, which include Chancellor College, Domasi College of Education (both University of Malawi) and Mzuzu University. Other private universities and colleges have recently started training secondary school teachers; these include the University of Livingstonia, the African Bible College and the Catholic University.

The lack of training for teachers wanting to specialise in Physical Education is certainly not aided by the fact that there is also a dearth of good quality facilities to support the teaching of the subject, particularly in the rural areas. Kondwani, a church leader noted that 'all the schools we have, they have no infrastructure – except at a few secondary schools'. Many respondents suggested that this was linked to the country's weak economy, therefore making it difficult for the Ministry of Education to provide adequate teaching and learning facilities for ancillary subjects such as Physical Education.

Moreover, from a government perspective, Luguno also spoke about how the challenges for school sport lay not only with infrastructural constraint, but also with the collective mindset:

> It's because it's a government policy, whatever is sport, I think it is not a priority. But it's an inborn instinct – the child will start dancing at an early age, looking at what the parents are doing. So, you can see if that culture can be brought in [to schools] at least in the right manner, we'll get something. It must be the culture that we must develop in sport.

Such insight leads to the idea that both formal and informal training is required; this knowledge transfer includes both external partners coming to Malawi to run workshops and internal partners sharing their knowledge and encouraging the local people to become involved in physical activity. This 'training of trainers' was explained by Mlengalenga, a church leader:

> The other thing is the training of trainers. As a church representative I'm fully trained ... I'm local and on the ground. I can also pass on the knowledge to my fellow leaders ... and in part it would boost their knowledge because now it will be on the ground, man to man, and we understand each other.

Integrating sport and physical activity into the local worldview and developing curricular provision within the education system emphasises the significance of contextualising sport development and SDP in a way that builds on the historical circumstances of the country. Chikoso, a community coach in Blantyre, reflected on the historical and cultural importance of sport for Malawians:

> The whole point that [be]comes very clear is [that] the way we regard sport has been critical. For Malawians, we need sport. You go back down in history, even they, they synchronised the sports; we are brought into our life believing that we have sports. Which was casual and local, because we spent the night, whenever there was a moon, we played and we would have games. That's the concept of sport ... [it's] part and parcel of what we are.

Here, Chikoso appears to allude to a time when sport and physical activity was taken more seriously in Malawi or at least carried more cultural kudos.

At a certain point, however, something changed; he went on: 'not necessarily the culture as such, because the culture had no problems with children playing at night ... getting busy with their sporting careers'. Chikoso continued to explain how, with the rise of formal institutionalised education, physical activity and sport became downgraded in terms of their importance within society. Consequently, sport is now seen by many Malawians as a relatively worthless pastime. This current (and dominant) view was echoed by Wilson, a member of the academic staff at Mzuzu University:

> One of the challenges is that we are now operating in an environment that does not have a proper background in terms of sporting activities and so it becomes difficult to convince everybody [of its importance]. Even as a parent, if my son is very good at football, I will stop him and tell him to work hard at school ... . Every quarter of society has to be educated [on the importance of sport].

By reflecting on such sentiments, Sport Malawi workers have been able to contextualise programme delivery in order to situate it in line with public perceptions of sport and physical activity. As a consequence, local partners have begun to take ownership of the Sport Malawi philosophy (i.e. the promotion of sport), and the benefits of sport and physical activity have subsequently come to be more accepted (and embedded) in local cultures and amongst those working in the country's education system.

Sport, community and religion

Across the spectrum of participants involved with Sport Malawi, a consensus has been established around the broad sport-for-development vision which directs the programme's objectives, namely addressing community needs through sport. This includes using sport to help achieve gender equality, and fight the HIV/AIDS pandemic in an environment of chronic poverty. Chambers (1993) describes poverty as a web of five reinforcing factors. These comprise: lack of resources, vulnerability, isolation, powerlessness and physical weakness. Sport is implicated within this toxic web. From the data gathered, two aspects of the Sport Malawi initiative appear to stand out within the minds of programme participants: first, emancipation through knowledge sharing and, second, the inclusion of the local church in programme activities. This was summed up by a community coach living in Lilongwe:

> The first thing that Sport Malawi is trying to address initially is the knowledge that people lack – training and knowledge; how to manage sport and develop it. Another thing I think that Sport Malawi is trying to do is to relate the use of the church as part of the community where sport can be developed. It should be a collaborative issue with the Football Association of Malawi, [and] maybe [the] Ministry of Sports and Culture,

so that all these things must be taken [considered] because they are for the benefits of the youth in the country.

Of course, the relationship between sport and the church has a long colonial history (Mangan, 2006). In the late 1800s the arrival of missionaries in Africa was, at best, a mixed blessing. Many leaders collaborated with the would-be-colonisers against the interests of their purported congregation, and the use of violence was commonplace. The Scottish Missions in Malawi were a welcome exception in this respect (Hokkanen and Mangan, 2006). Inspired by Livingstone's humanitarian values and his respect for local peoples, they made great efforts to end tribal wars and to curb slavery, often risking their own lives in the process. Today around 80 per cent of the country's population subscribe to Christianity as a worldview and many of the local partners of Sport Malawi hold the modern missionary movement in high regard. Indeed, Malawian churches continue to play an important role in facilitating community sports programmes. The role of spirituality is not absent from the narrative of Sport Malawi, its roots belonging to the Chaplaincy and Faiths Department of the University of Gloucestershire. At the outset of the project these underpinnings were recognised in Malawi, where a core group of individuals (all involved with churches and faith-based organisations) worked to generate close links between the Sport Malawi representatives and the country's education and sport sectors. Partners from all these sectors have collaborated to provide the human resources, structure, vision and determination to enable the programme to meet its targets. In this sense, Sport Malawi has experienced the benefits of multi-stakeholder collaboration.

Hokkanen (2005: 748) notes that, even though the early Scottish missionaries had a less prominent ideology of athleticism than some of their counterparts, they were 'important intermediaries for modern sport in Malawi'. In turn, Sport Malawi seeks to act in an intermediary role to broker renewed relationships between sport and church communities in order to encourage young people to see physical activity as a valuable pursuit in and of itself, and, more importantly, to enlighten them in relation to broader social concerns. Kondwani, a church leader in Lilongwe, articulated his interpretation of this process:

> Sport Malawi is trying to make the church in Malawi understand that we too can use sport for outreach and development because we have been looking at sport as something social, not intended to do special things. But Sport Malawi is trying to make us understand that the values in sport can also be applied.

Mlengalenga, another church leader, added,

> Their [the youths'] behaviour out there is not all that pleasant. I'm sure that through sports we are going to address some of the needs: the

spiritual part of it which we always strive for, and the social part of it, which is also an attraction to a lot of youths in the churches. So sports will address such challenges and needs where we can educate the youths for career development, issues to do with HIV/AIDS and other social activities which are taking place in communities. Such are the challenges which Sport Malawi will address in collaboration with the church.

Many SDP organisations that work nationally and internationally often view faith-based interventions which utilise sport with an element of suspicion and refuse to fund organisations that are seen to propagate a certain world-view. Hochachka (2009: 133) has noted that, 'when working in community development, one does not need to have the same spirituality or religion of the community, but one does need to understand and respect the indigenous belief systems, and give them space to emerge in the development process'.

Sport, church and spirituality

From their work in developing sports leaders within communities, Sport Malawi representatives recognise and appreciate that worldviews and social norms mesh with the deeply held beliefs of local people and are shaped by a variety of traditions and customs. Interviews with respondents revealed a deep yearning to 'go back to the way it used to be – encouraging youth to take part in sports' (Anthony). Since the time when sports participation was encouraged amongst young people in Malawi, the collective mindset has been altered. The following account by Emmanuel illustrates this well:

So many pastors now, and church leaders, don't see the connection between sports and Christianity, or sports and development; people still think that sports are evil. Let me give you my testimony. I became a Christian when I was still playing football and one of the Christians advised me to stop playing because it was 'sinful'. Actually he advised me to repay my football sins because I was making damage going this way. So, you can see that really there is a challenge. But when I went to the African Bible College I took a course in Sports Evangelism and then my eyes were opened, and I saw the link between sports and Christian life, and sports and development.

Emmanuel's experiences reflect a puritanical theology of sport (see Watson *et al.*, 2005; Erdozain, 2010) that is still prevalent in some Malawian communities. Often, traditional church leaders propagate the view that sport is not the best way for young people to spend their time, because competitive sports at the local level take place on Saturdays and Sundays and are often seen as a distraction from church attendance. Furthermore, modern-day sport is seen to promote unacceptable values with sportsmen and women, both local and global, being associated with behaviour that could encourage drinking, gambling and keeping bad company, sentiments which reflect wider Western concerns (see Hoffman, 2010; Krattenmaker, 2010). However, many faith-based youth leaders not only have a theology which values sport for its inherent beauty, but hold more utilitarian views mirroring those underpinning sport-for-development. This approach was epitomised by Kondwani, a young pastor in Blantyre:

> There isn't a lot of entertainment out there [for the youth], and if there's no sporting activity what do these young people do? You know, so they involve themselves in really bad things. It could be stealing, it could be smoking Indian hemp, they could be having unprotected sex, getting pregnant, getting kicked out of school. So, for me, I think that there's a need for behavioural change, and one thing that Sport Malawi can really do is to be able to reach out in that sense.

To change mindsets relating to the potential of sport for positive change requires community sports leaders to authentically connect with local people and to foster dialogue and ownership to build new meaning around cultural and historical circumstance. Without this, no amount of money or external know-how is sufficient to bring about change within communities. Sports outreach interventions and training should aim to understand and build on a nation's historical and cultural heritage to bring about fundamental social transformation that money, projects, or external partnerships alone can neither stimulate nor sustain.

Conclusion

The aim of this chapter has been to provide an empirical account of the complexities of sport-for-development within the context of one international, sport-based initiative, Sport Malawi. In this concluding section we summarise the key points of the chapter and make suggestions for future work in this substantive area.

Our discussion has focussed on three main issues. To begin we have outlined current debates around sport-for-development as a concept, emphasising the political tensions in play and the need for researchers to adopt appropriate and sensitive approaches to their scholarly and practical work. In turn, we have provided an overview of the Sport Malawi project, focussing specifically on the underpinning principles around which the project was initially conceived and is continually implemented. Central here is the involvement of local Malawian people in project design and delivery. Our empirical analysis then presented evidence of the ways in which such understandings have subsequently allowed the Sport Malawi programme to be acknowledged and accepted across various sectors and communities and how this has led to sport becoming a medium for broader social transformation.

For sport-for-development programmes across Africa and further afield, it is important for project leaders (and workers) to consider how participants feel when outside organisations do not fully take into account broader social norms, customs and traditions. Does this lead to local people perceiving themselves as objects of intervention, where scientific knowledge is valued over and above personal experience, where established 'ways of knowing' are deemed less valuable and reliable, and where cultural sensitivities are overlooked during project planning, implementation, evaluation and reporting: where the supposed recipients of such interventions are silenced? It is commonplace for sport-for-development programmes in Africa to be subjected to objective assessment by 'outside' professional agencies in relation to the technical and managerial effectiveness, efficiency and viability of intervention work. Nevertheless, without appropriate understanding of cultural heritage, such programmes may unwittingly be designed and implemented without any real input from prospective participants and/or their representatives and, therefore, fail to relate to their everyday needs in a way that is most meaningful to them.

Notes

1 See: www.un.org/wcm/content/site/sport/home/unplayers/memberstates/pid/6229.
2 See: www.sportmalawi.org.
3 Prior to the onset of the research, ethical approval was gained from the charitable organisations involved in programme delivery and from the University of Gloucestershire Research Ethics Sub-Committee.
4 To preserve anonymity, pseudonyms have been used throughout.

References

Akindes, G. and Kirwan, M., (2009), 'Sport as International Aid: Assisting development or promoting under-development in sub-Saharan Africa?', in R. Levermore and A. Beacom (Eds) *Sport and International Development*. London: Palgrave Macmillan, pp. 215–245.

Annett, E. (2011), 'We're All Ears: Towards an indigenous understanding of making Sport Malawi a sustainable community, national and international sport-for-development initiative'. MA Dissertation: University of Gloucestershire, UK.

Banda, D. (2011), 'Sport in Action: Young people, sex education and HIV/AIDS in Zambia', in B. Houlihan and M. Green (Eds) *Routledge Handbook of Sports Development*. London: Routledge, pp. 323–336.

Beacom, A. and Levermore, R. (2008), 'International Policy and Sport-in-Development', in V. Girginov (Ed.) *Management of Sports Development*. Oxford: Elsevier, pp. 109–126.

Beacom, A. and Read, L. (2011), 'Right to Play: Sustaining development through sport', in B. Houlihan and M. Green (Eds) *Routledge Handbook of Sports Development*. London: Routledge, pp. 337–354.

Bendell, J. (2005), 'In Whose Name? The accountability of corporate social responsibility'. *Development in Practice*, 15 (3–4): 375–388.

Black, D. (2010), 'The Ambiguities of Development: Implications for development through sport'. *Sport in Society*, 13(1): 121–129.

Chambers, R. (1993), *Challenging the Professionals: Frontiers for rural development.* London: Institute of Development Studies.

Coalter, F. (2010), 'The Politics of Sport-for-development: Limited focus programmes and broad gauge problems?'. *International Review for the Sociology of Sport*, 45 (3): 295–314.

——(2009), 'Sport-in-development: Accountability or development?', in R. Levermore and A. Beacom (Eds) *Sport and International Development*. London: Palgrave Macmillan.

——(2007), *A Wider Role for Sport: Who's keeping the score?* London: Routledge.

Darnell, S. (2010), 'Power, Politics and "Sport for Development and Peace": Investigating the utility of sport for international development'. *Sociology of Sport*, 27(1): 54–75.

Darnell, S. and Hayhurst, L. (2012), 'Hegemony, Postcolonialism and Sport-for-development: A response to Lindsey and Grattan'. *International Journal of Sport Policy and Politics*, 4 (1): 111–124.

——(2011), 'Sport for Decolonization: Exploring a new praxis of sport for development'. *Progress in Development Studies*, 11 (3): 183–196.

Di Cola, G. (2005), *ILO's Youth Sport Programme and Common Framework on Sport and Development*. Geneva: International Labour Organisation.

Erdozain, D. (2010), *The Problem of Pleasure: Sport, recreation and the crisis of Victorian religion*. London: The Boydell Press.

Hochachka, G. (2009), 'Depth and Dynamism of Integral Applications in International Development'. *Journal of Integral Theory and Practice*, 4 (2): 125–150.

Hoffman, S.J. (2010), *Good Game: Christianity and the culture of sports*. Waco, TX: Baylor University Press.

Hokkanen, H. (2005), '"Christ and the Imperial Games Fields" in South-Central Africa – Sport and the Scottish Missionaries in Malawi, 1880–1914: Utilitarian compromise'. *International Journal of the History of Sport*, 22 (4): 745–769.

Hokkanen, M. and Mangan, J.A. (2006), 'Further Variations on a Theme: The games ethic further adapted – Scottish moral missionaries and muscular Christians in Malawi'. *International Journal of the History of Sport*, 23 (8): 1257–1274.

Jarvie, G. (2011), 'Sport, Development and Aid: Can sport make a difference?'. *Sport in Society*, 12 (2): 241–252.

Jeanes, R. (2010), 'Zambian Young People's View on HIV/AIDS Education Through Sport'. *Leisure Studies Association Newsletter*, 85: 44–49.

Jeanes, R., and Kay, T. (2010), 'Developing Through Sport and Leisure? Critical perspectives from the international development context'. *Leisure Studies Association Newsletter*, 85: 34–36.

Kay, T. (2011a), 'Sport and International Development Introduction: The unproven remedy', in B. Houlihan and M. Green (Eds) *Routledge Handbook of Sports Development*. London: Routledge, pp. 281–284.

——(2011b), 'Development Through Sport? Sport in support of female empowerment in Delhi, India', in B. Houlihan and M. Green (Eds) *Routledge Handbook of Sports Development*. London: Routledge, pp. 308–322.

——(2009), 'Developing Through Sport: Evidencing sport impacts on young people'. *Sport in Society*, 12 (9): 1158–1176.

Kidd, B. (2008), 'A New Social Movement: Sport for development and peace'. *Sport and Society*, 11 (4): 370–380.

Krattenmaker, T. (2010), *Onward Christian Athletes: Turning ballparks into pulpits and players into preachers*. New York: Rowman and Littlefield.

Levermore, R. (2011), 'Evaluating Sport-for-development: Approaches and critical issues'. *Progress in Development Studies*, 11 (4): 339–353.

Levermore, R. and Beacom, A. (2009), *Sport and International Development*. London: Palgrave Macmillan.

Lindsay, I. and Grattan, A. (2012), 'An "International Movement"? Decentring sport-for-development within Zambian communities'. *International Journal of Sport Policy and Politics*, 4 (1): 91–110.

Lindsay, I., Namukanga, A., Kakome, G., and Grattan, A. (2010), Adventures in Research: Enabling community impact through sport for development research. *Leisure Studies Association Newsletter*, 85: 56–60.

Magee, J. (2010), 'Developing People Through Sport: Personal and professional reflections on the Homeless World Cup'. *Leisure Studies Association Newsletter*, 85: 50–56.

Mangan, J. (2006), 'Christ and the Imperial Playing Fields: Thomas Hughes's ideological heirs in empire'. *The International Journal of the History of Sport*, 23 (5): 777–804.

Mwaanga, O. (2010), 'Sport for Addressing HIV/AIDS: Explaining our convictions'. *Leisure Studies Association Newsletter*, 85: 44–49.

Sport and Development First International Conference (2003), *The Magglingen Declaration and Recommendations*. UNSDP and Swiss Academy for Development, Geneva.

Sport and Development Second International Conference (2005), *The Magglingen Call for Action*. UNSDP and Swiss Academy for Development, Geneva.

Sport for Development and Peace International Working Group (2006), *Sport for Development and Peace, From Practice to Policy*. Toronto: UNSDP.

United Nations (UN) (2003), *Sport as a Means to Promote Education, Health, Development and Peace*. Resolution 58/5. United Nations General Assembly, Geneva.

Watson, N.J., Weir, S. and Friend, S. (2005), 'The Development of Muscular Christianity in Victorian Britain and Beyond'. *Journal of Religion and Society*, 7 (1): 1–25.

Part III
Participation

Part III
Participation

8 Physical activity and sedentary behaviour among adolescents

*Christopher S. Owens, Diane Crone,
David V. B. James*

Introduction

There is widespread concern about the low levels of physical activity and high rates of sedentary behaviour in adolescents[1] in the UK (Department of Health, 2011). Lifestyle choices, such as physical activity participation, are established and embedded as people proceed through adolescence; thus the amount of physical activity undertaken by adolescents in their teenage years is increasingly recognised as a key determinant of physical activity levels in adulthood (Hallal *et al.*, 2006a). Additionally, adequate participation in physical activity during childhood and adolescence may play a significant role in the prevention of chronic disease later in life (Twisk *et al.*, 2002). In recognition of these behavioural patterns and health implications, specific physical activity recommendations, which include taking part in sport, for children and young people have recently been published in a UK-wide Chief Medical Officers' report (Department of Health, 2011). Due to concerns over sedentary behaviour among children and young people, this report also proposed a recommendation for limiting sedentary behaviour (sitting) time (Department of Health, 2011). However, this recommendation did not quantify the amount of sedentary behaviour that constitutes a suitable limit, but perhaps this is not surprising given that research in the area of sedentary behaviour is in its infancy (Gorely *et al.*, 2009). Nevertheless the existing evidence that an increasing proportion of the population are failing to meet guidelines for physical activity and sedentary behaviour through the course of adolescence suggests that future research effort needs to focus on factors associated with changes in physical activity and sedentary behaviour through adolescence. This research effort will require prospective longitudinal observational studies that examine individuals over time to understand fully the patterns of behaviours and associated factors.

The aims of the present chapter are to: (i) explain why it is important to have an understanding of physical activity and sedentary behaviour during adolescence; (ii) outline current recommendations for physical activity and sedentary behaviour and policies aimed at reducing the decline in physical activity and the increase in sedentary behaviour through the course of adolescence; (iii) summarise evidence from studies using self-reported data focusing on the levels and the trends or changes in the levels of each behaviour with increasing age; and (iv) explain the need for further prospective longitudinal observational studies examining these behaviours throughout adolescence and the factors associated with changes in these behaviours.

Physical activity participation and sedentary behaviour among adolescents – why is it an issue?

Physical inactivity (i.e. not meeting a criterion amount of physical activity) is recognised as a global public health concern for all ages (World Health Organization, 2010). Consequently, increasing physical activity among adolescents to a level that meets health-related physical activity guidelines is a major public health challenge (Allison *et al.*, 2007). The increasing interest in adolescent physical activity is primarily a consequence of public health considerations, since it is believed that physical activity in the future adult population and associated health benefits might be improved by encouraging improved habits of leisure-time physical activity among children and youths (Anderssen *et al.*, 2006). Many studies consistently show that physical activity declines sharply during adolescence (e.g. Eiðsdóttir *et al.*, 2008). However, levels of participation are mixed at the age range associated with this decline and appear to depend upon the country in which research is conducted. For example, in the UK, the decline has been shown in ages 11–16 years, with a reduction in the mean number of days of vigorous physical activity per week in boys and girls of 1.06 days and 1.82 days, respectively (Henning Brodersen *et al.*, 2007). Conversely, in Finland, the decline has been shown in ages 16–18 years, with only 46.7 per cent of boys and 46.3 per cent of girls who participated in physical activity daily at age 16 years also doing so at age 18 years (Aarnio *et al.*, 2002).

There is also growing global concern regarding trends of increasing sedentary behaviour among adolescents (Salmon *et al.*, 2011). Indeed, sedentary behaviour has become a major focal area in obesity research, interventions and policies (Boone *et al.*, 2007). Sedentary behaviour is not defined simply as a lack of physical activity, but is a collection of individual behaviours where sitting or lying is the main posture and where energy expenditure is very low (Department of Health, 2011). For example, key sedentary behaviours include screen time (television viewing, videogames and computer use), motorised transport and sitting to read, talk, do homework or listen to music (The Sedentary Behaviour and Obesity Expert Working Group, 2010). Most research into sedentary behaviour among adolescents has focused on highly visible and prevalent behaviours such as television viewing and the wider concept of screen time (Mark *et al.*, 2006). More specifically, television viewing is the most commonly studied marker because it represents the single largest share of adolescents' sedentary behaviour (Biddle *et al.*, 2009). It has been reported that television viewing is in fact the dominant 'screen behaviour', comprising approximately 70 per cent of all screen time for adolescents (Olds *et al.*, 2010). To place this in context, 'total screen time' has been reported to represent 40 per cent of total sedentary time among adolescents (Olds *et al.*, 2010). There is consistent evidence in studies from around the world that time spent watching television and other screen time is associated with a number of negative health outcomes among adolescents, including overweight and obesity (Vicente-Rodriquez *et al.*, 2008). Additionally, research into the determinants and correlates of adolescents' sedentary behaviour is developing, with studies predominantly examining television viewing as the 'proxy' for sedentary behaviour (Salmon *et al.*, 2011).

In relation to the measurement of physical activity and sedentary behaviour among adolescent populations, subjective and objective measures are used throughout the literature in this area. Objective measures such as accelerometers are commonly deployed with smaller groups of participants. However, subjective measures such as self-report are more practical among large groups of adolescents (Biddle *et al.*, 2004). Further advantages of using self-report include the ability to simply assess compliance with guidelines (Dollman *et al.*, 2009). For example, in relation to an adolescent population in the UK, compliance with physical activity guidelines would refer to the proportion of adolescents 'meeting' the UK recommended guidelines of at least 60 minutes (and up to several hours) of moderate-to-vigorous-intensity physical activity on each day of the week (Department of Health, 2011). For the purposes of the present chapter, studies using self-report methods[2] to measure physical activity or sedentary behaviour will be the central focus.

Recommendations and policy for physical activity and sedentary behaviour among adolescents

Current UK guidelines for physical activity propose that all children and young people, aged 5 to 18 years, should engage in moderate-to-vigorous-intensity physical activity for at least 60 minutes and up to several hours every day (Department of Health, 2011). These guidelines are the first to be applied to the UK as a whole, building upon previous recommendations for physical activity among children and young people which differed slightly between the four 'home' nations (e.g. Department of Health, 2004). This 60-minute recommendation is now widely accepted by the scientific community worldwide (e.g. Department of Health and Ageing, 2005; US Department of Health and Human Services, 2008; EU Working Group, 2008; Canadian Society for Exercise Physiology, 2012).

Despite the proliferation and consensus of such recommendations for physical activity, there are few published reports which present specific guidelines for the amount of sedentary behaviour that is recommended for young people (Marshall and Welk, 2008). The most regularly used and adopted recommendation is from the American Academy of Pediatrics (2001) which focuses mainly on television viewing or general categories such as 'media usage' (Marshall and Welk, 2008). In accordance with this, recommendations include that parents should limit children's total entertainment media time to no more than two hours of quality programming per day. Despite these recommendations being published in 2001, to date, only two countries (Australia and Canada) have issued guidelines regarding the amount of time young people should spend engaged in sedentary behaviour. In 2005 the Australian Government recommended that 'Children and young people should not spend more than 2 hours a day using electronic media for entertainment (e.g. computer games, Internet, TV), particularly during daylight hours' (Department of Health and Ageing, 2005: para. 1). Further, the Canadian Society for Exercise Physiology has developed the Canadian Sedentary Behaviour Guidelines for Youth (aged 12 to 17 years) (Canadian Society for Exercise Physiology, 2012). The final recommendations of this report stated that, for health benefits, youth should minimise the time that they spend being sedentary each day, which may be achieved by: (i) limiting recreational screen time to no more than two hours per day; and (ii) limiting sedentary (motorised) transport, extended sitting time and time spent indoors throughout the day. From a UK perceptive, recent guidelines suggest that children and young people, aged 5 to 18 years, should minimise the amount of time spent being sedentary (sitting) for extended periods (Department of Health, 2011). This recommendation does not specify a time limit for sedentary behaviour due to insufficient evidence, but does suggest reducing total sedentary time and breaking up extended periods of sitting. Overall, relatively few countries have recommendations for sedentary behaviour and, although many have issued guidelines concerning the limitation of sedentary time, these are not quantified (The Sedentary Behaviour and Obesity Expert Working Group, 2010).

In recent years policy documents have emerged in the UK with the aim of increasing participation in physical activity and decreasing/limiting sedentary behaviour among adolescents/young people. For example, in 2007, the UK Government's *Foresight* report adopted a cross-government 'systems' approach to issues of obesity, setting out a number of key challenges for government, individuals, families, the business community and society as a whole regarding the need to view obesity as a complex system that required integrated, multi-level solutions (Government Office for Science and UK Government's Foresight Programme, 2007). As a consequence, in 2009, the Government published *Healthy Weight, Healthy Lives: One Year On* which focused on the promotion of physical activity across the life-course and which also made a commitment to addressing sedentary behaviour (through the setting up of an expert working group on sedentary behaviour – including screen time) and issues relating to overweight and obesity (Cross-Government Obesity Unit, 2009). The Sedentary Behaviour and Obesity Expert Working Group then published a report in 2010 entitled, *Sedentary Behaviour and Obesity: Review of the Current Scientific Evidence*, which ultimately aimed to develop recommendations on limiting time spent being sedentary. This expert group considered the evidence for the development of specific recommendations on limiting time spent being sedentary, which sat alongside recommendations on physical activity produced by the Physical Activity Guidelines Editorial Group (Bull and the Expert Working Groups, 2010).

To support the publication of *Healthy Weight, Healthy Lives* (Cross-Government Obesity Unit, 2008), a physical activity strategy, *Be Active, Be Healthy* (Department of Health, 2009), was launched which included a framework for the delivery of physical activity (at the local, regional/sub-regional and national level) aligned with sport for the period leading up to the London 2012 Olympic and Paralympic Games. This strategy highlighted that, due to the fact that activity levels appeared to be falling dramatically after the age of 16, a partnership was to be formed between the Department of Health, the Fitness Industry Association and local authorities to pilot 'Fit for the Future', an incentive scheme offering 5,000 16–22-year-olds subsidised gym memberships linked to frequency of use. Further, the *Change4Life* public health campaign was launched in 2009 with the aim of getting the UK population more active through the '60 Active Minutes' campaign. This family-focused initiative, which used social media, television adverts and locally-based initiatives, was not exclusively aimed at children, but included a target that encouraged children to undertake at least 60 minutes of physical activity per day. In addition, the 'Up and About' campaign aimed to decrease the amount of time children spent in sedentary activities (Department of Health, 2010a). Following these initiatives, a Public Health White Paper *Healthy Lives, Healthy People* (Department of Health, 2010b) was published which pledged to (i) promote physical activity during adolescence through schools becoming active promoters of health education (e.g. through the Personal, Social and Health Education framework); and (ii) to support families to make informed choices about their levels of physical activity (via updated guidelines on physical activity).

The importance of tackling the reduction in physical activity levels of adolescents was reinforced by Sport England's Strategy 2008–2011 (Sport England, 2008), which emphasised Sport England's commitment to delivering a reduction in the post-16 decline in participation by 25 per cent in at least five sports by 2012–2013. Following this, *Start Active, Stay Active* (Department of Health, 2011), a report from the Chief Medical Officers of the UK's four home nations, proposed new guidelines on both physical activity and sedentary behaviour for children and young people (aged 5 to 18 years). Most recently, the Coalition government's strategy for sport, *Creating a Sporting Habit for Life* (Department for Culture, Media and Sport, 2012) has set out a series of measures for increasing youth participation in sport.

Overall, the recommendations proposed for physical activity by UK agencies have been widely accepted and have formed the basis of 'cut-off points' in the majority of research in order to define 'active' or 'inactive' in the area of adolescents' physical activity participation. The precise recommendations proposed for sedentary behaviour for adolescents are not widely agreed, but consensus is beginning to develop among researchers in the field. Regarding policy and strategy in the area of physical activity and sedentary behaviour among adolescents, there appears to be an enhanced effort in the UK to reduce the increase in unhealthy behaviours through the course of adolescence. As the next section will illustrate, there is presently a lack of evidence under-pinning these policies and proposals. Indeed, in order to develop strategies to reduce a decline in physical activity or an increase in sedentary behaviour, a better understanding of the factors associated with these changes is required.

Self-report data on physical activity among adolescents

Cross-sectional self-report studies

Most studies investigating physical activity among adolescents are cross-sectional in nature (Hallal *et al.*, 2006b). Whilst cross-sectional studies provide important contextual information, particularly in terms of international com-parisons, they do not provide evidence of the factors associated with changes in physical activity levels with increasing age. Importantly, the contextual infor-mation provided by cross-sectional studies may be used in the future to inform the design of prospective longitudinal observational studies and controlled intervention studies.

A number of scholars have investigated levels of physical activity among adolescents using a cross-sectional study design by assessing compliance with a recommended guideline. These studies have shown mixed compliance levels. For example, in Spain, Roman *et al.* (2008) analysed the prevalence of com-pliance with recommendations on physical activity and sports (60 minutes of moderate-intensity physical activity daily) within a population of 1,723 ado-lescents aged 6 to 18 years and found that only 47.5 per cent of participants complied. In contrast, Scully *et al.* (2007) provided an assessment of Australian adolescents' physical activity. A total of 18,486 participants aged 12 to 17 years were surveyed and it was shown that only 14 per cent of par-ticipants reported engaging in at least 60 minutes of moderate–vigorous activity each day in the previous week.

Longitudinal self-report studies

Longitudinal observational studies investigating physical activity levels of adolescents are increasing in number, with the main benefit being that they enable possible determinants of physical activity behaviour to be identified through exploring the factors associated with longitudinal changes in the behaviour of interest (Hallal *et al.*, 2006b). However, in comparison to cross-sectional studies, there are still relatively few longitudinal studies on physical activity conducted during adolescence.

Using a longitudinal study design, Kahn *et al.* (2008) examined trends in adolescent physical activity in the USA; a large sample size was involved – 12,812 boys and girls aged 10 to 18 years. Findings revealed a lower physical activity level in boys than girls in late adolescence and that this was partly due to a steeper decline in physical activity in boys compared to girls, especially between the ages of 15 and 18 years. In contrast, Sagatun *et al.* (2008) conducted a longitudinal study of 2,489 Norwegian adolescents at age 15 years and again at age 18 years and found that boys were more physically active than girls at age 15 and 18 years and that hours per week spent on physical activity declined as age increased. Henning Brodersen *et al.* (2007) undertook one of the few longitudinal studies to have been carried out in England, where the objective was to assess developmental trends in physical activity in adolescents in relation to gender, ethnicity and socio-economic status. Study duration was five years and followed a cohort (n = 5,863) of adolescents aged 11 to 12 years at baseline, and 15 to 16 years at follow-up. The researchers found that there were marked reductions in physical activity between ages 11 to 12 years and 15 to 16 years. Boys were more active than girls, with the decline in physical activity being greater in girls (46 per cent reduction) than in boys (23 per cent). Based on the limited number of longitudinal studies available, physical activity appears to decline during adolescence, and gender appears to be associated with this trend. Exploring factors associated with declines in physical activity through the course of adolescence should remain a priority for researchers, since little is currently known about the range of factors associated with this decline. Evidence-informed strategies and interventions are reliant on research findings in this area.

Self-report data on sedentary behaviour among adolescents

Cross-sectional self-report studies

Studies investigating sedentary behaviour among adolescents most commonly adopt a cross-sectional design. This is confirmed by The Sedentary Behaviour and Obesity Expert Working Group (2010: 50) who noted that 'better identification of changes in sedentary behaviour across time is needed' when referring to 'gaps in evidence'. Although cross-sectional studies are useful in terms of providing a 'snapshot' of levels of sedentary behaviour, they do not provide evidence of the factors associated with changes in sedentary behaviour levels with increasing age.

The evidence that is available on screen time (as a proxy measure of sedentary behaviour) among the adolescent population globally indicates that such behaviours are high and above the recommended levels and that the proportion of the adolescent population meeting the recommended guidelines is low. For example, Ullrich-French *et al.* (2010) used a cut-off point of less than two hours per day to classify the meeting of guidelines for non-school-related screen time in US adolescents aged 11 to 15 years. They reported that only a small percentage (23.5 per cent) of the sample met recommended levels. Conversely, studies examining only television viewing (as opposed to total screen time) have identified higher levels of compliance with recommended guidelines. For instance, Li *et al.* (2007) measured the time spent by

Chinese adolescents aged 11 to 17 years on weekdays and weekend days watching television, playing games, working on the computer, doing homework and carrying out other sedentary hobbies. Results showed that only 24 per cent of participants watched television for more than two hours per day. However, Li *et al.* did report that 79 per cent of participants spent more than two hours a day doing homework and, of these, 35 per cent spent more than four hours per day on homework.

Longitudinal self-report studies

Longitudinal studies have the distinct advantage (over cross-sectional studies) of identifying trends in sedentary behaviour with increasing age and factors associated with those trends. Sedentary behaviour studies among adolescents adopting a longitudinal design are, to date, somewhat sparse.

Referred to earlier in relation to physical activity, the work of Henning Brodersen *et al.* (2007) also measured longitudinal changes in the levels of screen time (as a proxy measure of sedentary behaviour) with increasing age in English adolescents. Sedentary behaviour (screen time) was measured by asking participants how many hours they watched television, or played computer or video games, on school days and weekends, with responses added to generate an estimate of total hours of sedentary behaviour (screen time). They found that there were marked increases in screen time between ages 11 to 12 years and 15 to 16 years, with an average increase of 2.52 hours per week in boys and 2.81 hours per week in girls. Conversely, other longitudinal studies have established no change in screen time among adolescent populations over time. Aires *et al.* (2010) undertook a three-year longitudinal analysis of changes in screen time among a cohort of Portuguese adolescents aged 11 to 19 years. Participants reported how much time they normally spent watching television or used a computer for work and for leisure during the day for weekdays and during weekends. Results revealed that participants spent more time watching television than using a computer over the three-year period, although there were no statistically significant changes with regards to screen time over the three-year period. Based on the limited number of longitudinal studies available investigating screen time and other sedentary behaviours, it is difficult to conclude whether or not there is an overall trend towards an increase, decrease or no change during adolescence. Furthermore, there is a lack of longitudinal studies exploring factors associated with changes in sedentary behaviour through the course of adolescence.

Summary of evidence and future needs

By summarising current empirical evidence in the area of physical activity and sedentary behaviour in adolescents it is evident that: (i) the levels of physical activity among adolescents are mixed, with some studies showing less compliance with guidelines than others; (ii) physical activity levels decline during the period of adolescence and the magnitude of this decline may be associated with gender; (iii) findings for screen time and television viewing (as proxy measures of sedentary behaviour) levels are mixed, with some studies showing less compliance with guidelines than others; and (iv) although screen time (as a proxy measure of sedentary behaviour) has been shown to increase during the period of adolescence, conflicting findings exist. It has also been identified that there is a need for more prospective longitudinal observational studies examining both physical activity and sedentary behaviour throughout adolescence. Furthermore, it is recommended that studies adopting this particular design should examine potential factors associated with each behaviour (e.g. gender, ethnicity, socio-economic status). The adoption of this type of study design should reveal factors of importance in future policies and strategies. Population-based longitudinal observational designs are becoming more popular within applied research settings in public health in order that a greater level of under-standing is gained about the characteristics of behaviour in large cohorts (e.g. James *et al.*, 2009). Despite this, to date, cross-sectional studies are far more prevalent than longitudinal studies, mainly because longitudinal studies are more difficult to conduct, for numerous reasons, including participant attrition.

Despite these challenges, a recent study undertaken in the UK has adopted a prospective longitudinal observational design and investigated both physical activity and sedentary behaviour (using screen time as a proxy measure of sedentary behaviour) concurrently, as well as the factors associated with these behaviours (cross-sectionally and longitudinally) among adolescents (Owens, 2012). This study focused on the important transition out of compulsory education. Adolescents completed a questionnaire at baseline (when in Year 11) and approximately six months later, at follow-up, post-compulsory education. This questionnaire ascertained adolescents' physical activity over a seven-day period (in relation to the Department of Health (2004) recom-mended guidelines of a total of at least 60 minutes of at least moderate-intensity physical activity each day) and the amount of screen time on a weekday and weekend day (in relation to recommended guidelines of no more than two hours a day for screen time) (e.g. Australia – Department of Health and Ageing, 2005) at baseline and follow-up. The findings of the study demonstrated the following: (i) a decline in physical activity through the transition (10.1 per cent of adolescents who were meeting guidelines at base-line were not meeting guidelines at follow-up); (ii) a high proportion (70.6 per cent) of adolescents not meeting guidelines for screen time at either baseline or follow-up; and (iii) associations between gender and physical activity during this transitional period (i.e. females were less likely than males to show a decline; and females were less likely than males to meet guidelines at follow-up).

Conclusion

Physical activity and sedentary behaviour among adolescents is of interna-tional interest for governments, health professionals and researchers, given the present and future public health implications. Varying definitions, particularly for sedentary behaviour, along with limitations of self-report data, make inter-study comparisons difficult. However, drawing on an extensive international base of cross-sectional studies, it is possible to conclude that a substantial portion of the adolescent population globally are physically inactive (i.e. not meeting recommended guidelines for physical activity), and that sedentary behaviour (e.g. screen time, television viewing) levels are of concern from a health perspective. Furthermore, longitudinal studies show that physical inactivity and sedentary behaviour increases through adolescence. Although the health-enhancing recommendations for sedentary behaviour remain less well developed compared to recommendations for physical activity, future research efforts should shift towards an investigation of the key factors associated with a decline in the proportion of adolescents meeting recommendations both for physical activity and sedentary behaviour. Understanding more about these issues will enable policy makers to better develop related policies and strategies and assist in creating effective interventions to address this growing area of concern. To shed light on this important area, and to understand more about the factors affecting these behaviours, prospective longitudinal observational studies need to be adopted by researchers on a wider scale.

Notes

1 For the purposes of this chapter, the term 'adolescents' includes individuals aged between 12 and 18 years.
2 For a review of the merits of different approaches, see Tudor-Locke and Myers (2001).

References

Aarnio, M., Winter, T., Peltonen, J., Kujala, U. and Kaprio, J. (2002). Stability of lei-sure-time physical activity during adolescence: a longitudinal study among 16-, 17- and 18-year-old Finnish youth. *Scandinavian Journal of Medicine and Science in Sports*, 12 (3), 179–185.

Aires, L., Andersen, L. B., Mendonca, D., Martins, C., Silva, G. and Mota, J. (2010). A 3-year longitudinal analysis of changes in fitness, physical activity, fatness and screen time. *Acta Paediatrica*, 99 (1), 140–144.

Allison, K. R., Adlaf, E. M., Dwyer, J. J. M., Lysy, D. C. and Irving, H. M. (2007). The decline in physical activity among adolescent students: a cross-national comparison. *Canadian Journal of Public Health*, 98 (2), 97–100.

American Academy of Pediatrics (2001). Policy statement/Committee on Public Education. Children, adolescents, and television. *Pediatrics*, 107 (2), 423–426.

Anderssen, N., Wold, B. and Torsheim, T. (2006). Are parental health habits trans-mitted to their children? An eight year longitudinal study of physical activity in adolescents and their parents. *Journal of Adolescence*, 29 (4), 513–524.

Biddle, S. J., Gorely, T. and Stensel, D. J. (2004). Health-enhancing physical activity and sedentary behaviour in children and adolescents. *Journal of Sports Sciences*, 22 (8), 679–701.

Biddle, S. J., Gorely, T., Marshall, S. J. and Cameron, N. (2009). The prevalence of sedentary behavior and physical activity in leisure time: a study of Scottish adolescents using ecological momentary assessment. *Preventive Medicine*, 48 (2), 151–155.

Boone, J. E., Gordon-Larsen, P., Adair, L. S. and Popkin, B. M. (2007). Screen time and physical activity during adolescence: longitudinal effects on obesity in young adulthood. *International Journal of Behavioral Nutrition and Physical Activity*, 4, 26.

Bull, F. C. and the Expert Working Groups (2010). *Physical Activity Guidelines in the U.K: Review and Recommendations*. British Heart Foundation National Centre for Physical Activity and Health: School of Sport, Exercise and Health Sciences, Loughborough University.

Canadian Society for Exercise Physiology (2012). *Canadian Physical Activity Guidelines and Canadian Sedentary Behaviour Guidelines – Your Plan to Get Active Every Day*. Ontario: Canadian Society for Exercise Physiology.

Cross-Government Obesity Unit (2008). *Healthy Weight, Healthy Lives: A Cross Government Strategy for England*. London: Department of Health.

——(2009). *Healthy Weight, Healthy Lives: One Year On*. London: Department of Health.

Department for Culture, Media and Sport (2012). *Creating a Sporting Habit for Life*. London: Department for Culture, Media and Sport.

Department of Health (2004). *At Least Five a Week: Evidence on the Impact of Physical Activity and its Relationship to Health. A Report from the Chief Medical Officer*. London: Department of Health.

——(2009). *Be Active, Be Healthy: A Plan for Getting the Nation Moving*. London: Department of Health.

——(2010a). *Change4Life: One Year On*. London: Department of Health.

——(2010b). *Healthy Lives, Healthy People: Our Strategy for Public Health in England*. London: Department of Health.

——(2011). *Start Active, Stay Active: A Report on Physical Activity from the Four Home Countries' Chief Medical Officers*. London: Department of Health.

Department of Health and Ageing (2005). *Australia's Physical Activity Recommendations for Children and Young People*. Department of Health and Ageing [online], [accessed 26-02-2012]. Available from www.health.gov.au/internet/main/publishing.nsf/Con tent/health-pubhlth-strateg-active-recommend.htm.

Dollman, J., Okely, A. D., Hardy, L., Timperio, A., Salmon, J. and Hills, A. P. (2009). A hitchhiker's guide to assessing young people's physical activity: deciding what method to use. *Journal of Science and Medicine in Sport*, 12 (5), 518–525.

Eiðsdóttir, S. P., Kristjánsson, A. L., Sigfúsdóttir, I. D. and Allegrante, J. P. (2008). Trends in physical activity and participation in sports clubs among Icelandic adolescents. *European Journal of Public Health*, 18 (3), 289–293.

EU Working Group 'Sport and Health' (2008). *EU Physical Activity Guidelines – Recommended Policy Actions in Support of Health-Enhancing Physical Activity*. Brussels: European Commission.

Gorely, T., Biddle, S. J., Marshall, S. J. and Cameron, N. (2009). The prevalence of leisure time sedentary behaviour and physical activity in adolescent boys: an ecological momentary assessment approach. *International Journal of Pediatric Obesity*, 4 (4), 289–298.

Government Office for Science and UK Government's Foresight Programme (2007). *Foresight – Tackling Obesities: Future Choices – Project Report*. London: Government Office for Science and UK Government's Foresight Programme.

Hallal, P. C., Victora, C. G., Azevedo, M. R. and Wells, J. C. (2006a). Adolescent physical activity and health: a systematic review. *Sports Medicine*, 36 (12), 1019–1030.

Hallal, P. C., Wells, J. C. K., Reichert, F. F., Anselmi, L. and Victora, C. G. (2006b). Early determinants of physical activity in adolescence: prospective birth cohort study. *British Medical Journal*, 332 (7548), 1002–1007.

Henning Brodersen, N., Steptoe, A., Boniface, D. R. and Wardle, J. (2007). Trends in physical activity and sedentary behaviour in adolescence: ethnic and socioeconomic differences. *British Journal of Sports Medicine*, 41 (3), 140–144.

James, D., Mills, H., Crone, D., Johnston, L. H., Morris, C. and Gidlow, C. J. (2009). Factors associated with physical activity referral completion and health outcomes. *Journal of Sports Sciences*, 27 (10), 1007–1017.

Kahn, J. A., Huang, B., Gillman, M. W., Field, A. E., Austin, S. B., Colditz, G. A. and Frazier, A. L. (2008). Patterns and determinants of physical activity in US adolescents. *Journal of Adolescent Health*, 42 (4), 369–377.

Li, M., Dibley, M. J., Sibbritt, D. W., Zhou, X. and Yan, H. (2007). Physical activity and sedentary behavior in adolescents in Xi'an City, China. *Journal of Adolescent Health*, 41 (1), 99–101.

Mark, A. E., Boyce, W. F. and Janssen, I. (2006). Television viewing, computer use and total screen time in Canadian youth. *Paediatric Child Health*, 11 (9), 595–599.

Marshall, S. J. and Welk, G. J. (2008). Definitions and measurement. In *Youth Physical Activity and Sedentary Behavior: Challenges and Solutions* (edited by A. Smith and S. J. H. Biddle), pp. 3–29. Champaign, IL: Human Kinetics.

Olds, T. S., Maher, C. A., Ridley, K. and Kittel, D. M. (2010). Descriptive epidemiology of screen and non-screen sedentary time in adolescents: a cross-sectional study. *International Journal of Behavioral Nutrition and Physical Activity*, 7, 92.

Owens, C. S. (2012). Sport and Physical Activity Participation and Sedentary Behaviour among Adolescents: Exploring the Transition from Compulsory Education. Unpublished PhD thesis: University of Gloucestershire, UK.

Roman, B., Serra-Majem, L., Ribas-Barba, L., Pérez-Rodrigo, C. and Aranceta, J. (2008). How many children and adolescents in Spain comply with the recommendations on physical activity? *The Journal of Sports Medicine and Physical Fitness*, 48 (3), 380–387.

Sagatun, A., Kolle, E., Anderssen, S. A., Thoresen, M. and Sogaard, A. J. (2008). Three-year follow-up of physical activity in Norwegian youth from two ethnic groups: associations with socio-demographic factors. *BMC Public Health*, 8, 419.

Salmon, J., Tremblay, M. S., Marshall, S. J. and Hume, C. (2011). Health risks, correlates, and interventions to reduce sedentary behavior in young people. *American Journal of Preventive Medicine*, 41 (2), 197–206.

Scully, M., Dixon, H., White, V. and Beckmann, K. (2007). Dietary, physical activity and sedentary behaviour among Australian secondary students. *Health Promotion International*, 22 (3), 236–245.

The Sedentary Behaviour and Obesity Expert Working Group (2010). *Sedentary Behaviour and Obesity: Review of the Current Scientific Evidence*. London: Department of Health and Department for Children, Schools and Families.

Sport England (2008). *Sport England Strategy 2008–2011*. London: Sport England.

Tudor-Locke, C. E. and Myers, A. M. (2001). Challenges and opportunities for measuring physical activity in sedentary adults. *Sports Medicine*, 31 (2), 91–100.

Twisk, J. W., Kemper, H. C. and Van Mechelen, W. (2002). Prediction of cardiovascular disease risk factors later in life by physical activity and physical fitness in youth: general comments and conclusions. *International Journal of Sports Medicine*, 23 (suppl. 1), S44–S49.

Ullrich-French, S. C., Power, T. G., Daratha, K. B., Bindler, R. C. and Steele, M. M. (2010). Examination of adolescents' screen time and physical fitness as independent correlates of weight status and blood pressure. *Journal of Sports Sciences*, 28 (11), 1189–1196.

US Department of Health and Human Services (2008). *2008 Physical Activity Guidelines for Americans*. Washington, DC: US Department of Health and Human Services.

Vicente-Rodríguez, G., Rey-López, J. P., Martin-Matillas, M., Moreno, L. A., Wärnberg, J., Redondo, C., Tercedor, P., Delgado, M., Marcos, A., Castillo, M. and Bueno, M. (2008). Television watching, videogames, and excess of body fat in Spanish adolescents: the AVENA study. *Nutrition*, 24 (7–8), 654–662.

World Health Organization (2010). *Global Recommendations on Physical Activity for Health*. Geneva, Switzerland: World Health Organization.

9 Moving forward from the Physical Education, School Sport and Young People Strategy

Don Vinson and Matt Lloyd

Introduction

Physical education and school sport (PESS) in the UK has changed considerably since the inception of the Physical Education, School Sport and Club Links (PESSCL) strategy in 2002 and the subsequent Physical Education, School Sport and Young People (PESSYP) strategy in 2008. These initiatives featured unprecedented funding for PESS, with over £2 billion being invested by government between 2002 and 2010 (Armour *et al.*, 2011). The evolution of PESS has witnessed a number of radical changes including the emergence of School Sport Partnerships (SSPs). This development ensured that, by 2006, all schools in England were part of an SSP which featured secondary, primary and special schools working collaboratively to enhance PESS provision for young people (Ofsted, 2011). SSPs were developed to improve the amount and quality of PESS on offer, targeting participants specifically through seven outcomes devised by the Youth Sport Trust (YST):

- increased participation in high-quality PE;
- increased participation in high-quality informal activity (e.g. playground);
- increased participation in high-quality out-of-school-hours learning;
- increased participation in high-quality competition and performance;
- improved attitude, behaviour and attendance in PE, sport and whole school;
- increased attainment and achievement in and through PE, out-of-hours learning and sport;
- increased participation in community-based sport.

(YST, 2005 cited in Flintoff, 2008: 397)

The purpose of this chapter is to highlight two areas which PESS practitioners (e.g. teachers, coaches and support staff) have developed over the course of the last decade. These two approaches represent key elements of that which was 'best' about this period and which will aid the profession as it attempts to 'move forward' into this new era. Alongside the promotion of holistic and lifelong learning through physical education (PE), the period

2002–2010 witnessed a philosophical shift in the way that young people were encouraged to maintain active, healthy lifestyles. This was partly as a result of the inception of PESSCL/PESSYP initiatives, but also due to the content of the 2008 National Curriculum for Physical Education (NCPE) (Qualifications and Curriculum Authority (QCA), 2007). By considering this philosophical shift in light of participant development and pedagogic literature, this chapter also provides some suggestions as to how practitioners might continue to build on the progress of the PESSCL/PESSYP era. We begin with a brief outline of the key aspects of PESS-related policy development since 2002.

Policy, PESSCL/PESSYP and the future

The PESSYP 2008 strategy focused primarily on creating a world class PE and school sport system (Department for Children, Schools and Families (DCSF)/Department for Culture, Media and Sport (DCMS), 2008), packaged within the 'Five Hour Offer'. The Five Hour Offer was a commitment by government that all 5–16-year-olds would have access to two hours of high-quality curriculum PE per week and further opportunity to access an additional three hours of sporting activities, through school, voluntary and community providers (DCSF/DCMS, 2008). Data reported within the national PESSCL survey (Quick *et al.*, 2009), drawn from all 450 SSPs (over 21,000 schools), indicated a consistently upward trend since the inception of PESSCL in terms of increased participation in high-quality PE and extra-curricular activity. This suggests that SSPs were, at least in part, achieving some of their primary goals. Following the Coalition government's comprehensive spending review of October 2010, the Department for Education (DfE) announced that ring-fenced funding for SSPs would not continue after March 2011. After this time schools would no longer be required to operate within an SSP and, despite a partial (and temporary) funding reprieve until 2013, at the time of writing their existence appears highly uncertain (Ofsted, 2011). Yet, amidst such uncertainty, the PESSCL/PESSYP era appears to have left PESS in an encouraging position. Ofsted (2009) remarked that, since 2002, schools had made the most of the opportunities that were offered as a result of national policy and strategy aimed at developing PESS provision. Such findings were in stark contrast to the bleak assessment of the World Summit on PE in 1999 when it was suggested that there had been a severe decline in the global standing of PESS (Bailey and Dismore, 2004). Secretary of State for Education Michael Gove appeared to recognise this as an encouraging platform from which to work. In December 2010 he stated:

> It's time to ensure what was best in school sport partnerships around the country is fully embedded and move forward to a system where schools and parents are delivering on sports with competition at the heart.
>
> (Department for Education (DfE), 2011)

The remainder of this chapter discusses two aspects of the SSP era which could be considered as 'best practice' elements. The first of these elements relates to the heightened prominence of fundamental movement skills as a pedagogic strategy and it is to this concept that we now turn.

Policy, sampling and fundamental motor skills

Michael Gove's assertion that competitive sport lies at the heart of a well rounded physical education (DfE, 2011), with a particular emphasis on team games, echoes the philosophy of previous government offerings in this area, namely those of the Conservative administration of the early 1990s (Department of National Heritage (DNH), 1995). The Coalition have recently reinforced their position on such matters in their policy document *Creating a Sporting Habit for Life* (Department for Culture, Media and Sport (DCMS), 2012) which features an Olympic-style 'School Games' as the headline policy, augmented by school–club links for which the national governing bodies (NGBs) of football, cricket, rugby union, rugby league and tennis are cited as illustrative drivers. Gove also believes that quality provision of competitive sport will encourage lifelong sporting participation (DfE, 2011); thus the forthcoming revision to the NCPE, due for implementation from September 2014, is expected to reinforce the emphasis on traditional, competitive, sports (Fellows, 2012).

The period of development under PESSCL and PESSYP saw an increase in the promotion of a wider variety of activities for young people, in some cases resulting in less curriculum time devoted to the more traditional sports (DCSF/DCMS, 2009). Indeed, it is our view that a more diverse curriculum benefits, rather than detracts from, the sporting competence of young people and the likelihood of lifelong participation. The current NCPE encourages a transformation in experiences of sport and physical activity, placing lifelong participation high on the agenda alongside the development of movement competency: a key thread running throughout (Frapwell, 2009). There is a danger that the emphasis on traditional competitive sports within current policy (and the forthcoming NCPE) will slow the development of PESS provision which has occurred over the last decade (Fellows, 2012; Kirk, 2012). By understanding the importance of diverse movement competence, the PESS community will be able to move forward, building on the progress and developments of the previous decade, rather than taking a backwards step. Consideration of participant development frameworks can aid the understanding of the importance of diverse movement competencies and it to this subject that we now turn.

The concept of participant development remains relatively under-theorised and suffers from a lack of empirical evidence (Ford *et al.*, 2011). Nevertheless, numerous models have been produced in order to aid practitioners in their development of young people's sporting potential. Such models are useful in providing frameworks aimed at applying empirical research which are usually easily comprehended (Bailey *et al.*, 2010). Participant development models have been structured in numerous ways from traditional pyramid approaches, where mass participation is considered an antecedent to heightened elite performance, to more staged approaches which may, for example, be based on age-dependent chronological progression (Bailey, 2005). Arguably the two most prominent models in contemporary practice are Balyi and Hamilton's (2004) Long-term Athlete Development (LTAD) model and Côté's (1999) Developmental Model of Sport Participation (DMSP). Numerous other models doubtless have much to offer our understanding of the development of young people, but a comprehensive review of these frameworks is beyond the scope of this chapter. In considering LTAD and DMSP, a better understanding of young people's sporting development can be gained.

The first participant development concept which we wish to discuss relates to Côté's (1999) principle of 'sampling', which features as the first step in the DMSP (Côté *et al.*, 2003). In the context of developing expert decision makers in and through sport, Côté (1999) suggests three distinct phases: the sampling years (6–12), the specialising years (13–15) and the investment years (16+). Within the DMSP, the sampling years are characterised by involvement in a wide variety of activities, developing a range of fundamental motor skills (FMS) and embracing the joy of sports participation. FMS are gross physical movements providing a basis for the progression to more intricate and specialised skills. FMS comprise:

- management of the body – stability skills (e.g. stop, twist, turn, bend);
- moving in different directions – locomotor skills (e.g. dodge, hop, skip);
- control and manipulation of objects such as hoops and bats and balls (e.g. strike, kick, throw).

(Murphy and Ni Chroinin, 2011: 145)

Murphy and Ni Chroinin (2011) suggest that participant development should be focused on the application of movement in diverse contexts in order to enhance the relevance, enjoyment and meaning of skills. Côté, Lidor, and Hackfort (2009) propose seven postulates (or requirements) concerning youth sport activities that lead to both elite performance and continued participation – the two key elements of recent government proposals on the development of school sport. Amongst these postulates is a recommendation concerning the diversification of activities and an emphasis on retaining a sense of deliberate play as the learning mechanisms valuable to a holistic developmental process. These principles of diverse sporting activities are also evident in the late specialisation version of the LTAD model (Balyi and Hamilton, 2004) which underpins much of the work of the UK's national (sport) governing bodies with young people. Within the LTAD framework, the first stage focuses on 'FUNdamentals', where children between the ages of 6 and 8 (for girls) or 6 and 9 (for boys) are encouraged to sample a wide range of fun, playful, activities. It should be noted that all the age categories cited here, within both models, are age-typical, not age-dependent – i.e. they should not be considered as absolutes: every child develops uniquely (Morley, 2009). The emphasis for development within these stages should be on FMS, rather than sport-specific techniques (Stafford, 2005). One of the numerous packages that has emerged in the last decade which offers materials to aid the progression of FMS (in line with development models such as DMSP and LTAD) is the concept of 'Multi-skills'.

Multi-skills programmes became extremely popular throughout the PESSCL/PESSYP era (Morley, 2010), focusing on the development of FMS such as balance, co-ordination, reaction and timing. Appropriate involvement with Multi-skills environments can provide the kind of sampling described by Côté, Baker and Abernethy (2009) and reduce the likelihood of athlete burn-out and subsequent withdrawal from a particular sport which may have become, for example, overly-pressurised or tedious (Baker *et al.*, 2009). The prominence of the Multi-skills phenomenon is best illustrated by the popularity of Multi-skills Clubs and Multi-skills Academies across the UK. The DCMS funded approximately 650 Multi-skills Clubs in 2005, targeting young people between the ages of 7 and 11. Sessions on the 'ABCs' (agility, balance and co-ordination) of movement were delivered by a community coach or teacher, generally outside normal school hours and at a wide variety of different venues (Morley, 2009). Part of the purpose of Multi-skills Clubs was to provide a pathway for appropriately talented young people to access local sports clubs (Youth Sport Trust (YST), 2006). Multi-skill Academies were funded through the DCSF and were aimed at children aged 10–12, being typically delivered as extra-curricular activities (Morley, 2009). The 450 Multi-skill Academies were focused on developing children's FMS, understanding of games principles and identifying talent to refer to NGBs (YST, 2006). This extensive network of FMS-based opportunities represents one of the developmentally appropriate systems which, we believe, should not be lost to funding cuts or the transition to a more competitively based PESS environment.

Another concept which has contributed to the advancement of PESS provision over the past decade, affording a better understanding of developmentally appropriate sporting provision for young people is Physical Literacy (Ford *et al.*, 2011). Physical Literacy was conceptualised by Whitehead (2001) and is now an internationally recognised term with a working definition that provides a basis for research in a number of fields:

> The motivation, confidence, physical competence, knowledge and understanding to maintain physical activity throughout the lifecourse.
>
> (Whitehead, 2010: 11–12)

It is noteworthy that, despite the concept of Physical Literacy being in the academic and practitioner domain for over a decade, no reference is made to it in the current NCPE at either Key Stage 3 or 4. This is somewhat surprising given that the alignment of the outcomes of curriculum entitlement for young people at school are centred on the values, concepts and, ultimately, the achievement of Physical Literacy. Whitehead (2007a) contends that a positive PESS experience can be a crucial and substantial contributor to the development of Physical Literacy, although there is relatively little empirical evidence to support such an assertion (Ford *et al.*, 2011). The concept of Physical Literacy is not intended to be in competition with, or act as a kind of replacement for PE, but is put forward as a wider concept to enable teachers and coaches to better understand their contribution to the long-term development of their pupils and participants (Whitehead, 2010). Physical Literacy embraces some of the notions of transferability of FMS apparent within Multi-skills, promoting a broader role for PESS than the development of sport-specific competencies. Kirk (2006) suggests that appropriate practice by teachers should feature authentic learning experiences resulting in an increased likelihood of young people developing the confidence and competence to become involved in lifelong physical activity. Much of this is embedded within Physical Literacy, in particular the promotion of self-esteem. The work by Killingbeck *et al.* (2007) attempts to contextualise the role of Physical Literacy in PE, arguing that distinct activities are likely to make a richer contribution to the development of young people and to offer a more authentic learning experience. Whitehead (2007b) suggests that motivation to take part in PE through the development of self-esteem and confidence must be an important consideration in curriculum planning. In reality, the attainment of physical competence might not always be immediately pleasurable and motivating; it can require considerable effort (Tinning, 2007). Nevertheless, there is evidence to suggest that current practices in PESS are not always successful in providing this motivation, self-belief and confidence (Bailey, 2005). Lifelong participation in physical activity relies upon an inherent self-belief concerning movement competence (Jess, Dewar and Fraser, 2004). Whitehead and Murdoch (2006) suggest that achieving Physical Literacy can result in high intrinsic motivation and self-confidence, both of which are key indicators in reducing the likelihood of avoidance of physical activity environments due to such considerations as poor peer acceptance, social isolation and low self-esteem (Bailey, 2005). Kirk (2005a) further suggests that the development of the perception of competence is a key part of the willingness to participate in physical activity and that PESS has often been relatively ineffective in this role. The emergence of the concept of Physical Literacy can aid PESS practitioners to plan curricular models which provide a broad base of movement competence which will, in turn, underpin both elite sport talent development and physical activity throughout the life-course. To this end, it is our contention that the concepts of FMS, Multi-skills and Physical Literacy should remain high on the PESS practitioner's agenda, regardless of the direction of future policy.

Dualism, NCPE and the future of holistic pedagogies in PESS

For many years, school sport has been restricted from fulfilling its holistic developmental potential by a kind of mind-body dualism (Kirk, 2005b), that is, a separation of the physical and cognitive elements which is evident in PE's theoretical/practical divide. However, most PESS practitioners consider competent games performance as inseparable from efficient and effective decision making (Baker *et al.*, 2003; Turner, 2005). As Oslin (2005: 128) has stated:

> Skilfulness goes beyond the execution of a particular skill within the game; it includes other components that relate to game play, such as support, movement off the ball, defensive actions and decision making.

Participants should be enabled and encouraged to think analytically about the sensory input to which they are exposed in physical activity and sports settings, comparing it to what they already know or to other ideas that are being put to them (Barnum, 2008). These challenging pedagogic demands are currently a requirement of the NCPE (QCA, 2007), as well as being an essential component of participant development (Light and Dixon, 2007). According to Light and Dixon (2007: 160):

> Contemporary societies require professionals and citizens who are lifelong learners, problem solvers, reflective independent learners, and creative and innovative thinkers.

The argument in support of the importance of developing cognitive skills within PESS is underlined by research such as that of Blomqvist *et al.* (2005), which examined secondary school students' decision making and game playing ability in soccer. In Blomqvist *et al.*'s (2005) study, students aged 14–15 years participated in video-based game-understanding tests as well as playing three different types of 3 vs 3 modified soccer matches for 10 minutes. Findings demonstrated that participants in such settings make more tactical decisions than technical executions. Furthermore, writers such as Barnum (2008) and Light (2004) have suggested that enhancing declarative knowledge can benefit procedural application. PESS has a large part to play in helping participants adopt such mindsets and to develop the requisite skills, whilst at the same time requiring players to think for themselves and become authors of their own learning, aspects of physical activity development which are part and parcel of the current NCPE.

The transformation of the current NCPE in terms of demanding more holistic pedagogic approaches which embrace cognitive skills alongside the well established physically-based outcomes reaches far beyond the minor revisions of 1995 and 2000 (Frapwell, 2009). Although curriculum change has traditionally failed to significantly impact the day-to-day practice of teachers (see, for example, Evans and Clarke, 1988), over the past decade there has been a much broader and deeper desire amongst PESS practitioners to transcend games-centred pedagogic models, to appreciate how and why young people participate in physical activity and to break from traditional approaches which encourage young people to associate sport with exclusive competition and performance (Dismore and Bailey, 2010). Despite this, Frapwell (2009) suggests, curricula are still too commonly designed around what teachers want to teach, rather than what young people need to learn, suggesting that the journey to a more holistic, child-centred, pedagogic approach is far from complete.

Existing pedagogic literature points to participant-centred pedagogies as being the way forward (Jones, 2006; Kirk, 2005a; Roberts, 2007). There are many participant-centred models in sport pedagogy, and it is beyond the scope of this chapter to describe these in detail. However, there are a number of common elements and resource implications which are paramount to the success of all these models and should be taken forward as a meaningful legacy of the past decade. In each case, the learner's role should become more active, probably through students working in small groups, being dependent upon one another and being cognitively and physically challenged to solve the problems presented by the environment in which they find themselves. The role of the PESS practitioner is to construct that environment in such a way as to maximally benefit the holistic development of participants. Situations need to be constructed to provide authentic sporting experiences that enable the pedagogist to step back, allowing participants the freedom to make decisions in whatever activity with which they are engaged. Participants should also be posed carefully constructed and challenging questions to assess and develop their understanding of the activites which they are undertaking. Such approaches may be considered as constructivist and are fundamentally different from the linear, technique-based models which tend to dominate sport-based curricula (Turner, 2005). Such constructivist theories reject the mind-body dualism to which sport pedagogy has, for so long, been tied (Light and Dixon, 2007). PESS practitioners should consider the social context in which they operate, the previous experiences and knowledge of their participants (including that drawn from sport-media coverage) and the intended actions and expected outcomes of session delivery in order to gain an altogether more balanced perspective on how participant understandings are constructed. In turn, they must be careful to avoid an over-reliance on formalised and linear teaching styles, should the range and content of the forthcoming NCPE revert to the traditional activity areas of bygone years.

There is evidence to suggest that recent developments in the area of holistic pedagogies and more learner-centred approaches have begun to impact on the experiences of young people in PESS (Wild, 2009). Such progress is apparent in the move away from activities such as games and gymnastics to a process of learning featuring flexible range and content such as 'identifying and solving problems to overcome challenges' (QCA, 2007: 194). The NCPE requires PESS practitioners to plan a curriculum experience that is focused on the needs of individual pupils, rather than sporting tradition. Examples of contemporary curriculum planning include pupils being taught the art of 'outwitting opponents' through football, handball and Rock-It-Ball, whilst exploring concepts, ideas and emotions through street dance and parkour. Although there may be a danger that some novel activities have been included in curricula for the sake of doing 'something different' (Fellows, 2012) and that the implementation of such activities without sufficient educational underpinning may only see a short-term benefit (Frapwell, 2009), it is the impact of embracing the range and content of the current NCPE which represents the greatest legacy for the forthcoming generation. Ofsted (2009) noted that, although most teaching in secondary school PE departments is good with outstanding elements, there is considerable room for improvement in the meeting of learners' individual needs. Garcia López *et al.* (2009) suggest that, rather than focusing on specific activities, a thematic approach to curriculum planning should be adopted that can be transferred into a specialised context as pupils progress through their school years.

Conclusion

The aim of this chapter has been to highlight some of the major developments in school sport provision during the PESSCL/PESSYP era. In many ways, the period from 2002 to 2010 represented a time of unprecedented change to national policy, educational reform and funding support which is unlikely to be replicated within the foreseeable future. Out of this period emerged numerous concepts built on the principles of sampling (Côté *et al.*, 2003) and FUNdamentals (Balyi and Hamilton, 2004), which allowed PESS practitioners to gain some appreciation of the importance of developing broad movement competencies. Emerging packages such as Multi-skills, and pedagogical concepts such as Physical Literacy have enhanced practitioners' ability to develop young peoples' FMS. Should the forthcoming NCPE revert to a more traditional range and content of activity areas, it is our contention that PESS practitioners should seek to build on the developmental work of the previous decade, confident in the value of broad movement competencies to form the foundation of sporting excellence as well as to enhance the likelihood of developing lifelong engagers in physical activity.

Contemporary pedagogic literature evidences considerable development in PESS practice. The adoption of more holistic pedagogic practices, reflecting the enhanced, cognitively focused content of the current NCPE, is also part of the legacy which PESS practitioners should not readily abandon. Non-linear pedagogic approaches such as constructivism enhance participant understandings, further aiding skill transferability between activities. Non-linear pedagogic approaches are also well suited to developing both elite performance and a richer engagement in physical activity through the lifecourse. Whilst the considerable reduction in funding and the likely demise of the SSPs may challenge many PESS practitioners to see policy developments as a progression, it is perhaps in these two elements of practice that the legacy of the PESSCL/PESSYP era can live on.

References

Armour, K., Sandford, R. and Duncombe, R. (2011). Right to be active: looked-after children in physical education and sport, in K. Armour (Ed.) *Sport Pedagogy: an introduction to teaching and coaching*, Harlow: Pearson Education, 214–225.

Bailey, R. P. (2005). Evaluating the relationship between physical education, sport and social inclusion, *Educational Review*, 57 (1), 71–90.

Bailey, R. and Dismore, H. (2004). *Sport in education (SpinEd) – the role of physical education and sport in education*. Project report. Paper presented at the 4th International Conference of Ministers and Senior Officials Responsible for Physical Education and Sport (MINEPS IV), December, Athens, Greece.

Bailey, R., Collins, D., Ford, P., MacNamara, Á., Toms, M. and Pearce, G. (2010). *Participant Development in Sport: an academic review*, Leeds: NCF.

Baker, J., Cobley, S. and Fraser-Thomas, J. (2009). What do we know about early specialization? Not much!, *High Ability Studies*, 20 (10), 77–89.

Baker, J., Côté, J. and Abernethy, B. (2003). Sport–specific practice and the development of expert decision-making in team ball sports, *Journal of Applied Sport Psychology*, 15 (1), 12–25.

Balyi, I. and Hamilton, A. (2004). *Long-term Athlete Development: Trainability in childhood and adolescence, windows of opportunity, optimal trainability*, Victoria: National Coaching Institute British Columbia and Advanced Training and Performance Ltd.

Barnum, M. G. (2008). Questioning skills demonstrated by approved clinical instructors during clinical field experiences, *Journal of Athletic Training*, 43 (3), 284–292.

Blomqvist, M., Vänttinen, T. and Luhtanen, P. (2005). Assessment of secondary school students' decision making and game-play ability in soccer, *Physical Education and Sport Pedagogy*, 10 (2), 107–119.

Côté, J. (1999). The influence of the family in the development of talent in sport, *The Sport Psychologist*, 13 (4), 395–417.

Côté, J., Baker, J. and Abernethy, B. (2003). From play to practice: a developmental framework for the acquisition of expertise in team sports, in J. L. Starkes and K. A. Ericsson, (Eds) *Expert Performance in Sport: Advances in research on sport expertise*, Leeds: Human Kinetics, 89–113.

——(2009). *The PE and Sport Strategy for Young People: how do we make the five hour offer relevant to every young person?* London: DCSF/DCMS.

Côté, J., Lidor, R. and Hackfort, D. (2009). ISSP position stand: to sample or to specialise? Seven postulates about youth sport activities that lead to continued participation and elite performance, *International Journal of Sport and Exercise Psychology*, 9 (1), 7–17.

Department for Children, Schools and Families (DCSF)/Department for Culture, Media and Sport (DCMS) (2008). *PE and Sport Strategy for Young People*, London: DCSF/DCMS.

——(2009). *The PE and Sport Strategy for Young People: a guide to delivering the five hour offer*, London: DCMS/DCSF.

Department for Culture, Media and Sport (DCMS) (2012). *Creating a Sporting Habit for Life – a new youth sport strategy*, London: HMSO.

Department for Education (DfE) (2011). *A New Approach for School Sports – decentralising power, incentivising competition, trusting teachers*. Retrieved 3 June 2012, from   www.education.gov.uk/inthenews/inthenews/a0071098/a-new-approach-for-school-sports-decentralising-power-incentivising-competition-trusting-teachers.

Department of National Heritage (DNH) (1995). *Raising the Game*, London: Cabinet Office.

Dismore, H. and Bailey, R. (2010). 'It's been a bit of a rocky start': attitudes toward physical education following transition, *Physical Education and Sport Pedagogy*, 15 (2), 175–191.

Evans, J. and Clarke, G. (1988). Changing the face of physical education, in J. Evans (Ed.) *Teachers, Teaching and Control in Physical Education*, London: Falmer Press, 125–143.

Fellows, A. (2012). The importance of teaching: teaching for achievement, assessment for change, *Physical Education Matters*, 7 (1), 10–12.

Flintoff, A. (2008). Targeting Mr Average: participation, gender equity and school sport partnerships, *Sport, Education and Society*, 13 (4), 393–411.

Ford, P., De Ste Croix, M., Lloyd, R., Meyers, R., Moosavi, M., Oliver, J., Till, K. and Williams, C. (2011). The long-term athlete development model: physiological evidence and application, *Journal of Sports Sciences*, 29 (4), 389–402.

Frapwell, A. (2009). A blue moon story, *Physical Education Matters*, 4 (1), 11–13.

Garcia López, L. M., Contreras Jordán, O. R., Penney, D. and Chandler, T. (2009). The role of transfer in games teaching: implications for the development of the sports curriculum, *European Physical Education Review*, 15 (1), 47–63.

Jess, M., Dewar, K. and Fraser, G. (2004). Basic moves: developing a foundation for lifelong physical activity, *British Journal of Teaching in Physical Education*, 35 (2), 23–27.

Jones, R. (2006). How can educational concepts inform sports coaching? in R. Jones (Ed.) *The Sports Coach as Educator: re-conceptualising sports coaching*, London: Routledge, 3–13.

Killingbeck, M., Bowler, M., Golding, D. and Gammon, P. (2007). Physical education and physical literacy, *Physical Education Matters*, 2 (2), 20–24.

Kirk, D. (2005a). Future prospects for teaching games for understanding, in L. L. Griffin and J. I. Butler (Eds) *Teaching Games for Understanding: theory, research and practice*, Leeds: Human Kinetics, 213–227.

——(2005b). Physical education, youth sport and lifelong participation: the importance of early learning experiences, *European Physical Education Review*, 11 (3), 239–255.

——(2006). Sport education, critical pedagogy, and learning theory: toward an intrinsic justification for physical education and youth sport, *Quest*, 58 (2), 255–264.

——(2012). Physical education futures: securing the conditions for radical reform, *Physical Education Matters*, 7 (1), 29–31.

Light, R. (2004). Coaches' experiences of game sense: opportunities and challenges, *Physical Education and Sport Pedagogy*, 9 (2), 115–131.

Light, R. and Dixon, M. A. (2007). Contemporary developments in sport pedagogy and their implications for sport management education, *Sport Management Review*, 10 (2), 159–175.

Morley, D. (2009). Multi-skills: contexts and constraints, *Physical Education Matters*, 4 (3), 19–23.

——(2010). Multi skills: the competence and confidence constraints, *Primary Physical Education Matters*, 5 (1), VII.

Murphy, F. and Ni Chroinin, D. (2011). Playtime: the needs of very young learners in physical education and sport, in K. Armour (Ed.) *Sport Pedagogy: an introduction to teaching and coaching*, Harlow: Pearson Education, 140–152.

Ofsted (2009). *Physical Education in Schools 2005/08: working towards 2012 and beyond*, Manchester: Ofsted.

——(2011). *School Sport Partnerships: a survey of good practice*, Manchester: Ofsted.

Oslin, J. L. (2005). The role of assessment in teaching games for understanding, in L. L. Griffin and J. I. Butler (Eds), *Teaching Games for Understanding: theory, research and practice*, Leeds: Human Kinetics, 125–136.

Qualifications and Curriculum Authority (QCA) (2007). *Physical Education: programme of study for key stage three and attainment target*. London: QCA.

Quick, S., Dalziel, D., Thornton, A. and Simon, A. (2009). *PE and School Sport Survey 2008/9*, London: TNS-BMRB.

Roberts, S. (2007). The motivational effects of incorporating teaching games for understanding pedagogy within a sport education season, *Physical Education Matters*, 2 (2), 41–46.

Stafford, I. (2005). *Coaching for Long-term Athlete Development*, Leeds: Coachwise Business Solutions/The National Coaching Foundation.

Tinning, R. (2007). Aliens in the gym? Considering young people as learners in physical education, *ACHPER Australia Healthy Lifestyles Journal*, 54 (2), 13–18.

Turner, A. (2005). Teaching and learning games at the secondary level, in L. L. Griffin and J. I. Butler (Eds), *Teaching Games for Understanding: theory, research and practice*, Leeds: Human Kinetics, 71–90.

Whitehead, M. (2001). The concept of physical literacy, *British Journal of Teaching Physical Education*, 32 (1), 6–8.

——(2007a). Physical literacy: philosophical considerations in relation to developing a sense of self, universality and propositional knowledge, *Sport, Ethics and Philosophy*, 1 (3), 281–298.

——(2007b). Physical literacy in the context of physical Literacy in the secondary school. *Physical Education Matters*, 2 (2), 24.

——(2010). Introduction, in M. Whitehead (Ed.) *Physical Literacy through the Lifecourse*: London: Routledge, 3–9.

Whitehead, M. and Murdoch, E. (2006). Physical literacy and physical education: conceptual mapping, *Physical Education Matters*, 1 (1), 6–9.

Wild, A. (2009). Implementation of the new secondary curriculum, *Physical Education Matters*, 4 (3), 15–18.

Youth Sport Trust (YST) (2006). *Multi-skill Clubs and Multi-skill Academies*, Loughborough: YST.

10 Sports coaching and young people in the twenty-first century

Simon Padley and Don Vinson

Introduction

Sports coaching is a valued vocational activity which, in recent years, has enjoyed a significantly heightened policy profile within the UK (Taylor and Garratt, 2010). Indeed, the past decade has witnessed the publication of several key policy documents which have brought considerable challenges both to the coaching workforce and to sports governing bodies. By 2016 it is the intention of Sports Coach UK (SCUK – the strategic agency for sports coaching in Britain), to have professionalised the industry and established a world-leading coaching system (National Coaching Foundation (NCF), 2008). The process of professionalisation requires a step-change in the investment of coaches in relation to their own development and is especially challenging considering the traditionally reproductive and intuitively informed working conventions of most practitioners (Jones, 2006). Recent policy development in this area began with the publication of *The Coaching Task Force – Final Report* (Department for Culture, Media and Sport (DCMS), 2002), which called for an integrated and unified system for developing coaching in the UK. In turn, SCUK's 3-7-11 Action Plan for Coaching (NCF, 2008) was designed to provide a framework by which professionalisation could be achieved. The term '3-7-11' refers to the number of years each stage of the Action Plan comprises, i.e. 'Building the Foundations (2006–2008)', 'Delivering the Goals (2006–2012)' and 'Transforming the System (2006–2016)'. Falling at the midpoint of the 3-7-11 Action Plan, this chapter discusses the challenges currently facing those involved in the professionalisation of coaching, focussing specifically on the impact of the requisite developments in coaching practice on young peoples' experience of sport. The scope of this issue is considerable, given that around 1.68 million hours of sport are delivered each week to over 5 million participants in the UK, two-thirds of whom are children (North, 2009). Furthermore, the widely espoused potential of appropriate sporting experience to cultivate many aspects of young people's development reinforces the coach's role in a powerful and serious endeavour (Morgan, 2006). This chapter challenges coaches to consider the experience of young people by exploring the implications of current policy and contemporary learning theory and by providing a philosophical critique of twenty-first-century sports coaching. The chapter concludes by suggesting that, by embracing contemporary pedagogic theory, coaches can balance the demands of competitively based UK sports policy with more holistically focussed coaching strategies.

How does sports policy impact on the young performer?

Amongst the foremost attributes of SCUK's coaching vision, outlined in policy such as *The Coaching Task Force – Final Report* (DCMS, 2002) and the UK Action Plan for Coaching (NCF, 2008), lies a commitment to an ethical, participant-centred system of coach and athlete development. This challenges coaches to deliver much more than fun, safe and inclusive sessions: a trilogy of expectations which are commonly considered to be the extent of 'good practice' in youth sport. Current policy demands that coaches re-evaluate the experiences of young people by considering the individual developmental pathway of participants, regardless of their perceived performance potential. Furthermore, The UK Action Plan for Coaching (NCF, 2008: 1) heightens the responsibility on sports coaches in terms of their broader developmental role:

> Sports coaching is central to developing, sustaining and increasing parti-cipation in sport. It drives better performances and increased success as well as supporting key social and economic objectives throughout the UK. At all levels of society, coaches guide improvement in technical, tactical, physical, mental and lifestyle skills, contributing to personal and social development.

The National Occupational Standards for Coaching (Skills Active, 2010) are the benchmark against which UK national governing bodies (NGBs) map content for coaching qualifications. These reinforce that the participant must be at the centre of the coaching process, stipulating that all NGBs adhere to this ethos in order to receive SCUK accreditation. The UK Coaching Framework (NCF, 2008), the reference point for NGBs, further encourages coaching programmes to consider and prioritise the '5Cs' of participant development: competence, confidence, connection, character and creativity (Bailey and Ross, 2009). Inherent within these aims is a sense that current policy still recognises the potential of competitive sports to develop positive character traits.

The 5Cs illustrate the holistic perspective of contemporary coaching policy, which raises challenging questions and demands in relation to the extent to which coaches engage in a regular, broad and deep review of their own prac-tice. Cassidy *et al.* (2009) suggest that the majority of coaches are pre-dominantly focussed on psychomotor development, with little attention paid to cognitive or affective elements. Understanding the holistic needs of perfor-mers requires the coach to go beyond the physical and mental components of sports performance, to address the social and perhaps even the spiritual aspects of personal development (Watson and Nesti, 2005). As with many aspects of coaching policy in the twenty-first century, such a focus is undoubtedly aspirational (North, 2009). Below, we examine three of the most challenging issues concerning holistic perspectives: (i) early specialisation; (ii) professionalisation and 'master' youth coaches; and (iii) coaching for cognitive and affective development in competitive environments.

Coaching young people from a holistic perspective: early specialisation

A holistic appreciation of coaching necessitates challenging the commonly held belief that early specialisation in sport is a prerequisite of elite performance. Engaging young people in suitable development pathways that are designed to enable progression to elite performance and also minimise the likelihood of burn-out or drop-out, should feature high on coaches' agendas, especially considering that long-term predictors of talented athletes are unreliable (Côté, *et al.*, 2009). Contrary to popular practitioner opinion, early skill development research (e.g. Ericsson *et al.*, 1993) and current practice (Côté *et al.*, 2009), contemporary literature opposes the notion that late starters are almost guaranteed to be unable to overcome the advantage of those performers who have amassed many hundreds of hours of deliberate practice by specialising in their chosen activity at a young age.

Encouraging early specialisation pathways is based upon a series of assumptions surrounding the relationship between deliberate practice and elite performance. Many sports in the UK draw on the Long Term Athlete Development (LTAD) framework (Balyi and Hamilton, 2004), which features four (for early specialisation sports) or six (for late specialisation sports) stages designed to aid the athletic development of participants. These stages are concerned with young people's initial involvement with their chosen sport, the process of learning to train and their relationship with competition through to retirement. Despite the widespread adoption of this model by UK NGBs, there are very few studies supporting LTAD's assertion that 10,000 hours of specialised training is required to develop expert performance. In fact, Côté *et al.* (2007) highlight that expert performance can be achieved with just 3,000 to 4,000 hours of sport-specific training. Drawing on a wide range of literature, Côté *et al.*, (2009) propose seven postulates concerning youth sport activities that lead to both elite performance and continued participation. These postulates rest upon the premise that early diversification in sports where peak performance is reached after maturation does not hinder elite sports participation but links to longer sports careers and positively affects youth development.

Côté *et al.*'s (2009) notion of diversification encompasses the abandonment of pyramidic models[1] of talent identification, i.e. those characterised by drop-out and high-performance burn-out and in which upward progression is the only valued outcome. Instead, they recommend the adoption of a participant needs-led approach to coaching, featuring varied pathways to excellence and a focus on individual, personal goals via a broad range of activities. Baker *et al.* (2003) suggest that the early specialisation of expert performers should not be seen as a prerequisite of expert performance, as a consequence of the potential early transfer of cognitive and kinesthetic appreciation and because some of the many thousands of hours required to attain expert status can be transferred by understandings elicited in other activities. On this basis, young people, it seems, should be encouraged to sample a wide range of activities in their formative years before choosing whether to specialise in a particular activity or continuing to be an 'all-rounder' or simply to be a recreational sportsperson. In sum, the need to see beyond the production-line style approach to talent identification and development is essential if coaching policy is to have a meaningful impact on practice.

Coaching young people from a holistic perspective: professionalisation and 'master' youth coaches

The impact of current coaching policy on young peoples' experiences of sport is further challenged when considering Sports Coach UK's (NCF, 2009) Coach Development Model (CDM – see Figure 10.1) which calls for

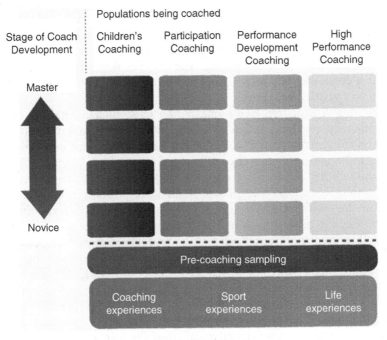

Figure 10.1 Coach development model (NCF, 2009: 8)

specialist, 'master', youth coaches. The CDM challenges the traditional notion of expert coach practice being almost universally associated with elite, adult, performance. Currently, the United Kingdom Coach Certificate (UKCC) recognises four levels of practice: (i) Assistant Coach (Level 1); (ii) Session Deliverer (Level 2); (iii) Annual Planner (Level 3); and (iv) Long-term, Specialist and Innovative Coach (Level 4). However, following the logic of the CDM, coaches will (over time) be able to choose their intended area of expertise from any one of the four strands (i.e. children's/participant/performance development/high performance) and specialise in working with that particular athlete population. SCUK recognise that the CDM is aspirational (North, 2009) and that considerable work has to be done in order to define the criteria for each stage. Unquestionably, coaching practice will not look the same at each of the 'master' stages, requiring consideration of appropriate pedagogy for each population group.

The CDM reinforces Cushion's (2007) assertion that seeking a common model for coaching practice is probably neither possible nor desirable. Coaching is a highly complex social practice and the industry should be ready to accept that each and every coaching context is different to every other (Jones, 2006). If we acknowledge that coaching is a highly contextualised process, then this necessitates an in-depth and critical consideration of how coaches guide participant development. While disagreeing with Cushion (2007) and Jones (2006), Lyle (2007) reinforces the contextual nature of the coaching process, arguing that non-linearity prevents practitioners from considering their work to be without planning or reason. Acknowledging the complexity of human interaction, Lyle (2007) believes that coaches should focus attention on a critical examination of their practices, rather than the factors that affect their intentions. Irrespective, both schools of thought require a connoisseurial appreciation of the impact of contemporary learning theory on coaching pedagogy.

Professionalisation represents one of the most fundamental concerns of contemporary coaching policy (DCMS, 2002; Taylor and Garratt 2008). Jones (2006) also asserts that coaching has been stifled by an over-reliance on bio-scientific underpinnings (e.g. physiology, psychology, biomechanics) and that, through the deepening of understanding relating to pedagogy, coaching will, in time, emerge as a legitimate stand-alone profession. Cushion (2007) suggests that, without an engagement with pedagogic theory and an appreciation that the process must equate to more than simply applying theories from other disciplines, coaching may never achieve broad acceptance as a profession. In turn, Taylor and Garratt (2008: 7) also highlight the importance of creating a 'distinct and specialised body of knowledge' as a basis for coaching practice. Jones (2006) believes that the reconceptualising of sports coaching as a predominantly educational process lies at the heart of professionalisation. If coaching is to embrace an educational perspective as part of its drive towards professionalisation, then the implications for specialist children's coaches are substantial. Kirk's (2006) consideration of critical pedagogy suggests such an approach would necessitate embracing notions of empowerment and cultural critique. Empowerment is a crucial aspect of rebalancing the coach-athlete relationship, which Jones (2006: 9) suggests has most frequently developed high degrees of participant dependency, where performers are heavily reliant on the decision making of their coach and their performances suffer through the inability to adapt to 'dynamic live environment[s]'. Such discussion highlights the need for all sports coaches (particularly specialist children's coaches, who deal with performers at their most important formative stages) to engage with contemporary pedagogic theory.

Coaching young people from a holistic perspective: coaching for cognitive and affective development in competitive environments

Numerous writers have noted that coaches may be ideally placed to engage with young people in a holistic developmental process due to favourable coach-to-athlete ratios and the extensive time that they spend together (see, for example, Bergmann Drewe, 1999; Jones, 2006). However, coaches are challenged in this respect due to the relationship between coaching and competition and the consequent preoccupation with physical skill development. The place of competition seems particularly explicit in the coaching environment and represents the predominant focus of the process, reinforcing the necessity to consider its nature and how this affects coaches' pedagogy. Furthermore, recent sports policy documentation from the Coalition government, *Creating a Sporting Habit for Life – A new youth sport strategy* (DCMS, 2012) places competitive sporting environments at the heart of youth athlete development. DCMS (2012: 3) establishes a national competition structure to build a 'lasting legacy of competitive sport in schools'. This structure is built around an 'Olympics-style' school games which enhances young people's opportunities to participate in intra- and inter-school competition. Of course, such ideas are founded upon the premise that competitive sporting environments provide an opportunity for self-discovery, the experiencing of excellence and the building of social relationships (Torres and Hager, 2007). Viewed from an educational perspective, competitive sports are often championed in order to engage individuals in a process of emancipation (including inclusion and equality), empowerment and critique (Kirk, 2006). However, it is also acknowledged that competitive sport has the power to develop a number of undesirable moral qualities (Bergmann Drewe, 1999).

For some, sporting competition represents the converse of morality, offering instead a training ground for a series of less desirable characteristics. As Spencer (2000: 143) notes:

> There is growing belief that sport, rather than encouraging moral value and spiritual values, promotes just the antithesis: man's inevitable fall from grace through egotism, cynicism, nihilism, an obsessive focus on

money, and win at all costs mentality that fosters disrespect for competitors and society.

With the increased focus upon competition as the vehicle for youth involvement in sport, and the recognition in research and policy of the need for a shift in the culture of coaching to a holistic, participant-centred process, one might expect the subsequent emergence of such matters in coach education. However, coaching practice is poorly informed by critical pedagogic scholarship (Jones, 2006). Taylor and Garratt (2010: 124) acknowledge that there are 'concerns regarding the lack of standards for coaching and strategies for training and employment, including guidance on the moral and ethical responsibilities, which have tended to evolve informally in concert with the many diverse traditions of sports coaching'. Current coaching policy advocates that the coach should be responsible for inculcating moral character in respect of young athletes' ability to demonstrate respect for social and cultural rules, possession of standards for correct behaviours, a sense of right and wrong and integrity, including showing respect for all (Bailey and Ross, 2009; NCF, 2009). In contradiction, Watson and White (2007) contend that the prevailing culture of coaching for competition is more akin to war-like preparation, where the opposition is recognised as the barrier to success and, at worst, the enemy. In order to counter this prevailing culture there is a need to learn from physical education practice (Jones, 2006). To this end, we turn now to an examination of the educational discourse of competition and moral development in order to elicit a number of practice-based recommendations for coaching. For coaches, the question arises: How might we best understand the complex social process of coaching in order to ensure the positive holistic development of the young people in our care, despite the potential pollution of inappropriately framed competitive environments? The answer, we would argue, lies in an examination of contemporary, constructivist pedagogic theory. In the following section we attempt to contribute to bridging the void between coaching practice and pedagogic theory by considering the potential of competitive sports experiences to provide opportunities for young people to experience moral development, a factor inherent in the 'C' of 'character', as presented by the UK Coaching Framework (NCF, 2008).

Sports coaching, young people and contemporary pedagogic theory

The majority of coaching practice in the UK remains dominated by direct pedagogies requiring the replication of movement such as skills and patterns of play, as directed by coaches (Jones, 2006). Cassidy *et al.* (2009) suggest that there are a number of concerns arising from such approaches: a lack of cognitive involvement, limited knowledge generation, participants devoid of active investment in the process, a dampening of creative problem-solving ability and inhibited social development. These issues are accentuated by an increasingly child-centred appreciation of pedagogy in schools, leading to an adjustment of young people's expectations of their involvement and investment in the learning process (Cassidy *et al.*, 2009). SCUK's Coaching Framework Consultation Report (Townend, 2009) reinforces this assertion by highlighting that, when discussing weaknesses in coaching provision, children are most likely to cite issues of 'over-coaching', i.e. sessions characterised by rigidity, coach-dominance and lack of play or expression. Light and Dixon (2007: 159) suggest that such practice is outdated:

> Within the context of rapidly changing social conditions in developed societies, traditional approaches to teaching and learning that view learning as a simple process of internalising a fixed body of knowledge have become outdated and ineffective. The traditional emphasis on content, or what we feel our students should learn, has become less important than the need to help them learn how to learn and to think critically about both content and process.

Constructivist pedagogies challenge the most common models of practice featuring the coach as knowledge dispenser and power holder. Such pedagogies criticise linear coaching processes based upon replication and reproduction (Light and Dixon, 2007) and challenge deliverers to help young people to become innovative and critical thinkers. Across the UK coaching landscape, didactic delivery dominates, inhibiting coaches' abilities to develop intellectual competencies and a sense of critical thinking (Cushion *et al.*, 2003). In seeking a participant needs-led approach, coaches (of young people at least) need to adopt more athlete-centred pedagogic practices. Such models share a number of common features. Athletes become increasingly dependent on one another whilst undergoing cognitive as well as physiological challenges. Coaches seek to create environments that facilitate the holistic development of the athletes. Situations are constructed in ways that provide authentic sporting experiences for athletes and allow coaches to place the educative burden on the activity and the environment (Gréhaigne *et al.* 2003). Within athlete-centred models, the importance of procedural knowledge is irrefutably upheld; however, technique should be introduced at developmentally appropriate stages, often after the athletes have come to understand 'why' the technique is important. Technique delivered prior to understanding leads to inhibited transfer between practice and performance (Butler and McCahan, 2005). Coaches must also appreciate that athletes do not all begin with the same knowledge-base, learn at the same rate, or acquire skills in the same way (Butler and McCahan, 2005). It should also be noted that enhancing declarative knowledge can precede and aid the development of the procedural (doing) (Barnum, 2008).

Contemporary sports pedagogy suggests that skilled performance is the result of a construction of the learner's life experiences (Light and Dixon, 2007). This perspective casts doubt upon the value of technique-led approaches to coaching, but also of guided-discovery pedagogies which lead athletes to a predetermined endpoint. Athletes should be considered 'legitimate peripheral participants' (Lave and Wenger, 1991: 28) i.e. they should be encouraged to develop a deeper, more mature and fuller sense of participation within their sporting community over time. Coaches should consider the social contexts and prior experiences of participants in order to develop a greater sense of how their athletes' understandings are constructed.

Constructivist pedagogic principles may sound idealistic, perhaps even unrealistic, given the present nature of coaching in the UK. However, evidence of such approaches infiltrating the coaching system through formal education courses (e.g. Roberts, 2010) suggests a step in the right direction. Whilst a comprehensive guide to the application of these principles is beyond the scope of this chapter, we have chosen an example of an athlete-centred coaching process which we believe represents an actionable component for coaches who are keen to explore the kind of principles that we have discussed. To this end, we present the following scenario as an example of how such a model might be implemented by a coach wishing to facilitate learning through educationally meaningful small-sided modified games.[2]

Participant needs-led coaching through situated learning

Within the context of sports coaching, 'situated learning' (Lave and Wenger, 1991) requires coaches to place participants alongside opponents in 'live' situations rather than in deliberate practice-style activities. Richard and Wallian (2005) suggest that there are two essential components to situated learning within sports coaching: (i) the observation of game play behaviours; and (ii) critical thinking through the debate of ideas and negotiated meaning. Athletes should be placed as active participants in the 'real' environments and given the opportunity to observe what goes on and explore their own role through involvement and experimentation. Mistakes yield excellent opportunities for the coach to aid development and should not merely be viewed as a consequence of incorrectly acquired technique. It is the role of the coach to prompt a deeper consideration by the participants of the environment through open-ended questioning (e.g. 'Why were group A more successful than group B?'). Learners are encouraged to answer such questions through a meaningful discussion of ideas and enabled to enact their own solutions to the problems in play by applying their thoughts to the 'real' live environment (Richard and Wallian, 2005). Within such situations, it is hoped that athletes will be able to construct their own understanding of effective performance – an illustration of a participant needs-led approach to coaching, rather than a content-based, coach-centred model (Gréhaigne *et al.*, 2003). Mallett *et al.* (2009) suggest that, through such an approach, the likelihood of a positive learning experience is greatly increased due to the emphasis on participant ownership of process and engagement (learning by doing), and the opportunity to apply solutions to emerging problems back into the real environment.

Debating ideas is an important pedagogical tool. Indeed, many studies have shown that the verbalisation of such thinking can enhance learning (Richard and Wallian, 2005). Whilst this may present difficulties for students who do not use language well, it is an important part of the development of critical thinking. Richard and Wallian (2005) describe three steps to the debating of ideas following the involvement and observation stages:

- Invite description of the events.
- Encourage participants to give their interpretations and explanations.
- Extrapolate efficient strategies.

Such a model of learning may comprise a radical shift for the majority of coaches. Pearson and Webb (2008) suggest that questioning is one of the most difficult elements of the coaching process to master, and undoubtedly facilitation of the debate of ideas will, for some, be similarly challenging. However, if sports coaches aspire to modify their everyday practices, then they must be willing to constantly review their practice in light of changing social constructs and contemporary theory. The implications of this constant process of review are both challenging and far reaching, but then this is the nature of professional practice. The final challenge for us here is to articulate how this appreciation of contemporary pedagogic theory complements the philosophical critique of the nature of the competitive environment as outlined above. Thus, in the final section of the chapter, we suggest how coaches might focus on 'real' environments, whilst embracing the notion of the opponent as one to strive *with* and not *against*.

Participant needs-led coaching through a re-evaluation of the nature of competition

Bergmann Drewe (1999: 14) stipulates that: 'although physical educators may not be able to change societal values regarding winning and losing, they can make progress in striving to diffuse the win at all costs mentality by stressing the striving together in the pursuit of excellence'. The key to such a shift lies in the original essence of the root words for competition – com-petitio (striving together) (Bergmann Drewe, 1999). The sense here is that competition cannot (and does not) exist without an opponent. To this end, the starting point for our morality in competitive sporting encounters must be the recognition of the inherent reliance upon the opponent for the experience to exist. This elevates the opponent above and beyond that of 'enemy' to a prerequisite asset in the pursuit of our best. As Morgan (2003: 187) states:

> The principle value of athletic competition is not in the winning but in the process of overcoming the challenge presented by a worthy opponent. What makes competition in sports morally defensible is seeing it as a mutual quest for excellence ... athletes ought to win (or lose) gracefully,

treat their opponents with respect, have respect for the rules of the game, and challenge their opponents.

Bergmann Drew (1999) argues that athletes will encounter moments during competition when decisions have to be made to discern whether or not certain behaviours would be morally defensible. For athletes to make such decisions they must have some underlying moral theory or framework to guide them; the coach has a responsibility to develop such frameworks. As outlined above the use of game-based 'live' environments within training allows athletes to experience moments of moral conflict. Hsu (2004) suggests that, when faced with problems of moral conflict within competitive situations, it is impossible for athletes to resolve these situations without critical thinking skills. Hsu (2004: 149) continues:

> Not all sports participants or relevant agents are wise enough or capable enough to think critically ... thus moral education regarding how to develop participants' critical thinking in sport plays a very important role. One important means by which a coach or a teacher can facilitate moral development is through example.

The role of the coach in modelling moral behaviour is important. However, this is not enough to ensure character development. Hsu (2004) recognises that a morally educated sports person will demonstrate behaviours not only in accordance with a specific principle (e.g. fair play) but also an appropriate disposition (e.g. respect for others and empathy), instigated by their critical thinking skills. As coaches, then, we must first recognise the need to instil in our athletes the value of not breaking rules but, in addition, we must also instil a sense of right and wrong based on a demonstrable set of underpinning values. Coaches must recognise the respect due to opponents, to the game itself and to fellow athletes who make our striving for excellence possible, and help the young people in their care to develop such an understanding for themselves. Coaches must therefore consider how they can develop realistic environments within coaching sessions whereby morality can be modelled, negotiated and developed within the athletic community.

Conclusions

In this chapter we have sought to argue that, by embracing contemporary pedagogic theory, coaches can balance the demands of competitively based UK sports policy with the more holistically focussed coaching strategies. We contend that embracing this kind of holistic approach will facilitate increased participation, reduce drop-out and enhance the enjoyment of young people in sporting environments (Cassidy *et al.* 2009). UK sports policy appears wedded to the value of competition; however, we have argued that this presents coaches with a number of problems. Coaches must seek to counter the notion that early specialisation is a prerequisite for reaching elite performance and to encourage a broad sampling of sports experiences. The coaching community also need to continue to invest in the notion of 'master' children's coaches and challenge the conception of the most competent coaches always being aligned with expert, adult, performance. Furthermore, coaches need to recognise that competition is often framed in a combative manner and that this can be detrimental to the ethical and moral development of young people. A truly ethical coaching framework must consider participants' pathways in terms of their holistic development. Such consideration demands an examination of the environments in which young people devote much time and energy, often pursuing a system which so keenly reinforces a win-at-all-costs mentality. A literate sportsperson understands not only how to play, but also how to play within the rules, both written and unwritten. Likewise, it has been argued that a holistically-minded coach will seek to ensure that participants understand that sport is more than a tool for personal glory and reward.

In order to develop the necessary skills to aid young peoples' holistic development, coaches need to embrace contemporary pedagogic models, a principle which is commensurate with current coaching policy and the professionalisation agenda. For the majority of coaches in the UK, this represents a considerable shift both in practice and mindset. Nevertheless, by learning how to frame competitive situations authentically and appropriately through embracing pedagogic models such as situated learning, coaches will be more likely to produce athletes capable of making difficult decisions in these environments. The competitive ethos promoted within contemporary sports policy presents a considerable challenge for youth sports coaches and, in this sense, our aim has been to present a compelling case for embracing contemporary pedagogic principles in order to aid the holistic development of the young people in our care.

Notes

1 Pyramidic models of talent development are based on the notion that simply broadening the base (i.e. increasing the number of players/participants at grass-roots level) necessarily leads to the production of a greater numbers of elite performers and are usually institutionally focussed, i.e. concerned with specific sports.
2 See, for example, Slade (2010).

References

Bailey, R. and Ross, G. (2009) *Participant Development – Key research themes*. Leeds: Sports Coach UK.

Baker, J., Côté, J. and Abernethy, B. (2003) 'Sport-specific practice and the development of expert decision-making in team ball sports', *Journal of Applied Sport Psychology*, 15(1), pp. 12–25.

Balyi, I. and Hamilton, A. (2004) *Long-term Athlete Development: Trainability in childhood and adolescence, windows of opportunity, optimal trainability*. Victoria:

National Coaching Institute British Columbia and Advanced Training and Performance Ltd.

Barnum, M. G. (2008) 'Questioning skills demonstrated by approved clinical instructors during clinical field experiences', *Journal of Athletic Training*, 43(3), pp. 284–292.

Bergmann Drewe, S. (1999) 'Moral reasoning in sport: Implications for physical education', *Sport, Education and Society*, 4(2), pp. 117–130.

Butler, J. I. and McCahan, B. J. (2005) 'Teaching Games for Understanding as a curriculum model', in L. L. Griffin and J. I. Butler (Eds) *Teaching Games for Understanding: Theory, research and practice.* Leeds: Human Kinetics, pp. 33–54.

Cassidy, T., Jones, R. and Potrac, P. (2009) *Understanding Sports Coaching: The social, cultural and pedagogical foundations of coaching practice*, (2nd edn). Abingdon: Routledge.

Côté, J., Baker, J. and Abernethy, B. (2007) 'Practice and play in the development of sport expertise', in R. Eklund and G. Tenenbaum (Eds) *Handbook of Sport Psychology*, (3rd edn), Champaign, IL: Human Kinetics, pp. 184–202.

Côté, J., Lidor, R. and Hackfort, D. (2009) 'ISSP position stand: To sample or to specialise? Seven postulates about youth sport activities that lead to continued participation and elite performance', *International Journal of Sport and Exercise Psychology*, 9(1) pp. 7–17.

Cushion, C. (2007) 'Modelling the complexity of the coaching process: A response to commentaries', *International Journal of Sports Science and Coaching*, 2(4), pp. 427–433.

Cushion, C. J., Armour, K. and Jones, R. L. (2003) 'Coach education and continuing professional development: Experience and learning to coach', *Quest*, 55(3), pp. 215–230.

Department for Culture, Media and Sport (DCMS) (2002) *The Coaching Task Force – Final report.* London: HMSO.

——(2012) *Creating a Sporting Habit for Life – A new youth sport strategy.* London: HMSO.

Ericsson, K. A., Krampe, R. T., Tesch-Römer, C. (1993) 'The role of deliberate practice in the acquisition of elite performance', *Psychological Review*, 100(3), pp. 363–406.

Gréhaigne, J.-F., Richard, J.-F. and Griffin, L. L. (2003) *Teaching and Learning Team Sports and Games.* London: Routledge.

Hsu, L. (2004) 'Moral thinking, sports rules and education', *Sport, Education and Society*, 9 (1), pp. 143–153.

Jones, R. (2006) 'How can educational concepts inform sports coaching', in R. Jones (Ed.) *The Sports Coach as Educator: Reconceptualising sports coaching.* Abingdon: Routledge, pp. 3–13.

Kirk, D. (2006) 'Sport education, critical pedagogy, and learning theory: Toward an intrinsic justification for physical education and youth sport', *Quest*, 58(2), pp. 255–264.

Lave, J. and Wenger, E. (1991) *Situated Learning: Legitimate peripheral participation.* Cambridge: Cambridge University Press.

Light, R. and Dixon, M. A. (2007) 'Contemporary developments in sport pedagogy and their implications for sport management education', *Sport Management Review*, 10(2), pp. 159–175.

Lyle, J. (2007) 'Modelling the complexity of the coaching process: A commentary', *International Journal of Sports Science and Coaching*, 2(4), pp. 407–409.

Mallett, C. J., Trudel, P., Lyle, J. and Rynne, S. B. (2009) 'Formal vs informal coach education', *International Journal of Sports Science and Coaching*, 4(3), pp. 325–334.

Morgan, W. J. (2003) 'Enhancing performance in sport: What is morally permissible?', in J. Boxill (Ed.) *Sport Ethics: An anthology.* Oxford: Blackwell, pp.182–188.

——(2006) 'Philosophy and physical education', in D. Kirk, M. O'Sullivan and D. Macdonald (Eds) *Handbook of Physical Education.* London: Sage, pp. 97–108.

National Coaching Foundation (NCF) (2008) *The UK Coaching Framework: A 3-7-11 year action plan.* Leeds: Sports Coach UK.

——(2009) *The Coach Development Model: User guide.* Leeds: Sports Coach UK.

North, J. (2009) *Coaching Workforce Document 2009–2016.* Leeds: National Coaching Foundation.

Pearson, P. and Webb, P. (2008) 'Developing effective questioning in teaching games for understanding (TGfU)'. Paper presented at the First Asia Pacific Sport in Education Conference, Adelaide, 21 January.

Richard, J.-F. and Wallian, N. (2005) 'Emphasizing student engagement in the construction of game performance', in L. L. Griffin and J. I. Butler (Eds) *Teaching Games for Understanding: Theory, research and practice.* Leeds: Human Kinetics, pp. 19–32.

Roberts, S. (2010) 'What can coach education programmes learn from the teachers? Model-based instruction in a UK national governing body award course', *International Journal of Sports Science and Coaching,* 5(1), pp. 109–116.

Skills Active (2010) 'National occupational standards: Level 2 – coaching', accessed 29 July 2010: www.skillsactive.com/skillsactive/national-occupational-standards/level-2/item/3169; last updated: 27 July 2010.

Slade, D. (2010) *Transforming Play: Teaching tactics and game sense.* Leeds: Human Kinetics.

Spencer, A. F. (2000) 'Ethics, faith and sport', *Journal of Interdisciplinary Studies,* 12, pp. 143–158.

Taylor, B. and Garratt, D. (2008) *The Professionalisation of Sports Coaching in the UK: Issues and conceptualisation.* Leeds: National Coaching Foundation.

——(2010) 'The professionalisation of sports coaching: Relations of power, resistance and compliance', *Sport, Education and Society,* 15(1), pp. 121–139.

Townend, R. (2009) *UK Coaching Framework Consultation Report.* Leeds: National Coaching Foundation.

Torres, C. R. and Hager, P. F. (2007) 'De-emphasizing competition in organized youth sport: Misdirected reforms and misled children', *Journal of the Philosophy of Sport,* 34(2), pp. 194–210.

Watson, N. J. and Nesti, M. (2005) 'The role of spirituality in sport psychology consulting: An analysis and integrative review of literature', *Journal of Applied Sport Psychology,* 17(3), pp. 228–239.

Watson, N. J. and White, J. (2007) '"Winning at all costs" in modern sport: Reflections on pride and humility in the writings of C. S. Lewis', in J. Parry, S. Robinson, N. J. Watson and M. Nesti (Eds) *Sport and Spirituality: An introduction.* Abingdon: Routledge, pp. 61–79.

11 The next generation: Young people, sport and volunteering

Hannah Mawson and Andrew Parker

Introduction

The role of volunteering in the development and sustainability of UK sport has attracted much interest over the past decade. In England alone there are reported to be over 100,000 sports clubs staffed by some 5.8 million volunteers (Taylor, *et al.*, 2003), with sports volunteering being estimated to account for some 26 per cent of all volunteering activity nationally (Davis Smith, 1998; Taylor *et al.*, 2003). Sport England recognises the importance of volunteering from a community sports perspective; the presence and development of coaches, leaders and volunteers is vital to achieving its three key objectives: increasing sports participation, developing talent and improving levels of satisfaction amongst participants (Sport England, 2008). However, it is well documented that sports clubs continue to experience difficulty in recruiting and retaining volunteers (Davis Smith, 1998; Taylor *et al.*, 2003). Indeed, research has shown that the number of young people undertaking such roles decreased markedly during the 1990s; in 1991 55 per cent of 16–24 year olds formally volunteered at least once, but by 2001 this had dropped to 40 per cent (Davis Smith, 1998; Attwood *et al.*, 2003). More recent research has demonstrated an increase in volunteering amongst young people aged 16–19 (from 41 per cent in 2003, to 53 per cent in 2005). The same period witnessed a time of relative stability in the number of 20–24 year olds formally volunteering: down from 43 per cent in 2003 to 42 per cent in 2005 (Munton and Zurawan, 2003; Kitchen *et al.*, 2005). Whilst some of these findings refer to youth volunteering across a range of activities, they have compounded fears that many sports clubs face closure in future years unless a new generation of young sports coaches and volunteers emerge.

A number of organisations currently aim to train and deploy young people into volunteering opportunities across the UK. Many of these organisations, such as Vinspired ('V') and Sports Leaders UK (SLUK), encourage young people to take an active role in volunteering in their local communities and ensure the provision of training, support and opportunity. Sports Leaders UK, in particular, provides training for a wide range of people who then actively volunteer in their local communities, leading sport and physical activity sessions. Despite the ongoing work of such organisations, the past few years have been challenging with regard to the securing of funding and support from key partners, upon which charities such as Sports Leaders UK depend. Recent attempts by the Coalition government to reduce the UK's financial deficit by way of deep public sector cuts have inevitably impacted on third sector organisations. However, the Government's flagship strategy, the 'Big Society' (Cabinet Office, 2010), places the third sector and volunteers at the centre of a series of objectives concerning the devolvement of power from central government to local authorities and community groups (Cabinet Office, 2010). Against this wider backdrop, the present chapter provides an overview of the current position with regard to youth sports volunteering in the UK. A case study examination of the work of Sports Leaders UK is presented which provides demographic profiles of sports leaders who are currently undertaking SLUK awards. The chapter also discusses the potential role and impact of SLUK in contributing to community sport within the context of 'Big Society' objectives.

The changing nature of UK sports policy

Between 1997–2010, successive New Labour governments were pivotal in placing sport high on the political agenda (Green, 2006; Grix, 2010). Yet, this period also witnessed a significant shift in the nation's sporting priorities, with less of an emphasis on grass-roots participation and a sharper focus on elite performance (see, Bloyce and Smith, 2010). Following 13 years of Labour rule, the 2010 General Election spawned the emergence of a new Coalition government which, faced with the immediate challenge of reducing the UK financial deficit, was quick to propose plans to cut public spending (Evans, 2011). To counteract the potential effects of such action, Prime Minister David Cameron proposed a new strategy which has since become central to his party's political rhetoric – the 'Big Society'. At the time of writing, little has been published about the potential impact of the Big Society strategy, particularly from a sporting perspective. Indeed, exactly what is meant by the concept remains unclear (see Evans, 2011). The Coalition describe the Big Society as 'the belief that citizens should be empowered to solve problems at the local level in communities where they live' (Hansard Society, 2011, p.44). What is clear is that such strategies place an emphasis on extending the third sector – organisations such as charities, co-operatives and social enterprises – and encourage a localised devolvement of power.

The Big Society agenda (or 'ecosystem' as it is also known) comprises three levels of activity. First, citizens (individuals and community groups) are to have a greater role in the development of services at the local level. Second, social organisations in the public and private sectors are to collaborate to deliver services in the community and, third, local and national government will work with partners to organise, promote and deliver services in more innovative ways (Hansard Society, 2011). Through this interconnecting ecosystem (and through an accompanying reconfiguration in policy, practice and delivery), it is envisaged that people will feel more empowered to make decisions about (and shape) the communities in which they live (Hansard Society, 2011). In addition to this, the Prime Minister aims to reduce the bureaucracy which has stifled innovation and progress in recent years, thereby making it easier for third sector organisations to work with government and to receive the support and funding which they need for sustainability and growth (Alcock, 2010; Shibli, *et al.*, 1999).

Despite David Cameron's passion for the Big Society, the concept has not found favour in all quarters. Many critics have questioned its feasibility, seeing it more as a political ideology than a realistic and achievable set of objectives. Similarly, the notion that the Big Society is the government's answer to fixing 'Broken Britain' has been perceived by some as providing a smokescreen for the deep and widespread funding cuts which have hit the public sector (Evans, 2011). How then, we might ask, will the Big Society operate and how will volunteering fit into its overall landscape? The role of volunteers has been identified as central to creating the personal responsibility and civic action required at the citizenship level. As Evans (2011, p.167) suggests, a core aim of the Big Society is for people to 'help themselves and each other out of the goodness of their hearts or the fire in their belly' instead of waiting for the government to make things happen. Of course, the notion of citizens giving of their time to help others is nothing new. Volunteers have long since been the driving force behind UK sporting provision, a fact which suggests that sport, particularly at the community level, represents the epitome of Big Society ideals (Nichols, 2011). Similarly, organisations such as SLUK can potentially be seen to be key contributors to the Big Society agenda through encouraging young people to volunteer in sporting activities in their local communities which may, in turn, engender lifelong volunteering behaviours.

With the third sector regarded as being at the heart of delivering Big Society objectives, the Coalition government has outlined plans to endorse the 'creation and expansion of mutuals, co-operations, charities and social enterprises, and support these groups to have much greater involvement in the running of public services' (Cabinet Office, 2010, p. 2). However, in practice such government 'support' is already being questioned, given reductions in funding to a number of key third sector organisations. For example, Timebank, a charity which promotes, organises and encourages volunteering across the UK, recently had its government funding cut (Timebank, 2011). Similarly, Capacitybuilders, the non-governmental body which provided support and advice to third sector organisations, was dissolved in 2011 as part of the government's spending review. Likewise, organisations such as 'V' have seen their budgets shrink and placed under review. These decisions appear to contradict the broader aims of the Coalition, given the apparent commitment to developing the voluntary sector. Whilst the Big Society promotes volunteering as a more economical alternative to the existence of large, public bodies, it must also be recognised that the training and organisation of volunteers requires accountability, management and strong leadership which, in turn, requires investment. Needless to say, cuts to funding for organisations and charities which may be recognised as potential contributors to the Big Society have left many unclear as to who the key players (and partners) are in this process. Of course, only time will tell as to the impact of public sector curtailments on the development of sport within the UK, both in the shorter and the longer term. Perhaps more important, particularly to sport development professionals, will be the legacy of the 2012 Olympic and Paralympic Games and the momentum which this carries for the next generation of athletes, coaches and volunteers.

Youth sports volunteering in the UK

Despite changes in government policy over the past 20 years, one thing which is clear is the importance of volunteers to the existence of UK sport. As we have seen, the significance of volunteering to the everyday functioning of sports clubs has been well documented; however, more formal leadership programmes which include a volunteering role, such as those facilitated by SLUK, have commanded less attention. Other national, government-sponsored initiatives such as 'Step into Sport'[1] (Kay and Bradbury, 2009) and 'Millenium Volunteers'[2] (Davis Smith et al., 2002; Eley and Kirk, 2002) have been evaluated to explore their impact on the personal development of young leaders. Whilst these schemes incorporate SLUK awards, existing research is limited in demonstrating the impact of these awards on the development of leaders themselves and the extent to which they contribute towards community sport development outcomes, such as volunteering prevalence.

With regard to the personal profiles of volunteers, previous national surveys suggest that volunteering primarily tends to be undertaken by those aged 16–24 years from white, middle-class socio-economic backgrounds (Davis Smith, 1998; Gaskin, 2008; Measham and Barnett, 2007; Ockenden 2008; Russell Commission, 2005), with ethnic minorities being far more likely to volunteer in coaching or leadership roles in sport rather than managerial and/ or committee positions (SkillsActive, 2005). In turn, it has been suggested that low self-esteem and a lack of confidence deter certain groups from volunteering, i.e. those with disabilities (Low et al., 2007; Russell Commission, 2005). Such research also suggests that men are more likely to volunteer in sport than women, with twice as many being involved (Taylor et al., 2003). In fact, research findings indicate a marked under-representation of females in sport-based volunteering roles, with 70 per cent of coaches and face-to-face workers within community sports projects being male (SkillsActive, 2005). To this end, related strategies have emphasised the need to engage more women in sport (Sport England, 2008).

So, what are the barriers for young people in relation to volunteering? Research has found that a perceived high commitment in taking on a volunteering role can deter young people as they attempt to juggle the demands of academic study and/or wider lifestyle interests (Taylor *et al.*, 2003). The public image of volunteering has been the subject of considerable debate in recent years, with research also suggesting that some young people have negative perceptions of voluntary work, given its traditional profile as a middle-aged activity (Gaskin, 1998). However, with new initiatives (such as those promoted by 'V' and SLUK) aimed specifically at engaging young people, the hope is that this perception will change. Similarly, the Games Maker[3] recruitment drives for London 2012 proved especially popular, with nearly 250,000 applying for 70,000 places (LOCOG, 2012). Nevertheless, the age demographic of these volunteers has yet to be reported. Other barriers include a lack of awareness amongst young people of the volunteering opportunities available to them and a lack of understanding regarding the personal, social and occupational benefits of volunteering per se (Gaskin, 2004).

At the same time, there is evidence to suggest that volunteering can significantly enhance the life chances of young people. A survey conducted by the Institute of Volunteering Research showed that 94 per cent of 16–24 year olds recognised that volunteering was an ideal way to gain work experience (Gaskin, 1998). Such benefits are particularly important in the sport sector, at a time when gaining university places and employment in the sport industry remains competitive (ISPAL, 2010). In this sense, experience through volunteering can place individuals at a distinct advantage over those who have no work experience (see CASE, 2011; Ellis Paine *et al.*, 2010). Volunteering opportunities, particularly organised initiatives such as sports leadership awards and Step into Sport, not only encourage young people to get involved in volunteering but also provide them with key leadership skills and vocational qualifications to assist in gaining future employment in sport or other industries (Bloyce and Smith, 2010; SLUK, 2011a). Indeed, more recent changes to the 14–19 National Curriculum which have introduced a broader portfolio of both academic and vocational qualifications have created a series of alternative educational pathways beyond traditional academic courses. For many years SLUK has facilitated accreditation through vocational qualifications which appear to be increasingly popular for young people (SLUK, 2011a). Despite this growing popularity, there is concern over the relevance and credibility of these qualifications, particularly from the more traditional universities which still require A-Level grades rather than adopting the UCAS[4] points-tariff system (Hodgson and Spours, 2007). However, with 30 UCAS points now being attached to the SLUK Level 3 award, the benefits of pursuing vocational pathways are becoming more apparent (SLUK, 2011a). Wider research has suggested that volunteer and leadership programmes can aid unemployed workers through retraining and work experience – which can also lead to new employment opportunities (Obare and Nichols, 2001). From a sporting point of view, the most important benefit to society is that, without the large number of volunteers involved in leading, coaching and managing sport, there would be significantly fewer opportunities for people of all ages to participate (Taylor *et al.*, 2003). The indirect effect that this would have on society is far reaching with regard to sporting success, the health and well-being of citizens and the economic impact of sport. Nevertheless, this does demonstrate the wider benefits of volunteering both to sport and to society at large and it is to an examination of how one particular organisation – Sports Leaders UK – encourages more people to take on volunteering and leadership roles within sport, that we now turn.

Sports Leaders UK: contributing to the Big Society?

Sports Leaders UK plays a key role in the training and deployment of voluntary sports leaders. The remainder of this chapter presents the initial findings of research conducted between 2009–2012 to evaluate the prevalence of SLUK awards and their impact on the development of sports leaders and community sport (see also Mawson, Crone, Parker, Deane and James, 2011). The research was commissioned in 2009 by SLUK which has been delivering sports leadership awards to people across the UK for over 30 years. Amidst a shifting policy landscape and reduced funding, SLUK is adapting its structure and product portfolio in order to strategically facilitate the production of the UK's next generation of sports leaders and volunteers. The research considers the range and diversity of young people participating in the various SLUK award schemes and how their individual role as future sports leaders might go some way to contributing to Big Society outcomes, in particular through being volunteers.

SLUK is a charity which provides nationally recognised sports leadership qualifications and awards that help people, irrespective of their age or background, to develop essential life skills such as teamwork, communication and leadership (SLUK, 2011a). SLUK contributes significantly to the development of sports leadership in the UK, training over 200,000 leaders each year, and can therefore be seen as a vehicle through which to evaluate sports leadership at a national level. The concept of 'sports leaders' was originally developed by the Sport and Recreation Alliance (formerly the Central Council for Physical Recreation) in 1982 with the inception of the Community Sports Leaders Award (CSLA). Since then, SLUK has extended the awards that it offers to cover a range of participatory levels and activities, including dance, basic expedition skills and foreign languages.

Context and method

The past two decades have witnessed an increase in the promotion of sports leadership in the UK, especially for young people, primarily due to changes in sports policy, education and society. Government publications such as *Game Plan* (DCMS/Strategy Unit, 2002), outlining an increased focus on community sport development, presented an opportunity for SLUK to increase its profile and prevalence. The six core values of SLUK echo these policy shifts by centring on two key aims: (i) to educate and improve the personal development of leaders; and (ii) to impact on the wider social aspects of sport, such as social capital, citizenship and community sport development (SLUK, 2011a). These aims also correspond with more recent government policy such as *Creating a Sporting Habit for Life* (DCMS, 2012) and strategy documents from sporting bodies (for example, Sport England, 2008), suggesting that successful sports leadership programmes have the potential to impact upon a wide range of social, sport and educational objectives.

The present research explored the prevalence of SLUK awards and investigated the association between the socio-demographics of sports leaders and whether accredited leaders were actively volunteering. In addition, it sought to evaluate the subsequent impact that these leaders might have on the wider community sport context, in particular, levels of participation and volunteering, and the number of sporting opportunities which they facilitated. The study involved an analysis of candidates' socio-demographic details and their association with volunteering experience. SLUK records the personal details of all candidates who undertake their leadership awards, from registration through to completion. A sample of the organisation's database was analysed to examine the characteristics of the candidates undertaking SLUK awards. The sample included all candidates registered to undertake a Level 2 or a Level 3 award[5] between 1 September 2004 and 31 August 2009. All data were anonymised and candidates could be tracked by the assignment of a unique candidate identification number. Candidate data was entirely quantitative and included details such as date of birth, gender, disability, ethnicity, location of award participation, volunteering experience and whether specific awards were completed. An assessment of material deprivation was also carried out using candidate postcodes and the Townsend score (Townsend *et al.*, 1988). A total of 76,179 datasets were included in the analysis, each one representing an individual who had registered for either a Level 2 or a Level 3 SLUK award.

In addition to descriptive and frequency analyses, binary logistic regression (BLR) was deployed. BLR is a tool which is able to measure the influence of a number of independent or 'predictor' variables on the dependent or 'outcome' variable (Tabachnick and Fidell, 2007). In this study, the outcome variable was whether or not candidates had accrued volunteering experience (i.e. had given their time unpaid to assist or lead in a sporting activity or at a club on at least one occasion) on completion of their award(s). The other advantage of BLR is that it is able to test models which include a range of different predictor variables all at once; these variables can be categorical, continuous or dichotomous in nature (Tabachnick and Fidell, 2007). Therefore, all predictor variables could be input into the model at the same time, with the resultant output providing an overview of which independent variables are significant predictors of whether a sports leader is likely to volunteer.

Significant predictors of volunteering experience

Of the total sample (n = 76,179), 40.8 per cent were female (n = 31,112) and 59.2 per cent were male (n = 45,067), illustrating a higher proportion of males pursuing SLUK awards. This corresponds with the existing research findings which indicate that more males participate in volunteering in sport compared to females (Taylor *et al.*, 2003). The majority of candidates were aged 25 years or younger, with 90.7 per cent of the sample being aged between 16 and 23 years (n = 69,078). The ages with the largest representation were 20 and 21 years, which accounted for 21.7 per cent and 22.2 per cent of the total sample, respectively. This, too, supports previous research which suggests that young people are still actively involved in volunteering in sport, albeit at the coaching and leading level rather than in more senior positions such as committee members (Taylor *et al.*, 2003).

Only 304 of the 79,176 candidates included in the analysis reported having a disability, which accounted for only 0.4 per cent of the sample. This supports the notion that people from under-represented groups are not as likely to volunteer, possibly due to a range of barriers which may deter such activity (Hill and Russell, 2009). In terms of ethnicity, the vast majority (89.5 per cent) of candidates included in the analysis categorised themselves as 'White'. The BLR model fit was found to be statistically significant (χ^2 = 10.37, df = 8, n = 76,179, $P < 0.05$). Table 11.1 provides an overview of the BLR output for the outcome variable of whether candidates reported having had experience of volunteering.

There are a number of predictor variables which are indicated as being significantly associated with whether a sports leader has volunteered. The strongest predictor is whether they have registered for the SLUK Level 3 award. These results suggest that the odds of a candidate having volunteering experience is 1.97 times higher for those who registered for the Level 3 award compared to those who did not (OR = 1.97, 95 per cent C.I. = 1.38–2.81, P = 0.000). This is understandable given that, in order to register at Level 3, candidates must first have demonstrated that they had completed the SLUK Level 2 award or an equivalent qualification and are therefore likely to have had some volunteering experience.

Gender appears to be a significant predictor of volunteering experience, with the analysis indicating a greater likelihood of females having volunteered compared to males, as indicated by an odds ratio of less than 1, where 'male' is the reference category (OR = 0.75, 95 per cent C.I. = 0.72–0.77, P = 0.000). This is noteworthy, given that the sample comprised more males (59.2 per cent) than females (40.8 per cent), indicating that more males are choosing to register. With regards to ethnicity, the findings indicate that the only ethnic groups that are more likely to have had volunteering experience than those categorising themselves as 'White' are those of Indian and Pakistani heritage, albeit marginally. The odds of a candidate volunteering are shown to be 1.21 times greater for those from an Indian background compared to other ethnicities (OR = 1.21, 95 per cent C.I. = 1.07–1.37, P = 0.002). Indian ethnicity represented 1.5 per cent of the total sample; the third largest group after 'White' and 'Black-Caribbean'. So, whilst more Black candidates were registered to undertake an award, Asian candidates were more

Table 11.1 BLR output illustrating predictor variables associated with the volunteering experience of sports leaders

Predictor (independent) variable	β	S.E.	Wald	P	Odds Ratio	95% C.I. for Odds Ratio	
						Lower	Upper
Age	0.00	0.00	0.44	0.507	1.00	0.99	1.00
Gender (male)	−0.29	0.02	353.19	0.000*	0.75	0.72	0.77
Ethnicity (white)			22.42	0.004*			
1 = Bangladeshi	0.19	0.10	3.19	0.074	1.21	0.98	1.48
2 = Black – African	−0.02	0.06	0.12	0.726	0.98	0.86	1.11
3 = Black – Caribbean	0.08	0.05	1.90	0.168	1.08	0.97	1.20
4 = Chinese	−0.04	0.13	0.09	0.765	0.96	0.74	1.25
5 = Black – other	0.07	0.08	0.61	0.435	1.07	0.90	1.26
6 = Indian	0.19	0.06	9.15	0.002*	1.21	1.07	1.37
7 = Pakistani	0.17	0.07	5.69	0.017*	1.19	1.03	1.37
Disability (Y)	−0.01	0.12	0.01	0.922	0.99	0.78	1.25
Occupation (full-time education)			87.30	0.000*			
1 = In part-time education	−0.01	0.07	0.02	0.894	0.99	0.86	1.14
2 = Employed FT	0.03	0.05	0.50	0.480	1.04	0.94	1.14
3 = Employed PT	0.13	0.06	4.75	0.029*	1.13	1.01	1.27
4 = Unemployed	−0.46	0.05	72.58	0.000*	0.63	0.57	0.70
Centre type (school)			951.09	0.000*			
1 = FE college	−0.45	0.02	725.86	0.000*	0.63	0.61	0.66
2 = University/HE	−0.28	0.13	4.87	0.027*	0.76	0.59	0.97
3 = Local education authority	−0.29	0.05	41.12	0.000*	0.75	0.68	0.82
4 = Prison service	−0.90	0.05	268.05	0.000*	0.41	0.37	0.45
5 = Youth service	−0.60	0.13	20.56	0.000*	0.55	0.43	0.71
6 = Voluntary youth organisation	0.13	0.07	3.52	0.061	1.13	0.99	1.29
7 = Outdoor education centre	−0.21	0.13	2.80	0.095	0.81	0.63	1.04
8 = Local authority	−0.03	0.05	0.35	0.555	0.97	0.89	1.06
Registered level 2 (Yes)	−1.90	0.18	116.92	0.000*	0.15	0.11	0.21
Registered level 3 (Yes)	0.68	0.18	14.09	0.000*	1.97	1.38	2.81
Completed level 2 (Yes)	0.16	0.02	112.93	0.000*	1.18	1.14	1.22
Completed level 3 (Yes)	−0.22	0.18	1.55	0.213	0.80	0.56	1.14
Townsend score	−0.02	0.00	61.96	0.000*	0.98	0.97	0.98
Urban rural classification (Urban)	−0.05	0.02	7.49	0.006*	0.95	0.92	0.99

*Significant predictor variables at p < 0.05
Reference category in brackets

likely to have volunteered, supporting previous findings which suggest that there are more Asian than Black volunteers active in sport (Low *et al.*, 2007).

With regard to the occupation of leaders, those who were unemployed whilst registering for an award were less likely to have had volunteering experience compared to those who were in full-time education (the reference category) (OR = 0.63, 95 per cent C.I. = 0.57–0.70, P = 0.000). Again, this corresponds with previous research which suggests that those who experience more challenging circumstances in terms of socio-economic and employment status are less likely to volunteer (Gaskin, 2008). This could partly be due to low self-esteem and confidence levels amongst these candidates, which prevents them from volunteering (Hill and Russell, 2009).

Centre type (i.e. the location where candidates had undertaken their awards) was also found to be a significant predictor variable of volunteering experience. More specifically, all centre types which were found to be significant (FE college, HE/University, LEA, Prison Service and Youth Service) were also found to result in a lower likelihood of candidates having experience of volunteering. For example, there is a significant decrease in the odds of a candidate having volunteer experience if they undertake an award at a Further Education College, compared to those who undertake an award at school (OR = 0.63, 95 per cent C.I. = 0.61–0.66, P = 0.000). This may be due to the way that SLUK programmes are organised and delivered, as a number of FE colleges deliver the awards as part of Business and Technology Education Council (BTEC) sport courses to avoid duplication across subject areas and registration is therefore compulsory for all students on such courses (SLUK, 2011b). However, this may result in some students being registered for SLUK awards who are not in fact interested in volunteering and/or leading in sport, and therefore do not complete their voluntary hours.

Socio-economic classification, determined by the Townsend score, shows a significant association with whether a candidate is more likely to volunteer. From the evidence presented in Table 11.1, it can be seen that, as Townsend scores increase (i.e. a greater level of deprivation) the less likely a candidate is to volunteer, albeit marginally (OR = 0.98, 95 per cent C.I. = 0.97–0.98, P = 0.000). Again, this endorses the findings of previous research which suggest that volunteers are more likely to emanate from a 'higher' socio-economic background (Kitchen *et al.*, 2005; Gaskin, 2008). Finally, 'urban rural classification' was found to be a significant predictor variable, with those candidates living in an urban area slightly less likely to volunteer than those living in a rural area (OR = 0.96, 95 per cent C.I. = 0.92–0.99, P = 0.006). This is notable given that previous research has suggested that barriers to volunteering include the cost of transportation, which may be a common problem for rurally based candidates, especially those who are not able to drive themselves (Gaskin, 2008). It is also the case that there are likely to be fewer clubs and opportunities in rural areas through which to volunteer. However, it is also likely that the socio-economic status of those living in rural areas is higher than those inhabiting urban settings.

As has been noted, these findings support much of the existing literature surrounding youth volunteering, with regard to gender, age and socio-economic status. However, these data also provide a snapshot of candidates who have registered for SLUK awards over a five-year period, so it cannot be determined how many of those individuals remain active as leaders or as volunteers in sport or in other activities. Of the total sample, 58.7 per cent of leaders reported having had volunteer experience (n = 44,714). This demonstrates a large number of mainly young people who have given of their time to help lead and organise sports within their local communities. In addition, of the total number of candidates who registered for the Level 2 Community Sports Leaders Award (n = 74,914), 59.4 per cent went on to complete the award, suggesting that those participants enjoyed their role as a leader and saw value and worth in completing the award. Whilst these data provide insight into the possible demographic profiles of future sports leaders, they do not explain the motivations behind young people's choices to undertake leadership awards or to volunteer in sport, a topic around which further research is ongoing.

Conclusion

This chapter has provided an overview of youth sports volunteering in the UK amidst recent policy change. Despite the challenges concerning the future of UK sport, it has sought to highlight the way in which Sports Leaders UK continues to encourage young people to take up volunteering and leadership roles in order to service the needs of community sport. The Coalition government's flagship strategy, the Big Society, has been criticised by some as representing political ideology rather than a realistic set of objectives. However, the rhetoric surrounding what the Big Society stands for provides an ideal platform for sport development initiatives to flourish, particularly those which focus on volunteers and community empowerment. Indeed, in many ways amateur sports clubs epitomise Big Society ideals, and organisations such as Sports Leaders UK contribute to policy objectives of this nature through the recruitment, training and deployment of young sports leaders and volunteers. Furthermore, this chapter has provided insight into the factors which may impact volunteering levels among sports leaders. The coming years will be particularly important in examining the role of volunteers in sport post-London 2012. Of greater importance still is whether the legacy of the 2012 Games is effective in ensuring that today's young sports leaders will carry the torch for tomorrow's sporting opportunities.

Notes

1 Step into Sport is a Youth Sport Trust initiative which recognises and rewards the volunteering experience of young people. The scheme utilises SLUK awards as a means by which young people are appropriately educated as leaders.

2 Millenium Volunteers was a government-supported, UK-wide initiative, which ran in 2007–2008 and which was designed to encourage 16–24 year olds to take up volunteering roles in their local communities.
3 Games Makers were the official volunteering workforce of London 2012 whose job it was to assist athletes and spectators during the Games.
4 The UCAS (Universities and Colleges Admissions Services) tariff is a system used in the UK for allocating points to various qualifications for entry into Higher Education.
5 The SLUK Level 2 award provides learners with the skills to be able to lead groups of people in sport under indirect supervision, with candidates being required to complete 10 hours of voluntary leadership experience. The Level 3 award builds on these skills, enabling candidates to lead groups independently without supervision. Candidates at Level 3 must complete 30 hours of voluntary leadership experience to attain the award.

References

Alcock, P. (2010). Building the Big Society: a new policy environment for the third sector in England. *Voluntary Sector Review*. 1(3): 379–389.

Attwood, C., Singh, G., Prime, D., Creasey, R. *et al.* (2003). *2001 Home Office Citizenship Survey: People, Families and Communities.* London: Home Office.

Bloyce, D. and Smith, A. (2010). *Sport Policy and Development: An Introduction.* London: Routledge.

Cabinet Office (2010). *Building the Big Society.* London: Cabinet Office.

CASE (2011). *Understanding the Drivers of Volunteering in Culture and Sport: Analysis of the Taking Part Survey.* The Culture and Sport Evidence programme. London: Department for Culture, Media and Sport (DCMS).

Davis Smith, J. (1998). *The 1997 National Survey of Volunteering.* London: Institute of Volunteering Research.

Davis Smith, J., Ellis, A. and Howlett, S. (2002). UK-wide evaluation of the Millenium Volunteers Programme. *DfES Research Report 357.* London: DFES.

DCMS (2012). *Creating a Sporting Habit for Life. A New Youth Sport Strategy.* London: DCMS.

DCMS/Strategy Unit (2002). *Game Plan: A Strategy for Delivering Government's Sport and Physical Activity Objectives.* London: Cabinet Office.

Eley, D. and Kirk, D. (2002). Developing citizenship through sport: the impact of a sport-based volunteer programme on young sport leaders. *Sport, Education and Society* 7(2): 151–166.

Ellis Paine, A., Hill, M. and Rochester, C. (2010). A rose by any other name ... . Revisiting the question: 'What exactly is volunteering?'. IVR Working Paper Series, No. 1. London: Institute for Volunteering Research.

Evans, K. (2011). Big Society in the UK: a policy review. *Children & Society.* 25: 164–171.

Gaskin, K. (1998). Vanishing volunteers: are young people losing interest in volunteering? *Voluntary Action.* 1(1): 33–43.

——(2004). *Young People, Volunteering and Civic Service: A Review of the Literature.* London: IVR.

——(2008). *A Winning Team? The Impact of Volunteers in Sport.* London: IVR.

Green, M. (2006). From 'sport for all' to not about 'sport' at all?: Interrogating sport policy interventions in the United Kingdom. *European Sport Management Quarterly.* 6(3): 217–238.

Grix, J. (2010). From hobbyhorse to mainstream: using sport to understand British politics. *British Politics.* 5(1): 114–129.

Hansard Society (2011). *Audit of Political Engagement 8: The 2011 Report.* London: Cabinet Office.

Hill, M. and Russell, J. (2009). *Young People, Volunteering and Youth Projects: A Rapid Review of Recent Evidence.* Prepared for 'V'. London: IVR.

Hodgson, A. and Spours, K. (2007). Specialised diplomas: transforming the 14–19 landscape in England? *Journal of Education Policy.* 22(6): 657–673.

ISPAL (2010). On course for success. *Inform.* Spring, 9: 30–31.

Kay, T. and Bradbury, S. (2009). Youth sport volunteering: developing social capital? *Sport, Education and Society.* 14(1): 121–140.

Kitchen, S., Michaelson, J., Wood, N. and John, P. (2005). *2005 Citizenship Survey: Active Communities Topic Report.* London: Department for Communities and Local Government.

London Organising Committee for the Olympic and Paralympic Games (LOCOG) (2012). News. Available from: http://www.london2012.com/news/articles/london-2012-games-makers-honoured-queen-diamond-jubilee-awards.html.

Low, N., Butt, S., Ellis Paine, A. and Davis Smith, J. (2007). *Helping Out: A National Survey of Volunteering and Charitable Giving.* London: Cabinet Office.

Mawson, H., Crone, D., Parker, A., Deane, J. and James, D. (2011). 'Sports leadership and its role in the development of community sport', in H. Schulz, P.R. Wright, & T. Hauser (eds.) *Exercise, Sport and Health.* Chemnitz: University of Chemnitz, pp. 116–123.

Measham, T. and Barnett, G. (2007). Environmental volunteering: motivations, modes and outcomes. Available online at: www.csiro.au/outcomes/Environment/Population-Sustainability/SEEDPaper3.aspx.

Munton, T. and Zurawan, A. (2003). *Active Communities: Headline Findings from the 2003 Home Office Citizenship Survey.* London. Home Office.

Nichols, G. (2011). The contribution and limits of civic activism: the role of volunteers in promoting youth sport. Conference paper: LSA Conference, Southampton Solent. 5–7 July.

Obare, R. and Nichols, G. (2001). The full sporty – the impact of a sports training programme for unemployed steelworkers. *World Leisure.* 2: 49–57.

Ockenden, N. (2008). Environmental volunteering in the North East of England. London: Institute for Volunteering Research.

Russell Commission (2005). *A National Framework for Youth Action and Engagement.* London: The Russell Commission.

Shibli, S., Taylor, P., Nichols, G., Gratton, C. and Kokolakakis, T. (1999). The characteristics of volunteers in UK sports clubs. *European Journal for Sport Management.* 6: 10–27.

SkillsActive (2005). *Community and Sport Development Research Project Report.* London: Skills Active.

Sport England (2008). *Sport England Strategy 2008–2011.* London: Sport England.

Sports Leaders UK (SLUK) (2011a). What we do and why. Available from: www.sportsleaders.org/about-us/.

——(2011b). *Non Standard Learning Routes.* Available from: www.sportsleaders.org/run-a-course/non-standard-learning-routes.

Tabachnick, B. G. and Fidell, L. S. (2007). *Using Multivariate Statistics.* 5th ed. Boston: Pearson Education.

Taylor, P., Nichols, G., Holmes, K., James, M., Gratton, C., Garrett, R., Kokolakakis, T., Mulder, C. and King, L. (2003). *Sports Volunteering in England, 2002: Summary Report.* Sport England.

Timebank (2011). How we are funded. Available from: http://timebank.org.uk/how-were-funded.

Townsend, P., Phillimore, P. and Beattie, A. (1988). *Health and Deprivation: Inequality in the North.* London: Croom Helm.

12 Sport, volunteering and marginalised youth

*Samaya Farooq, Ben Moreland,
Andrew Parker and Andy Pitchford*

Introduction

Although there is a growing body of research on volunteering both within and beyond sporting contexts (Davis-Smith *et al.*, 2002; Deane *et al.*, 2010), the impact of formal youth volunteer programmes (YVPs) is not well documented. Existing research findings hint at the exclusivity of volunteer activity, indicating that young people from minority communities and poorer socioeconomic backgrounds are least visible in volunteering contexts (Adams and Deane, 2009; CASE, 2011). This chapter seeks to broaden debates in this area by exploring the volunteering experiences of a group of marginalised young men in the English West Midlands. It stems from 24 months of data collection into the delivery and operationalisation of a YVP which, since 2010, has been working to attract a 'new generation' of youth volunteers. Conceptually, this 'new generation' was to include young people (aged 14–19) from 'diverse socio-cultural backgrounds' as well as those experiencing 'various dimensions of social exclusion' (NatCen, 2010: 1–3). Findings depict how these increasingly stigmatised, marginalised and/or socially excluded young men perceived and engaged in volunteering. Hence, the discussion adds to the evidence base about youth volunteering, whilst considering the impact (both personal and social) that such engagement might on have those concerned. With these issues at its core, the chapter dovetails well with broader social and political agendas surrounding the mobilisation of marginalised youth (Hill and Russell, 2009; NatCen, 2010).

Volunteering: trends, issues and debates

Within the UK context volunteering has experienced almost a decade of paradoxical reform, with academic debate now exposing the two key, but often contradictory, features which appear to drive participation, namely: (i) philanthropic altruism; and (ii) individualised self-help (Davis-Smith, 2000). To this end, the traditional image of the volunteer participant is now juxtaposed to more contemporary understandings of such roles which carry a sense of 'contractual' exchange, whereby an 'input' of one's time, labour and/

or expertise is traded for a measure of personal gain (i.e. 'outputs') (Stebbins, 1996; Taylor, 2004). Hence, for some, volunteering continues to comprise an informal non-compulsory, unpaid and altruistic activity in which individuals might commit their time as a result of compelling personal, moral, ethical and/or social reasons (i.e. to 'give something back' to society) or to help their local environment (Ellis Paine *et al.*, 2010; Gaskin, 2004; Hill and Russell, 2009; NatCen, 2010). For others, it represents a transitional experience through which individuals might accrue a degree of personal, educational/ occupational (and ultimately financial) gain (Ellis Paine *et al.*, 2010). This is certainly evident in the rise of volunteering in secondary and tertiary educa- tion and the burgeoning of university-based initiatives that encourage stu- dents to volunteer to improve their life chances (Ofsted, 2011; V, 2008). These shifts have primarily emanated from government statements surrounding the merits and purposes of volunteering (CASE, 2011; McAll, 2011; Stott, 2011). Indeed, the rhetoric accompanying the Coalition government's 'Big Society' agenda has witnessed Prime Minister David Cameron championing volun- teering both as an innovative approach to developing local communities and as a civic duty (Cabinet Office, 2010).

Marginalised and invisible volunteers

Academic discussion around sport-based volunteers relates primarily to those in voluntary sports club settings (Central Council for Physical Recreation, 2003; Davis-Smith, 1998; Davis-Smith *et al.*, 2002; Taylor *et al.*, 2003; Taylor, 2004; Taylor *et al.*, 2003) and portrays a disproportionate and rather 'exclu- sive' sense that volunteering within this context is dominated by a particular demographic, i.e. white, middle-aged males (CASE, 2011; Deane *et al.*, 2010; Eley and Kirk, 2002; Gaskin, 2004; Institute of Volunteering Research (IVR), 2004; Marsh *et al.*, 2010). The Russell Commission (2008) confirms that young males (and females) from minority backgrounds do volunteer across a range of community and sporting initiatives and have a strong sense of civic obligation. It also indicates that religious communities offer ample opportu- nity for young ethnic minority males to volunteer and that this type of activ- ity is often, although not always, linked to their 'close-knit' ethnic, religious or faith networks. Hence, focusing on voluntary sports clubs can mean over- looking the activities, attitudes and perceptions of minority groups who may be volunteering outside traditional sporting spaces.

Of course, it would be naive to overlook the degree to which the exclusive nature of sport may curtail the involvement of minority groups. Indeed, there is a wealth of literature that alludes to the social, cultural and ideological constraints that minority groups face when accessing sports clubs in the UK (see Burdsey, 2007). There has also been a tendency in the sports volunteering literature to ignore the extent to which sports clubs are traditionally located in more affluent geographical locations that are perhaps also known to be predominantly populated by white, 'majority' communities. When coupled with more recent evidence which suggests that: (i) volunteering opportunities are far more accessible in non-deprived areas (CASE, 2011; Measham and Barnett, 2007; Ockenden, 2008; Russell, 2009); and (ii) that a greater proportion of Britain's minority ethnic population are ghettoised and segregated in areas facing higher-than-average social exclusion, poverty and deprivation (Alibhai-Brown, 2000; Wood *et al.*, 2006), it is perhaps unsurprising to learn that such groups are less visible as volunteers. In this chapter we broaden and diversify these initial debates about the voluntary participation of minority ethnic groups by focusing on the experiences of volunteer participants who find themselves on the periphery of mainstream society.

Context and method

The findings presented here are taken from a two-year research project into young people's views and perceptions of (and motivations towards) sports-based volunteering programmes. The research featured a mixed-methods approach. The quantitative aspect of the study used a questionnaire survey to determine the educational backgrounds of participants, motivations and barriers to volunteering, and personal perceptions about the programme itself. The qualitative aspect of the research comprised both focus group and one-to-one (semi-structured) interviews with past and present programme participants to facilitate a better understanding of young people's entry and exit routes into and out of volunteering, and how it impacted on their personal and social development, employability prospects and community engagement. In turn, interviews sought to identify the longitudinal impact of volunteering on young volunteers' sense of self, their capacity to be/feel socially included and/or accepted, and their community and inter-generational relationships, friendships and social networks. Focus groups were also conducted with voluntary, statutory and community-based partners (including parent groups), wider stakeholders and associated agencies to better understand how, if at all, they perceived volunteering to have impacted on the lives of the young people concerned.

Data were collected across seven UK project sites (five in London and two in the West Midlands). The present chapter focuses on findings from volunteer programmes delivered in the city of Rosall,[1] which is located in the English West Midlands, a region that has witnessed significant migration in recent years, resulting in almost 13 per cent of the city's 300,000 population having been born outside the UK. Participants were recruited from a number of different local statutory and voluntary youth and community-based services. A total of 50 young men (aged 14–25 years) completed project questionnaires and a further 25 took part in one-to-one interviews or focus groups.[2] Active volunteers engaged in a variety of sport-based YVPs in areas where a diverse range of young people (including those seeking asylum and those living as official refugees) were residing in areas of high crime and social deprivation.[3] Volunteers expressed ethnic and cultural affiliations with a diverse range of countries, including Afghanistan, Pakistan, Sri Lanka, Iraq, Libya, Somalia, Sudan, Nigeria, Latvia, Poland, Ukraine, Lithuania and Slovakia. Analysis of the data revealed a series of key themes relating to the way in which respondents perceived their experiences of volunteering. Here, we pay specific attention to two of these themes, both of which relate to the demographics of the participant group, namely, 'old migrant' volunteers and 'new migrant' volunteers. Before exploring these themes in more detail we provide a brief overview of the social circumstances around which these respondent experiences were lived out.

'Old migrants'

The volunteer sample was primarily made up of young people who had been born and raised in Britain and who, as a consequence, considered themselves to be 'British citizens' belonging to 'old' migrant communities. These predominantly included young Muslim males who further defined themselves as 'British Pakistani', 'British Gujrati' and 'British Bangladeshi' and were living with their immediate families. The majority of these British-born migrant volunteers were Muslim (64 per cent), had fewer than five GCSEs (73 per cent), and were living with both parents (83 per cent). Some were enrolled onto Further Education courses or involved with formal employability training programmes, but had been out of work for long periods of time prior to their experiences of volunteering. Many were participating in weekend volunteer placement schemes helping to coach or to run local Sunday League football teams. Their volunteer activities were closely affiliated to three local youth clubs, all of which were dominated by males.

Aside from the shared religious and cultural geographies amongst this cohort, what united the young Asian male volunteers was their desire to assert themselves as valuable, contributory citizens. Ali, a young man from the local Pakistani community, summarised the 'mood' of many of the 'boys' in the area as feeling like 'outsiders in (their) own homes ... and neighbourhoods'. During interview he spoke of how the extent to which his troubled experiences of schooling, of being 'excluded for fighting', of attaining poor GCSE grades, of not gaining entry into college or finding employment had left him feeling 'worthless'. Those around him often expressed their disappointment in his lack of educational attainment, especially his parents who would compare him to his more successful siblings. Ali felt excluded from his own family and from the social networks and the local community settings within and around which he lived:

> Everyone would jus' like look at me and my mates like we was nuffin' ... like riff raff ... it does get you down 'cos you know you've let yourself down, but no-one's there to give you a break ... instead they jus' wanna put you down more.

Ali's testimony typically reveals the kind of frustrations that, at a personal level, led to him feeling 'isolated ... and alone'. The subjective experience of always being made to feel 'inadequate' not only galvanised Ali's sense of isolation, but impacted his overall outlook on life, causing him to internalise such negative and derogatory viewpoints. Other Asian boys expressed similar sentiments alluding to troubled childhoods and growing 'postcode' rivalries between different groups of males in the city. There was a sense of fear and concern as to where some of these volunteers saw themselves fitting into the increasingly segregated socio-cultural fabric of local neighbourhoods, with inter-generational tensions between Asian boys from the same social, cultural, ethnic and religious groups becoming ever more apparent.

'New migrants'

A higher-than-average proportion of those engaged with YVPs were 'new' migrants who had been recruited from agencies and local services directly established to provide support for young people who were not engaged in mainstream education but whose age or social position dictated that they should receive some form of educational assistance and guidance with spoken English. Those seeking asylum were more vulnerable to (and at a greater risk of) social exclusion and sustained isolation than new migrants from the European Union (EU) and those who had been afforded refugee status and/or had exceptional leave to remain. This vulnerability stemmed from a multitude of factors, all of which rested on the uncertainty of their stay and the lack of entitlements to key resources, such as money, accommodation and the right to work.

Discussions with young people from these social groups indicated that the majority had travelled from (or fled) war-torn countries such as Afghanistan, Iraq and Libya. Some spoke of civil war and ethnic violence and how continued atrocities had forced them to leave their homes in places like Somalia, Sudan and Nigeria. The majority of Somalian, Sudanese and Nigerian volunteers were living with their own families, whilst many of the Afghani, Iraqi and Libyan teenagers had been placed in care. Often these young men were victimised as 'outsiders' and 'foreigners'. One young boy from Afghanistan spoke of how he was harassed by local British children for not having enough money to buy clothes which were deemed to be 'popular'. Many of the Afghani, Iraqi and Libyan volunteers claimed to feel doubly oppressed in Britain for, not only were they estranged from their families, friends and homelands, but they were also burdened by derogatory labels and stereotypes. Some presented emotional and behavioural difficulties, often struggling to control their aggression. Certainly such experiences of marginalisation impinged upon the young men's perceptions of themselves, thwarting their sense of self-esteem and value and affecting their ability and capacity to feel socially included or accepted. When coupled with the fact that their cultural practices, religious affiliations and skin colour marked them out as overtly 'different', it was somewhat unsurprising to learn of their perceived sense of isolation.

In contrast, there were those who found themselves in altogether more protected social circumstances. For example, a proportion of the school-aged males within the 'new migrant' group had travelled to the UK as EU citizens with their parents who were in search of employment and a better quality of life. The entitlement of their parents to access work and healthcare and for their children to attend a local school meant a reduction in the level of anxiety and concern experienced by those seeking asylum and/or living as refugees. The majority of these young men were also living with their families and siblings, had access to statutory services and training, and attended local agencies and support groups for additional assistance with their English language skills. Nevertheless, this group also expressed how they had struggled to make friends with other young people. Whilst some felt 'out-of-place' and spoke of bullying and harassment from their school peers and from people living in local neighbourhoods, others recounted more positive experiences of having made friends in Britain. Despite the social, cultural, ethnic/racial and generational differences between volunteers, what united them all was their social position as 'young migrants' and the extent to which they felt marginalised and socially excluded. Hence, it is to a closer analysis of how volunteering impacted on these feelings of social exclusion that we now turn.

'Old migrants' and volunteering

There is a substantial body of literature that exposes the civic merits of volunteering (Ellis Paine *et al.*, 2010; Kay and Bradbury, 2009), with some youth-based interventions championing volunteering as a 'magic bullet' to remedy social problems. The power of volunteering to increase youth citizenship, develop young people's employability skills, reduce anti-social behaviour and rehabilitate young offenders has also been recognised (Brewis *et al.*, 2010). There is, however, little empirical evidence surrounding the specific perceptions and motivations (or indeed the impacts) that volunteering might have for young people whose lives are compounded by multiple and complex social deprivations and whose access to opportunities and social and civic services may be limited for a number of reasons.

The use of volunteering as a vehicle to up-skill and (re)train young people gathered momentum with the onset of successive New Labour administrations post-1997 and stemmed from an attempt to reduce unemployment and reconceptualise full-time education for 14–19 year olds (*Youth Matters* Green Paper, DfES, 2005). The focus on empowering disadvantaged and marginalised groups implied the adoption of a positive youth philosophy, where young people, their position in society and their futures mattered (Russell Commission Report, 2005). A 'win-win' image of volunteering has since been at the forefront of government policy and third sector campaigns to market and incentivise volunteering as something beneficial to young people. Whilst this rests on the assumption that those concerned understand, or are at least made aware of, the benefits derived from volunteering, we found that not everyone that we met 'in the field' embraced this viewpoint. That said, the capacity for volunteering to nurture a range of positive personal skills to better equip young people was certainly recognised by youth leaders in the West Midlands, as Jeff (a YVP programme organiser) commented:

> When ... volunteers join ... they won't always know what benefits volunteering can have on them ... but once they're engaged and they participate in ... courses and training ... that's when they'll tell you they've learned a lot.

The majority of young British Asian (old migrant) volunteers recognised the merits of volunteering for their personal, social and employability/educational skills. In turn, they acknowledged an increase in levels of confidence and self-esteem, and improvements in their ability to make decisions, organise their time, be more goal-orientated and motivated, and adopt an approach to life whereby they generally wanted to make a contribution to their local neighbourhoods. Indeed, 73 per cent claimed that 'increasing their awareness of their actions on others' motivated them to volunteer. Similarly, the use of volunteering to 'keep busy' was something that a significant number (82 per cent) alluded to. Many also suggested that engaging as volunteers helped them to want to invest more positively in their own lives and openly confessed that the inclination to stay off the streets and away from joining gangs had also increased. Equally important were responses indicating that, as a consequence of their volunteering experiences, they felt that they now had things to 'look forward to'.

Despite positive changes to old migrant personal and social identities, questionnaire responses highlighted that overall perceptions and feelings of social inclusion had not improved. This was reflected in volunteer responses to questions concerning civic capacity, with many indicating that, although their willingness to make a contribution to civic life had increased, their ability to feel part of something special or important and/or their ability to engage in a range of local community campaigns had either remained the same, or decreased. Indeed, survey data findings indicated that old migrants felt either as disengaged from the local community as they had done before they began volunteering or even more so. According to volunteer testimonies, this stemmed from the overwhelming tendency of local people to position those from 'troubled' circumstances as a 'social waste' and to subject them to rigorous questioning about their contribution to society, as opposed to recognising (and rewarding) volunteers for their efforts. Ali alluded to this point, explaining how, when the YVP recruited volunteers, 'the locals' were bemused that 'all the riff raff' had been 'taken on'.

'What have you got to give?' Tha's all people were saying to begin with ... They didn't think we could do somefin' for other people ... cos' we let ourselves down ...

According to Ali, the view of local people was that adults or qualified professionals with university degrees and/or other academic qualifications had the ability to 'give something back' to the community, but that certain groups of young people (especially those who had 'disappointed' or 'fallen short' of parental expectations) were not in a position to either offer anything 'constructive', or assert themselves as potential 'do-gooders'. Hence, local perceptions of philanthropic service appeared to rest on a traditional (and one-dimensional) view of volunteering, whereby the individual 'gave' of their time, effort and energy, and the local community or neighbourhood simply 'received' (and/or 'benefitted' from) this. The notion that volunteering might act as a transformative process which provided an opportunity for an individual to change as a person was rarely embraced. Against this backdrop, Ali's parents were reluctant to view volunteering as 'positive', instead trivialising it as 'time-wasting'. His father explained that his own 'negative attitude' towards his son's engagement with the YVP stemmed from a deep scepticism about how (indeed whether) the programme could 'work' for Ali when so many 'previous efforts' had failed to encourage him to alter his lifestyle, adapt his behaviour and embrace a more positive outlook – a point which Ali recognised and accepted:

They did try everything with me ... anger management, community centre work ... I even did some project work through the mosque but the people didn't understand me ... they kept drilling information [into me] about being a better man and so on ...

Whilst the previous attempts to redirect Ali 'went right over (his) head', disengaging him yet further, the YVP approach had worked partly because he was 'good at sport' and partly because he found staff to be 'more positive (and) up-beat'. Ali explained how his programme leader had taken 'an interest and genuinely cared' about young people and had not simply been in the business of 'judging someone by the size of their CV'. For him, youth workers did not hold exclusionary or prejudiced views about entitlements to engaging in philanthropic service. In turn, Ali had responded positively to being 'taken seriously' and being 'treated like an adult' and suggested that the kind of support which he had received was much more empowering and more constructive than that which he had previously encountered. This kind of approach had allowed him to focus on improving his skills and enhancing a series of personal characteristics, all of which was conducive to attaining a more positive outlook on life, as opposed to working against the grain to 'prove himself to other people'. To this end, Ali saw his volunteer placement operating both as a vehicle for self-actualisation and as a medium through which he could become a 'better person'. Such evidence illustrates the power of volunteer placements to provide embodied and situated learning experiences through which young people might readily re-engage with discourses of citizenship and social responsibility.

'New migrants' and volunteering

The majority of new migrant volunteers confessed that they had not participated in volunteering before, either in their home countries or in Britain. Their understandings of what volunteering entailed was thus entirely reliant upon what they had learned from programme leaders, teachers, youth workers, and/or past volunteers. For asylum seekers and refugees, opportunities for task-mastery and the development of recognised skills were strong drivers to engage in volunteering. Central to this sense of self-enhancement was the chance to improve their reading and writing, technical and IT skills. The opportunity to find paid work, to identify a career path and to identify and enrol onto suitable college courses also provided a strong incentive. Questionnaire responses from this group indicated that, on the whole, a greater percentage of volunteers who were either seeking asylum or who had official refugee status were motivated by these factors. Conversely, those from Eastern European communities were enthused by altruistic and social/civic factors. In particular, they were drawn to volunteering as a way to increase the size and range of their friendship networks (84 per cent) and the people whom they could meet from different backgrounds (82 per cent), as well as their involvement in social gatherings (73 per cent). The chance to assess and evaluate their role in the community (57 per cent) and their contribution to local neighbourhoods (82 per cent) were similarly cited as motivational aspects of the voluntering experience. Given that the majority of these participants reported experiencing a significant amount of harassment and bullying in their day-to-day lives, the need to increase friendship networks and to participate in local events that increased their self-worth was unquestionably an important facet of their YVP engagement.

Although volunteering has been recognised both by government and by academics as an effective vehicle to enhance the skills required to succeed in an increasingly competitive neo-liberalist world of work (Low et al., 2007; Rochester et al., 2009), providing employment preparation opportunities was not directly at the forefront of the Rosall YVP campaigns. Rather, delivery was built around the ethos of developing young people and was based on the view that enabling participants to access paid employment required them to be equipped with a broad range of both 'essential' and 'desirable' skills.

These findings sit in stark contrast to previous research on volunteering which suggests that the potential to become employed through volunteering is not always recognised as a key driver for participants (see Low et al., 2007). Such differences in motivation appeared to stem from the disadvantageous position of non-Eastern European volunteers. For example, a greater percentage of those seeking asylum, or those attaining refugee status, were living alone and without entitlements to formal mainstream education and work. This highly vulnerable position meant that these individuals looked to volunteering to help them gain the kinds of skills that they believed could (and would) facilitate upward social mobility. Asa, an asylum seeker from Afghanistan, alluded to the empowerment and freedom that came from being in a position to finance his own life:

> Money is important ... it make life better ... I no ask people to give me money ... I work ... I have own money ... I buy own clothes ... I go where I like ... I do what I want to do with friends ... freedom.

Asa was clearly drawn to volunteering in order to find paid employment and accrue work-related skills which he had not been able to attain in his home country or through formal school-based education. The desire to improve his own circumstances through skill-acquisition cannot be underestimated given that, for those whose lives are placed in the hands of others, being able to do things for oneself, having recognised skills and qualifications or 'things to put on a CV' are potentially life-changing events that can better locate such individuals within mainstream society. Indeed, for some, such opportunities can be a prerequisite to their social inclusion. Yet much of this was dependent upon the overall entitlement rights of individuals to paid employment and often meant that, despite having participated in volunteer campaigns some young people still struggled to find work. Neverthless, 51 per cent of new migrant volunteers claimed that their financial situation had improved as a result of participating in YVP campaigns, primarily because participants had been able to find part-time work (e.g. newspaper rounds and jobs as retail shop assistants). However, this related mainly to young volunteers from Eastern Europe and not those living as asylum seekers or refugees.

Conclusions

By framing our discussion around the subjective experiences of volunteer participants on YVP programmes in the English West Midlands, we have attempted to uncover the perceptions and motivations of what might be described as an 'invisible' group of volunteers. In so doing we have explored the various impacts that active volunteering had on the personal and social positions of those concerned. Despite the alleged merits of volunteering, subjective testimonies indicate that such activities alone do not always serve to empower young people, particularly those experiencing multiple social deprivations. Certainly, opportunities for self-enhancement and social and civic responsibility are open to volunteers. However, what this research reveals is that the wider aspects of social disadvantage and exclusion may curtail the degree to which some marginalised young people are able to fulfil their potential through volunteering. For example, our findings highlight how Asian male volunteers were able to accrue a level of respect and a social standing through volunteering, but this did not always apply to asylum seekers or those living as refugees. On the contrary, many of the young men from these latter communities talked about feeling isolated, alienated and not being understood by those around them.

Social and civic benefits were alluded to by volunteers across different cultural groups. Whilst the social capacity of volunteering was more alluring to Eastern European migrants, this aspect did not always appeal to (or indeed serve to attract volunteers from) asylum seeker or refugee communities who were keen to up-skill themselves, recognising the extent to which their lives could improve if they had 'real' qualifications, opportunities for paid work and access to social support. That is not to say that friendship networks were not valued amongst non-EU participants. However, asylum seekers and refugees accepted that friends alone could not necessarily contribute to (or improve) their overall marginalised and disadvantaged status. These views were largely shared by young people whose immediate circle of friends consisted of other new migrants living amidst poverty, destitution and deprivation in that asylum seekers and refugees appeared to be channelled through volunteer partnerships schemes with local agencies which only targeted 'new migrants'. According to youth leaders in the city, this segregated approach to programme recruitment stemmed from bureaucratic protocols that existed with regard to the integration of young people from these particular groups into mainstream volunteer settings.

Other practical barriers and constraints relating to the recruitment of volunteers stemmed from a lack of supporting evidence concerning personal identification. Issues around having 'no passport', 'no formal documents', 'no proof of age', 'no permanent address', 'no legal guardians on record', all meant that it became difficult to enrol certain volunteers, to initiate Criminal Records Bureau checks and to identify suitable work placements. Needless to say, when marginalised young people are given limited exposure to non-asylum and non-refugee communities and not granted access to the same kinds of opportunities and services as British-born young people, there is a danger that their sense of being underprivileged, isolated and socially excluded may not only become acute, but also normalised.

Notes

1 To preserve anonymity, pseudonyms have been used throughout.
2 Prior to the onset of the research, ethical approval was gained from the charitable organisations involved in programme delivery and from the University of Gloucestershire Research Ethics Sub-Committee.
3 The term 'old migrant' is used here to denote those who had been born in Britain and were fluent English speakers. 'New migrants', on the other hand, were young people who were newly arrived in the UK and for whom English was a second language.

References

Adams, A. and Deane, J. (2009), 'Exploring formal and informal dimensions of sports volunteering in England', *European Sport Management Quarterly* 9 (2): 119–140.

Alibhai-Brown, Y. (2000), *Who do we think we are? Imagining the New Britain*, London: Penguin.

Brewis, G., Hill, M. and Stevens, D. (2010), *Valuing volunteer management skills*, London: Institute for Volunteering Research.

Burdsey, D. (2007), *British Asian and football: Culture, identity and exclusion*, London: Routledge.

Cabinet Office (2010) *Building the Big Society*, London: Cabinet Office.

CASE (2011), *Understanding the drivers of volunteering in culture and sport: Analysis of the Taking Part Survey*, The Culture and Sport Evidence programme. London: Department for Culture, Media and Sport (DCMS).

Central Council for Physical Recreation (2003), *Everybody wins: Sport and social inclusion*, London: CCPR.

Davis-Smith, J. (1998), *The 1997 National Survey of Volunteering*, London: National Centre for Volunteering.

——(2000), Volunteering and Social Development, *Voluntary Action* 3 (1): 9–23.

Davis-Smith, J., Ellis, A. and Howlett, S. (2002), *UK-wide evaluation of the Millennium Volunteers Programme*. DfES Research Report 357, London: DFES.

Deane, J., Mawson, H., Crone, D., Parker, A. and James, D. (2010), Where are the future sports volunteers? A case study of sports leaders UK, *Leisure Studies Association* 86: 29–32.

Department for Education and Skills (DfES) (2005), *Youth Matters*, London: DfES.

Eley, D. and Kirk, D. (2002), Developing citizenship through sport: The impact of a sport-based volunteer programme on young sport leaders, *Sport, Education and Society* 7 (2): 151–166.

Ellis Paine, A., Hill, M. and Rochester, C. (2010), A rose by any other name … . Revisiting the question: 'What exactly is volunteering?' IVR Working Paper Series, No. 1. Available at: www.ivr.org.uk/NR/rdonlyres/EDA41448-4B3F-4981-9C84-3CA8DE69D027/0/ArosebyanyothernameFINALJAN11.pdf. London: Institute for Volunteering Research.

Gaskin, K. (2004), *Young people, volunteering and civic service: A review of the literature*. A Report for the Institute for Volunteering Research, London: IVR.

——(2008), *A winning team? The impacts of volunteers in sport*, London: IVR.

Hill, M. and Russell, J. (2009), *Young people, volunteering and youth projects: A rapid review of recent evidence*, London, IVR.

Institute of Volunteering Research (IVR) (2004), *Volunteering impact assessment toolkit*, London: IVR.

Kay, T. and Bradbury, S. (2009), Youth sport volunteering: Developing social capital? *Sport, Education and Society* 14 (1): 121–140.

Low, N., Butt, S., Ellis Paine, A. and Davis Smith, J. (2007), *Helping out: A national survey of volunteering and charitable giving*, London: Cabinet Office.

Marsh, K., MacKay, S., Morton, D., Parry, W., Bertanou, E. and Sarmah, R. (2010), *CASE report: Understanding the drivers of engagement in culture and sport, technical report*. London: Department for Culture, Media and Sport (DCMS).

Measham, T. and Barnett, G. (2007), *Environmental volunteering: Motivations, modes and outcomes*. Available online at: http://www.csiro.au/Outcomes/Environment/Population-Sustainability/SEEDPaper3.aspx.

McAll, B. (2011), Big Society and the devolution of power, in M. Stott, *The Big Society challenge*, Thetford, Keystone Development Trust Publications.

National Centre for Social Research (NatCen) (2010), *Formative evaluation of V, the National Young Volunteers' Service*. Interim report: Executive summary, London: NatCen.

National Youth Agency (2008), *Youth action and engagement: Building intergenerational relationships*, London: Cabinet Office/NYA.

——(2010), *Exploring volunteering in a recession: Talking with youth*, London: NYA.

Ockenden, N. (2008), *Environmental volunteering in the North East of England*. London: Institute for Volunteering Research.

Ofsted (2011), *Choosing to volunteer*. Manchester: Ofsted.

Rochester, C., Ellis Paine, A., Howlett, S. and Zimmeck, M. (2009), *Volunteering and society in the 21st century*, Basingstoke: Palgrave MacMillan.

Russell Commission (2005), *A national framework for youth action and engagement*, London: The Russell Commission.

——(2008), *Ethnic minority young males and volunteering*, Wales Active Community/Russell Commission Fund.

Russell, J. (2009), *Making volunteering easier: The story of environmental volunteering in South West England*, Institute for Volunteering Research.

Stebbins, R. (1996), Volunteering: A serious leisure perspective, *Non-profit and Voluntary Sector Quarterly* 25 (2): 211–224.

Stott, M. (2011), (Ed.) *The Big Society challenge*, Thetford, Keystone Development Trust Publications.

Taylor, P. (2004), *Driving up participation: Sport and volunteering*. London: Sport England.

Taylor, P., Nichols, G., Holmes, K., James, M., Gratton, C., Garrett, R., Kokolakakis, T., Mulder, C. and King, L. (2003), *Sports volunteering in England. Summary report*, London: Sport England.

V. (2008), *Youth volunteering: Attitudes and perceptions*, London: V.

Wood, P., Landry, C. and Bloomfield. (2006), *Cultural diversity in Britain: A tool kit for cross-cultural co-operation*, London: Joseph Rowntree Foundation.

Afterword

Reconsidering youth sport, physical activity and play

Don Vinson and Andrew Parker

Introduction

We began this book by arguing that the volume and breadth of policy impacting on the lives of children and young people in the UK warranted further consideration. To this end, the preceding chapters have sought to offer comment on the direction and pace of contemporary policy, with a particular focus on how this is shaping youth sport, physical activity and play. It has been our aim throughout to bring to the attention of the reader a wide range of issues across these related sectors. By considering policy formulation, intervention strategies and participatory experience, the various contributors have richly illustrated the complex tensions which exist between the potential benefits of physical activity and the extent to which policy makers help or hinder this process.

At the time of writing we are approaching the mid-point of the Coalition government's term in office. Our contributors have argued that matters concerning sport, physical activity and play remain highly pertinent to the lives of young people, although recent Coalition policy appears to have muddied the waters in terms of the developmental pathways available through these activity areas. In drawing together the central themes collectively arising from this work, we ask the reader to consider in more detail three of these key tensions; these comprise: (i) the need for individualised understandings of development in policy making; (ii) past and present political ideology; and (iii) ongoing debates between sport for development and the development of sport.

The need for individualised understandings of development in policy making

Inherent in the challenge of effective policy making lies the need to create an all-encompassing strategy designed to shape the behaviour and development of a broad and diverse population. This challenge is evidenced by the fact that a number of our contributors highlight the importance of individualised, child-centred approaches to practice. Mark Elliot, Andy Pitchford and Celia Brackenridge are particularly lucid in this regard (chapter 6), discussing the FA's approach to enhancing notions of 'respect' within the footballing community. Whilst acknowledging the importance of the roles of spectators, coaches and referees within this process, Elliot *et al.* identify the FA's (2011) National Game Strategy as a point of reference, suggesting that the most fundamental tenets of this document lie in three core child-centred recommendations: (i) the development of flexible, child-centred competitions for primary school children; (ii) new player pathways for children built around small-sided game formats; and (iii) the development of an intervention programme which aims to counter the relative age effect (RAE). Similarly, in their chapter on sports coaching (chapter 10), Simon Padley and Don Vinson argue that an individualised, athlete-centred approach to engagement with competition is crucial for the holistic development of young people. Citing contemporary pedagogic theory (see Richard and Wallian, 2005) as a suitable framework for such practice, Padley and Vinson also suggest that coaches have a particular responsibility to shape the development of the young people in their care through appropriately framed experiences of sport.

This individualised theme is similarly picked up by Denise Hill and colleagues (chapter 4) in their discussion of the benefits of physical activity programmes for young people with low self-esteem – a chapter which also challenges the Coalition's 'competitive sports for all' mantra (DCMS, 2012). Hill *et al.* suggest that traditional competitive sports are unlikely to engage all young people and that, for the sake of their long-term physical and mental health, a more individualised approach to curriculum design should be adopted. Likewise, Don Vinson and Matt Lloyd (chapter 9) are cautious of Coalition policy on competitive sport, suggesting that movement-based approaches such as Multi-skills and Physical Literacy are more appropriate for young people than sport-specific curricula. A focus on movement-based delivery would more readily build upon the successes of the past decade by continuing to offer opportunities such as Multi-skills Clubs/Academies (see Morley, 2009) and retain an appreciation of the concept of Physical Literacy (see Whitehead, 2010). In turn, such approaches, they argue, should not be overlooked during forthcoming revisions to the National Curriculum, which is expected to revert back to a more traditional, games focus. Vinson and Lloyd agree that the move away from 'sport-based' curricular perspectives is beneficial for both the development of sports performance and for increasing the likelihood of creating a lifelong, physically active populace (Côté *et al.* 2009). To this end, policy makers need to ensure that delivery organisations are enabled and encouraged to implement a tailored and individualised approach to practice. This challenge becomes invariably more difficult as governments, together with their particular ideologies and philosophies, come and go. Indeed, it is to the policy-related challenges of negotiating the transition from (New) Labour (1997–2010) to the current Coalition government that we now turn.

Past and present political ideology

The contributors to this text collectively identify a number of areas which could potentially be labelled 'under threat' within the wider context of the current political regime. *Game Plan* (DCMS/Strategy Unit 2002) brought together performance-related sporting targets with a series of broader cultural factors relating to social exclusion and physical activity for health. Perhaps unintentionally, the health, social inequality and social justice-related implications of *Game Plan* (DCMS/Strategy Unit, 2002) furthered understandings of a more holistic appreciation of participant development through sport. A number of chapters within this volume have emerged, in no small part, due to the political expedience of subject areas such as physical activity for health (see Owens *et al.*), play work (see Lester and Russell), volunteering (see Farooq *et al.*; Mawson and Parker) and sport for development (see Annett and Mayuni). However, the publication of *Playing to Win* (DCMS, 2008) evoked some fundamental political and developmental questions; the overt separation of physical activity-based and performance-focussed participation marred the nature of the policy-related bond between sport, physical activity and play. The social inclusion agenda, so prevalent in *Game Plan* (DCMS/ Strategy Unit, 2002), had been entirely eliminated. For Green (2009) it was the (New) Labour principle of New Public Management (NPM) which led to a focus on podium athletes to the detriment of genuine holistic development and societal enrichment (Grix, 2009; Grix and Phillpots, 2011). This challenge was further taken up by *Playing to Win* (DCMS, 2008), where the outcome of sporting performance appeared to matter more than the holistic development of participants themselves.

The direction of late (New) Labour and current Coalition policy has seen a diminishing emphasis on the importance of holistic development. Subsequently, some disciplinary areas face a particularly challenging period. For example, Stuart Lester and Wendy Russell (chapter 3) highlight the way in which the Coalition has distanced itself from policies on play, considering them to be an area of responsibility for local communities, rather than central government. There appear to be both positive and negative connotations here. Almost all aspects of sport, physical activity and play need support and funding from government in order to grow and thrive, yet, because of this, they are typically challenged by utilitarianism and instrumentalism (Houlihan and White, 2002). Lester and Russell draw on Bauman's (2003) analysis of utopian projects, which elicits two key attributes of contemporary policy relating to children and young people. The first of these identifies the fixity and finality of vision in perfect states, whilst the second suggests that children are confined by territorialisation. Lester and Russell call on policy makers and playwork practitioners to reject the notion of play as totalising and to embrace the value of uncertainty and disorderliness and the complex interrelationships between children and their physical, social and cultural environments. By considering play spaces as spontaneous, unfinished *terrains vagues*, Lester and Russell encourage us to have faith in children to develop their own ideas, rather than feel the need to impose a particular purpose or outcome on their play. Given the Coalition's enthusiasm for pushing the playwork agenda in the direction of local communities, it is perhaps unsurprising that Lester and Russell identify potential resonance between current policy making and the broader remit of David Cameron's Big Society (see Cabinet Office, 2010).

Representing something of an elusive concept, the Big Society receives considerable attention in this text, most notably from Hannah Mawson and Andrew Parker (chapter 11), who question the government's emphasis on encouraging young people to volunteer (in whatever capacity), whilst at the same time cutting the funding of organisations who specialise in the facilitation of such roles. Mawson and Parker tentatively argue that, although the predictors of volunteering remain relatively constant, there is evidence to suggest that minority groups are more readily accessing these kinds of opportunities. Reinforcing this claim, Samaya Farooq and colleagues (chapter 12) offer a unique account which provides insight into the volunteering experiences of 'old migrant' and 'new migrant' youth in the UK. Farooq *et al.* suggest that, whilst there are personal and social benefits to volunteering, such roles do not always serve to empower those experiencing multiple social deprivations. This appears to be particularly true for new migrants such as asylum seekers and refugees. The uncertainty surrounding the future and direction of areas such as playwork and volunteering may simply be a hangover from the shifting policy priorities of (New) Labour and the result of an imperfect union of Liberal Democrat and Conservative philosophies. These tensions further illustrate ongoing debates as to whether government sees sport as a tool for development or as an end in itself. A number of our contributors postulate how these debates are playing out via contemporary policy making; these views are considered in the next section.

Ongoing debates between sport for development and the development of sport

The consensus throughout this book is that contemporary policy in the areas of youth sport, physical activity and play is not well aligned. Mike Collins (chapter 1) is especially critical of the current position, arguing that sport policy for young people over the past decade has been largely ineffective, particularly concerning participation and societal inequalities. Collins contends that there is a perception of gender equality within youth sport, but that this is an 'illusion' (see also Jeanes, 2011). Collins further suggests that the physical activity participation targets set over the past decade were, at best, naive. The lack of progress made towards these targets underlines the impact of the tension between a policy focus on sport for development as opposed to favouring the development of sport. Green (2009) argues that the systems of governance deployed by (New) Labour, featuring evidence-based policy making and accountability in exchange for freedom in decision making, did little to unite the UK's national governing bodies of sport (NGBs), which remain fiercely independent and exclusive. Further to this, there is still considerable confusion in the UK over which institutions are responsible for leading which aspects of sport policy (Grix, 2009). When placed alongside a lack of cohesive governance, such levels of independence directly hinder many areas of sport and physical activity. Collins refers to the work of de Bosscher *et al.* (2009), who propose that there is a 'global arms race for medals' (p. 41) that has led to an inappropriately narrow focus on youth development (see also Côté *et al.*, 2012). In this volume, Christophers. Owens and colleagues (chapter 8) have outlined why the loss of the holistic aspects of sport-related policy, evident in *Game Plan* (DCMS/Strategy Unit, 2002), but absent in *Playing to Win* (DCMS, 2008) and *Creating a Sporting Habit for Life* (DCMS, 2012), are potentially damaging to public health in the UK. Owens *et al.* summarise the empirical evidence surrounding physical activity and sedentary behaviours in adolescents, revealing how little data is available in this area. Existing research provides mixed findings relating to sedentary behaviours and a dearth of evidence emanating from longitudinal studies, all of which highlights a problematic relationship amongst adolescents between screen time and physical activity.

At a structural level, Mike Collins is also critical of the impact of policy on addressing questions surrounding inequality of provision in sport and physical activity for those of low socio-economic status, suggesting that this remains the most fundamental predictor of exclusion. Numerous other chapters address similar concerns, not least that of Andrew Parker and Rosie Meek (chapter 5), who discuss how sport might impact reoffending rates amongst young people. Focussing on the work of one particular sporting initiative in the South West of England, the 2nd Chance Project, their chapter illustrates the dramatic effect that involvement with meaningful sporting activity might have for individuals whose youth experiences have included periods of incarceration. Parker and Meek reveal the physical, social and psychological benefits of involvement with sport in custody and the kind of multi-agency support which can address some of the common shortcomings of a seemingly overloaded criminal justice system. One of the keys to the success of such initiatives appears to be an empowerment of those involved through the promotion of positive thinking, the rebuilding of broken (family) relationships and the enhancement of self-esteem. This discussion presents something of a contrast to Farooq *et al.*'s chapter in which new migrants to the UK appear insufficiently empowered by their engagement in volunteering roles to facilitate a change in their perceptions of marginalisation. On the basis of much of the work presented in this collection, it is clear that involvement in sport and physical activity can offer young people the opportunity to alter their life circumstances and chances, that is, sport for development can be an effective policy strategy. Despite this, it is clear that the relationship between offering marginalised youth the opportunity to engage with meaningful sporting experiences and the achievement of social stability and/or mobility is far from simple and requires considerable thought on the part of policy makers and practitioners alike.

A further setback for those advocates of a sport for development approach to policy making is the recent loss of the Physical Education, School Sport and Young People (PESSYP) strategy. It appears that this will be replaced by a more traditional emphasis on competitive games at all levels of education. Despite being confident in the merits of the Youth Sport Trust to ensure at least some financial support for PESS, Mike Collins agrees that the loss of funding for PESSYP could result in a significant step backwards for schools. Collins also expresses concern about the low profile of playwork within UK sport policy although, countering this, Nic Matthews (chapter 2) encourages us to look to the impact of the European Union (EU) in shaping sport, playwork and physical activity more positively. Matthews suggests that the EU has changed the relationship between Member States and the way that policy agendas are constructed. In particular, she contends that the health-related implications of the physical activity agenda and the human rights-related issues concerning the playwork debate have benefitted the young people of Europe in terms of policy focus. Elizabeth Annett and Samuel Mayuni (chapter 7) are equally positive about the impact of the 'Sport Malawi' initiative with which they are involved, a sport-for-development programme focussed on training local Malawian people in the power of sport to ignite economic development, relieve poverty, facilitate health benefits, build communities, promote equality and advocate justice. Like some of our other contributors, they address the relationship between faith/religion and sport for development. Annett and Mayuni highlight the importance of fully engaging local individuals and communities to ensure the effectiveness of sport development programmes, particularly emphasising the understanding of cultural norms, values and traditions in the phases of design, implementation and evaluation. Similarly, Farooq *et al.* suggest that the volunteering experiences of young migrants can often be linked to their respective ethnic, religious or faith groups. In turn, Collins notes that discussion surrounding physical activity provision, particularly in relation to young Muslim women, is an important policy-related issue. Collectively PESS, play and faith represent three areas which face particular challenges in the coming years within the context of uncertain policy focus and government support.

Summary

What the preceding discussion confirms is that numerous tensions surface when discussing policy in relation to youth sport, physical activity and play. Across all three of these sectors there is a need for policy makers to ensure that practitioners are encouraged to adopt child-centred approaches which embrace holistic development and tailored, individual provision. Meanwhile, the uncertainty surrounding future policy remains. For example, whilst it is apparent that the publication of the forthcoming revision to the National

Curriculum will answer some of the questions being posed by PESS practitioners, it is less clear how the Coalition government will tangibly empower local communities to operationalise objectives surrounding sport and physical activity within the context of the Big Society. Contributors to this text are critical of the effectiveness of policy in recent years and highlight the discrepancy in the underpinning philosophies of successive governments. This discrepancy has, it seems, exacerbated the ongoing debates between 'sport for development' and 'sport for sport's sake'. From the evidence presented here it appears that sport, physical activity and play are potentially effective tools in reaching some of the most vulnerable and marginalised young people in our society. It is, therefore, difficult to understand why sport for development has been so under-represented in recent iterations of UK sport policy. Indeed, the consensus within this volume is that sport, physical activity and play remain highly pertinent areas of development for young people both in the UK and beyond. Only time will tell whether policy makers will come to adopt a similar mind-set.

References

Bauman, Z. (2003), Utopia with no topos, *History of the Human Sciences*, 16 (1): 11–25.

Cabinet Office (2010), *Building the Big Society*, London: Cabinet Office.

Côté, J., Coakley C., and Bruner, M. (2012), Children's talent development in sport: Effectiveness or efficiency? in S. Dagkas and K. Armour (eds) *Inclusion and Exclusion through Youth Sport*, London: Routledge, pp. 172–185.

Côté, J., Lidor, R., and Hackfort, D. (2009), ISSP position stand: To sample or to specialise? Seven postulates about youth sport activities that lead to continued participation and elite performance, *International Journal of Sport and Exercise Psychology*, 9 (1): 7–17.

de Bosscher, V., Bingham, J., Shibli, S., van Bottenburg, M. and de Knop, P. (2009), *The Global Sporting Arms Race: An international study on sports factors leading to international sporting success*, Oxford: Meyer and Meyer Sport.

Department for Children, Schools and Families (2007), *The Children's Plan: Building brighter futures*, TSO: Norwich.

Department for Culture, Media and Sport (DCMS)/Strategy Unit (2002), *Game Plan: A strategy for delivering government's sport and physical activity objectives*, London: Cabinet Office.

Department for Culture, Media and Sport (DCMS) (2008), *Playing to Win: A new era for sport*, London: Cabinet Office.

——(2012), *Creating a Sporting Habit for Life – A new youth sport strategy*, London: HMSO.

The Football Association (2011), *National Game Strategy 2011–15*, London: Football Association.

Green, M. (2009), Podium or participation? Analysing policy priorities under changing modes of sport governance in the United Kingdom, *International Journal of Sport Policy*, 1 (2), 121–144.

Grix, J. (2009), The impact of UK sport policy on the governance of athletics, *International Journal of Sport Policy*, 1 (1): 31–49.

Grix, J. and Phillpots, L. (2011), Revisiting the 'governance narrative': 'Asymmetrical network governance' and the deviant case of the sports policy sector, *Public Policy and Administration*, 26 (1): 3–19.

HM Government (2011) *Open public services white paper*, Norwich: The Stationery Office.

Houlihan, B., and White, A. (2002), *The Politics of Sports Development: Development of sport or development through sport?*, London: Routledge.

Jeanes, R. (2011), Girls in sport, in I. Stafford (ed.) *Coaching Children in Sport*, London, Routledge, pp. 215–226.

Morley, D. (2009). Multi-skills: Contexts and constraints, *Physical Education Matters*, 4 (3): 19–23.

Richard, J.-F., and Wallian, N. (2005) Emphasizing student engagement in the construction of game performance, in L. L. Griffin and J. I. Butler (eds) *Teaching Games for Understanding: Theory, research and practice*, Leeds: Human Kinetics, pp. 19–32.

Whitehead, M. (ed.) (2010), *Physical Literacy through the Lifecourse*, London: Routledge.

Index

Locators in *italics* refer to figures and tables.